Installation, Storage, and Compute with Windows Server 2016: Microsoft 70-740 MCSA Exam Guide

Implement and configure storage and compute functionalities in Windows Server 2016

Sasha Kranjac
Vladimir Stefanovic

BIRMINGHAM - MUMBAI

Installation, Storage, and Compute with Windows Server 2016: Microsoft 70-740 MCSA Exam Guide

Copyright © 2019 Packt Publishing

Commissioning Editor: Kartikey Pandey
Acquisition Editor: Shrilekha Inani
Content Development Editor: Ronn Kurien
Technical Editor: Aditya Khadye
Copy Editor: Safis Editing
Language Support Editor: Mary McGowan
Project Coordinator: Jagdish Prabhu
Proofreader: Safis Editing
Indexer: Pratik Shirodkar
Graphics: Tom Scaria
Production Coordinator: Jyoti Chauhan

First published: February 2019

Production reference: 1280219

Published by Packt Publishing Ltd.
Livery Place
35 Livery Street
Birmingham
B3 2PB, UK.

ISBN 978-1-78961-945-4

www.packtpub.com

mapt.io

Mapt is an online digital library that gives you full access to over 5,000 books and videos, as well as industry leading tools to help you plan your personal development and advance your career. For more information, please visit our website.

Why subscribe?

- Spend less time learning and more time coding with practical eBooks and videos from over 4,000 industry professionals

- Improve your learning with Skill Plans built especially for you

- Get a free eBook or video every month

- Mapt is fully searchable

- Copy and paste, print, and bookmark content

Packt.com

Did you know that Packt offers eBook versions of every book published, with PDF and ePub files available? You can upgrade to the eBook version at www.packt.com and as a print book customer, you are entitled to a discount on the eBook copy. Get in touch with us at customercare@packtpub.com for more details.

At www.packt.com, you can also read a collection of free technical articles, sign up for a range of free newsletters, and receive exclusive discounts and offers on Packt books and eBooks.

Contributors

About the authors

Sasha Kranjac is a security and Azure expert and instructor with more than two decades of experience in the field. He began programming in Assembler on Sir Clive Sinclair's ZX, met Windows NT 3.5, and the love has existed ever since. Sasha owns an IT training and consulting company that helps companies and individuals to embrace the cloud and be safe in cyberspace. He is a Microsoft MVP, MCT, MCT Regional Lead, Certified EC-Council Instructor (CEI), and currently holds more than 60 technical certifications. Sasha is a frequent speaker at various international conferences, and is a consultant and trainer for some of the largest Fortune 500 companies.

Vladimir Stefanovic is a Microsoft Certified Trainer (MCT) and system engineer with more than 10 years of experience in the IT industry. Over his IT career, Vladimir has worked in all areas of IT administration, from IT technician to his current system engineer position. As a lead system engineer at Serbian IT company SuperAdmins and lead technician trainer at Admin Training Center, he successfully delivered numerous projects and courses. He is also an active conference speaker, having spoken at a long list of conferences, such as MCT Summits (in the USA, Germany, and Greece), ATD, WinDays, KulenDayz, and Sinergija (Regional Conferences). He is the leader of a few user groups and is an active community member, with the mission to share knowledge as much as possible.

About the reviewer

Mustafa Toroman is a program architect and senior system engineer with Authority Partners. With years of experience of designing and monitoring infrastructure solutions, lately he focuses on designing new solutions in the cloud and migrating existing solutions to the cloud. He is very interested in DevOps processes, and he's also an Infrastructure-as-Code enthusiast. Mustafa has over 30 Microsoft certificates and has been an MCT for the last 6 years. He often speaks at international conferences about cloud technologies, and he has been awarded MVP for Microsoft Azure for the last three years in a row. Mustafa also authored *Hands-On Cloud Administration in Azure* and co-authored *Learn Node.js with Azure*, both published by Packt.

Packt is searching for authors like you

If you're interested in becoming an author for Packt, please visit `authors.packtpub.com` and apply today. We have worked with thousands of developers and tech professionals, just like you, to help them share their insight with the global tech community. You can make a general application, apply for a specific hot topic that we are recruiting an author for, or submit your own idea.

Table of Contents

Preface

Welcome to *Installation, Storage, and Compute with Windows Server 2016: Microsoft 70-740 MCSA Exam Guide*!

This book is designed to give you a thorough understanding of fundamental installation skills and vital services in Windows Server 2016 to prepare you for Exam 70-740: Installation, Storage, and Compute with Windows Server 2016, which is part of the MCSA Windows Server 2016 Certification and MCSE Core Infrastructure Certification. The book will start with the installation of Windows Server 2016. Appropriate requirements and usage scenarios will be covered, followed by Windows Server Imaging and Deployment, where updates and image management will be covered. Next, configuration, implementation, and storage management will be described, after which virtualization with Hyper-V and virtualization building blocks in Windows Server 2016 will be explained. Afterward, Windows Containers will be introduced, and, subsequently, how to support business-critical workloads with high availability will be covered. Finally, implementing highly-available solutions with clustering will be explained, along with an outline of monitoring and maintaining server environments.

Who this book is for

This book is aimed at anyone who wants to learn about the installation, storage, and compute functionalities available in Windows Server 2016, and earn valuable Microsoft certifications. To better understand the content of this book, you should have a working knowledge of Windows Server operating systems, and preferably, experience of working with them.

What this book covers

Chapter 1, *Installing Windows Server 2016*, helps you to understand which version of Windows Server to install, and what types of hardware are essential for building a solid and reliable infrastructure.

Chapter 2, *Windows Server Imaging and Deployment*, addresses the assessment of existing environments, planning for workload deployments, and Windows Server image management and maintenance.

Chapter 3, *Configuring and Implementing Storage*, explains configuration and storage management, and introduces more advanced topics, such as Storage Replica and deduplication.

Chapter 4, *Getting to Know Hyper-V*, helps you to determine the hardware and software requirements for Hyper-V, before looking at how to install, configure, and manage it. We will configure the **virtual machine** (**VM**) memory and integration services, determine the appropriate usage scenarios of Generation 1 and Generation 2 VMs, install Linux-based VMs, and move and convert VMs.

Chapter 5, *Understanding Windows Containers*, describes containers in Windows Server 2016, the installation of container support in Windows, how to deploy Windows Containers, and how to manage them.

Chapter 6, *High Availability*, explains high availability and disaster recovery options in Hyper-V. Additionally this chapter will covers the implementation of Storage Spaces Direct and Network Load Balancing, which are both equally important technologies, along with other features for achieving highly available Windows Server infrastructure.

Chapter 7, *Implementing Clustering*, explains how to implement and configure failover clustering, configure failover settings and VM monitoring, perform workload migrations, and monitor clustered environments.

Chapter 8, *Monitoring and Maintaining Server Environments*, covers how to implement **Windows Server Update Services** (**WSUS**) and use it to manage system updates. You will also learn how to install and configure Windows Server Backup, how to protect services with this feature, and how to monitor Windows Server 2016 using built-in tools.

To get the most out of this book

Before you start with this book with a view to preparing for Exam 70-740, you should have an understanding of networking in Windows Server 2016, imaging concepts, storage technology, virtualization, and related services. Experience of configuring Windows Server 2012 and Windows Server 2016, as well as working with virtualization, is required to better understand storage and virtualization-related services. The following Windows Server roles and services will be used in this book:

- File and storage services
- Hyper-V

Conventions used

There are a number of text conventions used throughout this book.

`CodeInText`: Indicates code words in text, database table names, folder names, filenames, file extensions, pathnames, dummy URLs, user input, and Twitter handles. Here is an example: "By default, the location of the AD DS database is `C:\Windows\NTDS\ntds.dit`."

Any command-line input or output is written as follows:

```
Install-WindowsFeature AD-Domain-Services -IncludeAllSubFeature -
IncludeManagementTools
```

Bold: Indicates a new term, an important word, or words that you see onscreen. For example, words in menus or dialog boxes appear in the text like this. Here is an example: "Select **Operation Masters**."

 Warnings or important notes appear like this.

 Tips and tricks appear like this.

Get in touch

Feedback from our readers is always welcome.

General feedback: If you have questions about any aspect of this book, mention the book title in the subject of your message and email us at `customercare@packtpub.com`.

Errata: Although we have taken every care to ensure the accuracy of our content, mistakes do happen. If you have found a mistake in this book, we would be grateful if you would report this to us. Please visit `www.packt.com/submit-errata`, selecting your book, clicking on the Errata Submission Form link, and entering the details.

Piracy: If you come across any illegal copies of our works in any form on the Internet, we would be grateful if you would provide us with the location address or website name. Please contact us at `copyright@packt.com` with a link to the material.

If you are interested in becoming an author: If there is a topic that you have expertise in and you are interested in either writing or contributing to a book, please visit `authors.packtpub.com`.

Reviews

Please leave a review. Once you have read and used this book, why not leave a review on the site that you purchased it from? Potential readers can then see and use your unbiased opinion to make purchase decisions, we at Packt can understand what you think about our products, and our authors can see your feedback on their book. Thank you!

For more information about Packt, please visit `packt.com`.

Installing Windows Server 2016 1

In this first chapter, we will cover the installation of Windows Server and Nano Server, and migration to Windows Server 2016 from previous versions. We will start by determining the important installation requirements of Windows Server 2016, including which versions and Windows Server editions to install and what hardware is essential for a solid and reliable infrastructure. One important part is installing and configuring a special version of Windows Server without a GUI, Windows Server Core. We will see how to configure the installation of Windows Server 2016 using various options and tools.

Essential to Windows Server administration is the ability to perform server management remotely and use automation tools to reduce management errors and save time. We will then move on to the installation and configuration of Nano Server and the tools we need to build Nano Server images and configure Nano Server workloads. Finally, we will learn how to perform upgrades from previous versions and how to activate Window Server installations.

In this chapter, we will cover the following topics:

- Installing Windows Server 2016
- Installing and configuring Nano Server
- Upgrading and migrating servers and workloads

Technical requirements

You will need a version of Windows Server 2016. This can be a retail version, a volume-licensed version, or an evaluation version with which you can experiment. I suggest you set up your own lab, preferably in a sandboxed environment. You can set up your lab either in Hyper-V or in Microsoft Azure. Additionally, Hyper-V is available on Windows 10, or you can use any other virtualization platform to build your own lab: VMware, Amazon Web Services, VirtualBox, and so on. Be aware that Microsoft Azure does not support some Windows Server roles and features, including the following:

- **Dynamic Host Configuration Protocol** (**DHCP**) Server
- Hyper-V (at the time of writing, Hyper-V's role in Azure is supported in all v3 virtual machines, such as Ev3 and Dv3 virtual machines)
- Rights Management Services
- Windows Deployment Services

In upgrade scenarios, you will need Windows Server 2012 or an older version. Trial operating system versions are available at `https://www.microsoft.com/en-us/evalcenter/`.

Sometimes, when you click on **Windows Server 2016** under the **Products** menu, only a list of Windows Server 2012 products is displayed. This might be a temporary glitch. To display the Windows Server 2016 version, click on the plus sign next to any Windows Server 2012 version and expand the entry. After an automatic refresh, the list will show the Windows Server 2016 versions that are available for evaluation and download. There are three options available: **Azure**, **ISO**, and **Virtual Lab**. Choose whichever suits you best.

Installing Windows Server 2016

Windows Server 2016 is available in many different variants, but before choosing the appropriate version for your specific workloads and needs, you must be sure that your current or future hardware will be able to support it.

The following system requirements are minimum hardware requirements that are common to all Windows Server 2016 installation options and editions. The actual minimum hardware requirements are estimated and may vary depending on the planned roles and features. Obviously, for production environments and optimum server performance, you should plan to install Windows Server 2016 on hardware that exceeds these requirements.

Minimum system hardware requirements

Your system should have at least the following specifications:

- **Processor**:
    - 4 GHz 64-bit processor.
    - Support for **Second Level Address Translation** (**SLAT**) or nested paging. SLAT is a processor technology that is used in virtual-to-physical memory address translation. Both AMD and Intel support SLAT. AMD's implementation is called **Rapid Virtualization Indexing** (**RVI**) and Intel's implementation is called **Extended Page Tables** (**EPT**).
    - Support for **Data Execution Prevention** (**DEP**) and **No-Execute** (**NX**). DEP/NX is a processor feature that allows you to mark memory pages as either executable or non-executable. It also allows a processor to help prevent the execution of malicious data being placed into your memory. Note that a 32-bit processor is not supported.
- **RAM**: 512 MB, although the desirable minimum memory for a server with a GUI is 2 GB.
- **Disk/Storage**: 32 GB of disk space and a PCI Express storage adapter. Older architectures (such as PATA, ATA, IDE, or EIDE) are not supported.
- **Network**: PCI Express-compliant Gigabit Ethernet adapter that supports **Pre-boot Execution Environment** (**PXE**).

Optional requirements

The following are optional requirements for Windows Server installation; they are convenient to have but not are required:

- **Optical drive**: DVD drive, if you are installing Windows Server 2016 from a disk
- **Video**: SVGA 1024x768 video resolution
- **Input devices**: Keyboard and mouse
- **Internet:** Recommended
- **Other**: UEFI firmware and a **Trusted Platform Module** (**TPM**) chip

The optional requirements are exactly that, options, and are not necessarily needed to install Windows Server 2016 because the server administration should be performed almost exclusively remotely. Specific features may require additional hardware, such as BitLocker Drive Encryption, which requires a TPM chip. If you plan to use BitLocker, then hardware-based TPM chip must adhere to version 2.0 of the TPM specification. Additionally, it needs to support the SHA-256 encryption and the EK certificate.

Both Windows Server 2016 editions support a maximum of 24 TB of RAM, 12 TB of RAM per generation 2 VM (1 TB of RAM per generation 1 VM), 64 of 64-bit sockets, 512 physical (host) logical processors, and 240 virtual processors per VM.

Windows Server 2016 editions

Windows Server 2016 is available in two main editions and a few minor standalone editions. The two main editions are as follows:

- **Datacenter Edition**: This edition has the complete set of features and roles and is most appropriate for environments in need of unlimited virtualization or highly-virtualized, enterprise-scale workloads.
- **Standard Edition**: This edition is mostly appropriate for physical installations or non-virtualized, low-density environments. It supports Hyper-V as well but the number of virtualized workloads is limited compared to the Datacenter Edition.

The features that are exclusive to the Datacenter Edition include shielded virtual machines, **Software-Defined Networking (SDN)**, networking stacks, Storage Spaces Direct, and Storage Replica. The Standard Edition includes rights to two **Operating System Environments (OSEs**, or virtual machines) or Hyper-V Containers, whereas the Datacenter Edition includes unlimited OSEs and Hyper-V Containers. OSE is a Microsoft term that represents a Windows instance running either as a physical or a virtual installation. The Standard Edition therefore grants you the right to run a physical server OSE instance in addition to a virtual instance.

If a physical OSE is used exclusively to host and manage virtual OSEs, you can use two virtual OSEs in addition to the physical OSE. At first, the Standard Edition OSE limit might not look very attractive, but the price is an important factor to consider as well; currently, Datacenter Edition price is approximately six to seven times higher than Standard Edition. Unless you will run more than twelve to fourteen virtual machines, having a single Datacenter license might not be a good decision because you could spend less money buying Standard Edition licenses instead. Of course, licensing and money are not the only variables here. Should you decide to buy Standard licenses, you have to consider expense of buying the same amount of additional server hardware.

If you choose the Datacenter version, a high-end server with hardware characteristics powerful enough to run fourteen virtual machines might be more expensive than buying seven low- or mid-end servers suitable to host Standard versions of Windows Server. With in increased number of servers, the administrative burden increases as well.

The Datacenter and Standard Editions require every user or device that accesses a server to have a **Client Access License** (**CAL**). The following table gives you a comparison of the features of Windows Server 2016 editions:

Feature	Datacenter	Standard
Windows Server Core functionality	Yes	Yes
OSEs/Hyper-V Containers	Unlimited	Two (supports two OSEs or instances)
Windows Server Containers	Unlimited	Unlimited
Host Guardian Hyper-V Service	Yes	Yes
Nano Server	Yes	Yes
Storage features, including Storage Spaces Direct and Storage Replica	Yes	No
Shielded virtual machines	Yes	No
Networking stack	Yes	No
Software-Defined Networking	Yes	No

Table 1: Feature comparison between different editions of Windows Server 2016

Minor or standalone Windows Server 2016 Editions include the following:

- **Essentials**: Ideal for small businesses with up to 25 users and 50 devices. No CALs are required. Be aware that the Essentials edition does not support more users and devices once it's at its user or device limit.
- **Microsoft Hyper-V Server 2016**: A free edition that contains only Windows Hypervisor, the same technology as is in the Hyper-V role on Windows Server 2016. Like Server Core, it has no graphical interface.
- **Windows Storage Server 2016**: A dedicated file and print server in both Standard and Workgroup editions. This is available only with a purchase of dedicated hardware as part of an **Original Equipment Manufacturer** (**OEM**) offering.
- **Windows Server 2016 Multipoint Premium Server**: Available only through Volume Licensing for academic customers.

Although not listed as an exam objective at the time of writing, knowing a little bit about Windows Server 2016 licensing can be helpful in determining which Windows Server edition to use.

Installing Windows Server 2016

There are several different ways of installing Windows Server 2016, each of which are suitable for different scenarios. In this section, we will explain a clean installation, while upgrades and migrations will be described later.

The term *clean installation* describes how to install Windows Server 2016 either on new hardware or a virtual machine, or on old hardware or a virtual machine without retaining the old operating system.

Whether you install Windows Server 2016 on a physical server or as a virtual machine, the process is the same. The only difference is in how you supply the installation files. To install an operating system on a virtual machine in Hyper-V, you would provide a Windows Server 2016 ISO file. This can be used to burn a DVD or to make a bootable USB drive.

To burn a DVD or to make a bootable USB drive, consider using the *Windows 7 USB DVD Download Tool*, a lightweight, minimalistic, and simple-to-use imaging tool. Although the name suggests its main purpose is to make Windows 7 images and bootable drives, you can safely use it to make bootable USB and DVD media for all Windows Server and Windows Client operating systems, from Windows 7 to the most recent versions.

The Windows USB/DVD Download Tool web page has necessary information about the tool, installation instructions, software prerequisites and a download link:
`https://www.microsoft.com/en-us/download/windows-usb-dvd-download-tool`.
To go directly to the download page, where you can download multiple language versions of the tool, visit `https://www.microsoft.com/en-us/download/details.aspx?id=56485`.

If you have optical media available, you can use a DVD drive as an installation source either on a virtual machine or on bare metal:

1. After starting the Windows Server 2016 setup process, you are presented with pull-down menus that you can use to choose which language, time zone, currency format, and keyboard layout to use. You can change all these options after setup process is finished. However, depending on the installation file used, you might not be able to choose a different language.

2. Click **Next** and a simplistic setup window will appear. The **Repair Your Computer** option brings up recovery options, in which the **System Image Recovery** and **Command Prompt** options are available.

3. After you click **Install now**, Windows Setup will ask you to enter a product key and activate an installation. The product key you enter will determine which Windows Server version is used in the setup process.

4. If you do not have your product key, choose **I don't have a product key** and the operating system selection window will appear, as can be seen in the following screenshot:

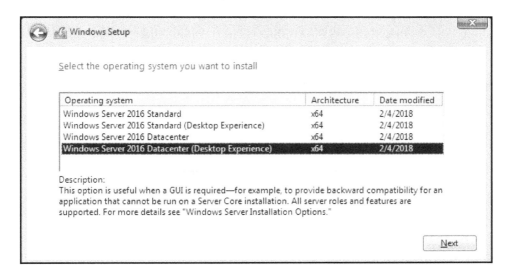

There are four choices available. There are two Windows Server 2016 versions, Datacenter and Standard, each of which is presented in two different configurations: with a GUI (Desktop Experience) or without it (Server Core). Unless you have a specific reason to install GUI elements, you should always choose to install the Server Core version.

In earlier Windows Server releases (in Windows Server 2012 and Windows Server 2012 R2 for example), you could choose either **Desktop Experience** or **Server Core version** and remove or install a GUI easily after installation. Windows Server 2016 releases do not support installing or uninstalling a GUI anymore. If you change your mind about which version you want to choose, you should do a clean installation:

1. On the next screen, after you accept the license terms, Windows Setup will ask you which type of installation you require: upgrade or custom. For now, we will choose custom install, as we will explain the upgrade option later in this chapter. You should choose custom install in the following situations:
    - You are performing a clean install, where an operating system is not present
    - An operating system is installed and you want to retain it, so that you can use multi-booting
    - You are unable to upgrade from an existing operating system
    - You want to delete all existing data and operating systems and perform a clean install

2. The custom installation option also allows you to make changes to drives, partitions, and load drivers:
    - **Refresh** will rescan hardware after you have provided a new driver
    - **Delete** enables you to delete existing partitions or ones that you created during the setup process
    - **Format** performs formatting of partition using NTFS file system, erasing all data
    - **New** creates a new partition, and **Extend** allows you to make partitions larger, if disk space adjacent to partition is unoccupied

3. If you have bought a new disk, it is not necessary to use these commands and prepare a disk. Windows Setup will do this for you. If you need to prepare the disk in a specific way, the `diskpart.exe` command executed in Command Prompt, will enable you to do so.

4. **Load driver** lets you load device drivers if Windows Setup doesn't recognize the installation disk and you need to enable the storage controller to choose the installation destination. The following screenshot shows **Windows Setup** options that appear if only one installation drive is available. You can also see the commands mentioned earlier that will help you manage the storage:

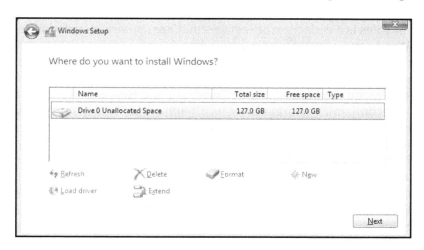

5. To open Command Prompt during setup, press *Shift + F10*. Here, you can use `diskpart.exe` to make advanced changes to disks and partitions, or use other commands that may help you to install and troubleshoot Windows Setup.
6. In the next step, the Windows installation begins. Once Windows Setup copies the necessary files, system restarts.
7. On the **Customize settings** screen, **Windows Setup** prompts you for the built-in administrator password. Enter this to sign in and the installation is complete.

Installing Windows Server 2016 roles and features

To enable Windows Server 2016 to perform a specific duty or to enhance it to support a particular task, you need to install server roles and features:

- Server roles is a collection of services that are usually installed together to enable the Windows Server to perform a certain function. Examples of server roles include DNS Server, DHCP Server, or Active Directory Domain Services. A Windows Server computer can perform one or more roles at the same time, depending on the installation environment and the number of users it supports. Smaller companies or organizations often have servers that perform many functions or roles, while larger companies or enterprises might have multiple servers configured with one dedicated role only. These dedicated servers are likely to be used more heavily, serving a larger number of users, devices, or requests.

- Features are services or additional programs that enhance a server's or a role's capabilities. They do not necessarily need a role as a prerequisite for installation or to perform a function. Examples of features include BitLocker Drive Encryption, Containers, and Network Load Balancing.

You can add, remove, and configure roles and features either locally, using Server Manager or Windows PowerShell, or remotely, using Server Manager, Windows PowerShell, remote server, or **Remote Server Administration Tools** (**RSAT**). You can install or uninstall roles and features on a physical computer, virtual machine, or on an offline **virtual hard disk** (**VHD**).

Installing roles and features using the Server Manager

To install roles and features, follow these instructions:

1. Start **Server Manager** and select **Manage** and **Add Roles and Features** in the upper-right corner:

2. The **Add Roles and Features Wizard** starts with **Before you begin** page. This contains initial information and helpful advice. If you want to skip this page in the future, tick **Skip this page by default** checkbox.

3. On the **Select installation type** page, select which installation type you want to perform, **Role-based or feature-based installation** or **Remote Desktop Services installation**:

4. The **Server Selection** tab gives you the option either to select a server or to select a virtual hard disk on which to install roles and features. The Server Pool contains a list of servers that have been added using **Add Servers** button in Server Manager. You can choose either local server or any of the discovered and listed servers in the Server Pool list. That way, you can install roles and features on a local server or on any remote server using the wizard on a local server. Although you cannot perform installations on multiple servers at once, you can do that easily using PowerShell:

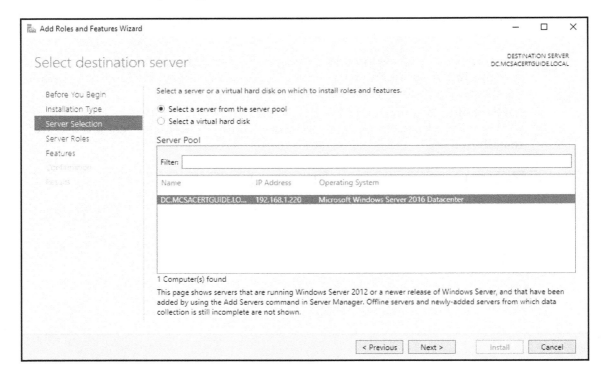

5. After selecting the server and hitting **Next**, the **Server Roles** page appears. On this page, you can select one or more server roles to install:

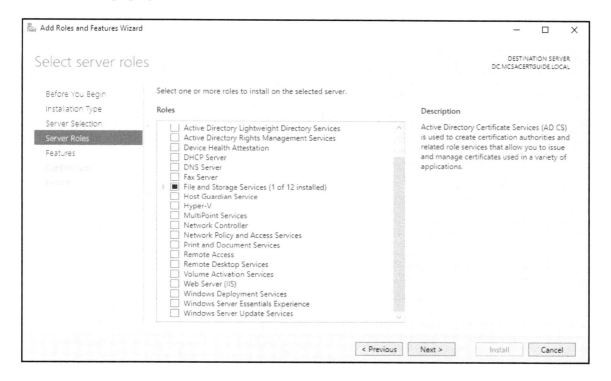

Some roles, such as the **Files and Storage Services** role, have role Services, which provide additional role functionalities and enhancements:

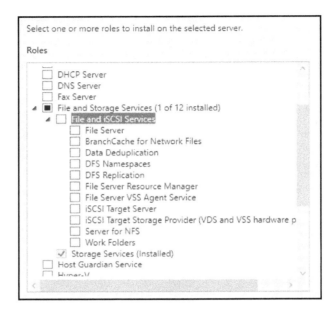

A window will appear if a role has any dependencies that also need to be installed.

The next page is the **Features** page, which allows you to select one or more features to install, along with any dependencies they may have:

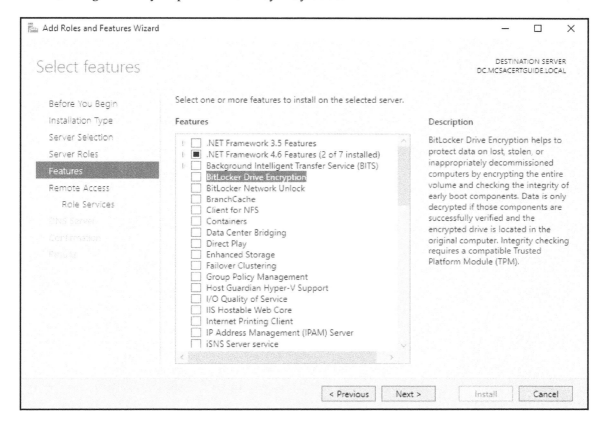

If the roles that you have selected support additional services, you will be able to select them on the **Role Services** page:

For example, **Remote Access** role selected in the previous screenshot has three individually selectable components, or **Role Services: DirectAccess and VPN (RAS)**, **Routing**, and **Web Application Proxy**.

Each of the selected roles and features might have their own configuration page. After performing eventual configuration tasks and entering required information, the **Confirm installation selections** button appears.

If the server requires a restart after installation, select this option, but ensure that the users are aware of possible interruptions in operations. The **Export configuration settings** button saves the steps performed by **Add Roles and Features Wizard** in an XML template file, which can be used later to perform identical installations using PowerShell.

If the Windows Server 2016 source files are incomplete or missing, the **Specify an alternate source path** option will tell the wizard the location of the `Install.wim` file that contains the required source files:

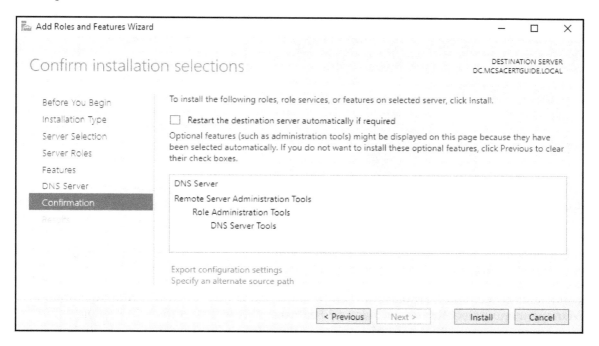

After clicking **Install**, you can close the wizard window without disturbing the installation. You can track its progress by clicking on the Notifications flag at the top of the **Server Manager** window:

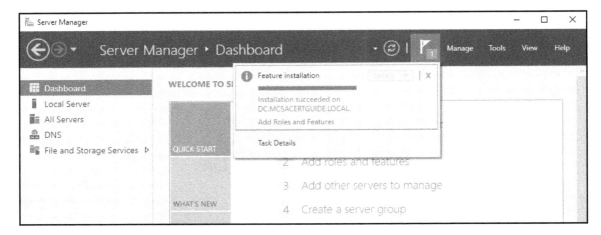

If the roles or features that you have installed require post-installation steps or additional configuration steps, the Notification flag will give you the relevant information and links.

Uninstalling roles and features is straightforward and simple. In **Server Manager**, under **Manage** menu, select **Remove Roles and Features**. This will start the wizard. Select the target server of the virtual hard disk, deselect the roles and feature that are no longer needed, and click **Remove** on the last screen. You can restart the server automatically as well.

Installing roles and features using Windows PowerShell

To install server roles and features on more than one server at the same time, or to script role and feature installations in more complex scenarios, using Server Manager is not practical, nor does it provide the desired functionality, such as managing multiple servers at once. This is where Windows PowerShell excels, controlling server with either GUI or Server Core version. PowerShell is a task-based command shell and scripting language developed by Microsoft for the purpose of configuration management and task automation. It is based on the .NET Framework, is open source, and can be installed on Windows, macOS, and Linux platforms.

To install server roles and features using Windows PowerShell, you need to run a PowerShell session with elevated user rights, unless you are installing them on a remote server.

To list roles and features that are available locally on a server, type `Get-WindowsFeature` or `Get-WindowsFeature -computerName <computer_name>`, where `<computer_name>` represents the name of the remote computer you are connecting to. The roles are listed first, followed by the features. In PowerShell terminology, the term *role* is not used, only *features*; cmdlets do not differentiate between the two. The following screenshot shows the output of the Windows PowerShell `Get-WindowsFeature` command:

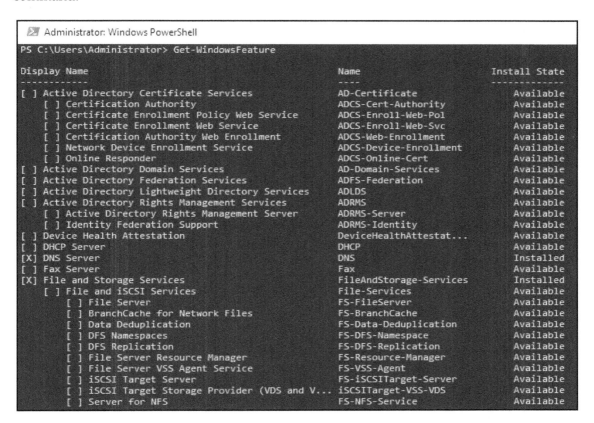

To install a server role or a feature type, enter the following command:

```
Install-WindowsFeature -Name <feature_name> -computerName <computer_name>
```

To install multiple roles and features, separate values using a comma. The management tools needed to manage installed roles and features will be also installed, and your computer will restart if required once the command completes. The following PowerShell command will install the DNS role and XPS Viewer onto a computer using FQDN SRV1.MCSAGUIDE.LOCAL:

```
Install-WindowsFeature -Name DNS,XPS-Viewer -ComputerName
srv1.mcsacertguide.local -IncludeManagementTools -Restart
```

To verify the installation, run the Get-WindowsFeature command or open **Server Manager**. On the **All Servers** page, right-click on a server and select **Add Roles and Features**.

If needed, list all currently installed features using Windows PowerShell on a target server with the Get-WindowsFeature command. To uninstall or remove roles and features, type the following command:

```
Uninstall-WindowsFeature -Name <feature_name> -computerName <computer_name>
-Restart.
```

The -Restart switch is not mandatory, but will initiate a computer restart if this is necessary to complete the removal process.

Installing and configuring Windows Server Core

Windows Server with a GUI is a fully-fledged server installation that is capable of supporting highly scalable, enterprise-grade workloads, but it also comes with a significant overhead and a burden: a GUI. Since servers are mostly managed remotely, especially in larger environments, having a GUI doesn't make much sense. The supporting files increase installation size, which makes patching and updating more complex and makes the server more vulnerable.

The solution to this problem was to introduce Server Core, which offered a significantly smaller footprint without the files that are required to support a GUI. Although some of the roles and features are not supported in Server Core, having a more secure server with less frequent updates is appealing. A typical Windows Server 2016 Datacenter installation with several roles installed can occupy between 5 and 10 GB of disk space. The Server Core installation, by contrast, could take up around 2 to 5 GB, while the Nano Server installation occupies around 200-500 MB.

Windows Server Core is the version of Windows Server 2016 that does not use graphical elements. Although this might sound like a disadvantage, it is actually quite the opposite.

User interface elements require additional files and hard disk space, they have more components, and they need updating more frequently. A web browser, for example, is not available in a Server Core installation, so all potential problems related to web browsers are eliminated. Overall, Server Core has a smaller number of files, it occupies less space, it needs less patching and updating, and it has a smaller security vulnerability footprint than its fancier graphical interface counterpart.

Setting up Windows Server Core uses same steps as setting up Windows Server with Desktop Experience, except that it is much faster, due to its smaller size.

When you start installing Windows Server 2016, as discussed previously, you can choose between Standard or Datacenter versions and whether or not you want a GUI. When you install Windows Server version 1709 and later, you have two options: **Windows Server Standard** or **Windows Server Datacenter**, as shown in the following screenshot:

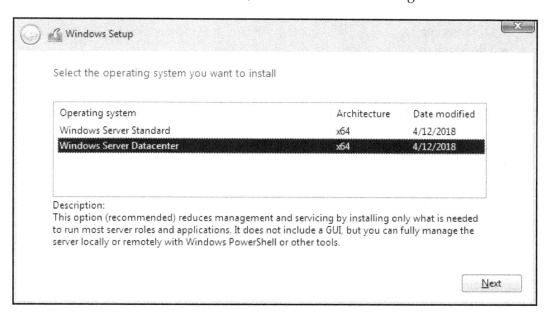

All the other installation steps are identical to those described in *Installing Windows Server 2016* section.

As there is no user interface in Server Core to interact with, you can manage a server using Windows PowerShell for local administration. Alternatively, you can use different tools for administering a server remotely, such as Server Manager, RSAT, Windows Admin Center, or Windows PowerShell.

Server Core supports the following server roles:

- Active Directory Certificate Services
- Active Directory Domain Services
- Active Directory Federation Services
- **Active Directory Lightweight Directory Services** (**AD LDS**)
- Active Directory Rights Management Server
- Device Health Attestation
- DHCP Server
- DNS Server
- File Services
- Host Guardian Services
- Hyper-V
- Network Controller
- Print and Document Services
- Routing and Remote Access Server
- Volume Activation Services
- Web Server
- Windows Server Essentials Experience
- Windows Server Update Services

Server Core supports the following features:

- .NET Framework 3.5 (includes .NET 2.0 and 3.0)
- .NET Framework 4.6
- ASP.NET 4.6
- TCP Port Sharing
- Background Intelligent Transfer Service (BITS)
- BitLocker Drive Encryption
- BranchCache

- Containers
- Failover clustering
- Group Policy Management
- **IP Address Management** (**IPAM**) server
- Directory Service Integration
- Routing service
- Network Load Balancing
- Telnet Client
- Windows Defender features
- Windows PowerShell
- Windows Server Backup
- WINS Server

Besides GUI elements and files, Server Core lacks the following features:

- Fax services
- Network Policy and Authentication Server
- Windows Deployment Services
- Remote Desktop Services roles (Connection Broker, Virtualization Host, Licensing)
- BITS
- Remote assistance
- Hyper-V Tools
- Many RSAT, RDS, and WDS features
- SMTP Server
- TFTP Client
- Biometric Framework
- Windows TIFF Filter
- Wireless networking
- XPS Viewer
- Accessibility tools
- No audio support
- No OOBE (out-of-box experience)

For a complete list of roles and features that are supported and those that are not, consult following resources:

- **Roles, Role Services, and Features included in Windows Server - Server Core:** https://docs.microsoft.com/en-us/windows-server/administration/server-core/server-core-roles-and-services
- **Roles, Role Services, and Features not in Windows Server - Server Core:** https://docs.microsoft.com/en-us/windows-server/administration/server-core/server-core-removed-roles

Although it is more secure, Server Core might not be the first option for some organizations. In Windows Server 2012 and Windows Server 2012 R2, you were able to shift between installing Server Core and a server with a GUI. In Windows Server 2016, this is no longer possible. Additionally, applications and services that previously relied on the GUI or other missing roles and features might not work with Server Core and might need further testing before servers are released in production.

Managing Windows Server installations

When Server Core starts, you will see the following screenshot. As there is no GUI, here in the console window is where you perform local management of a server:

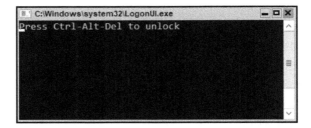

Typically, Server Core is managed remotely, but it has tools that are built for managing a server locally as well. You can manage Windows Server Core using Server Manager, Windows PowerShell, a remote server, or RSAT.

The typical first steps you need to take to configure and manage Server Core usually involve the following:

1. Establishing connectivity—setting IP address, subnet mask, and default gateway
2. Configuring the firewall
3. Activating the server
4. Configuring the name resolution
5. Joining a domain
6. Enabling PowerShell remoting and remote access

After Server Core has been installed, the first task is to change the administrator password.

 If you close the Command Prompt window by accident, don't panic! You don't have to restart the server to get the console back. Press the *Ctrl + Alt + Del* key combination and the command window will return.

Windows PowerShell is one of the most common management tools for local management, and especially for remote management. Understandably, these commands also work with other server versions, not just with Server Core. To start a PowerShell session, type `powershell` at a command prompt.

The `Get-NetIPConfiguration` command retrieves the current network configuration, including network interfaces, IP addresses, and DNS servers. The `Get-NetIPAddress` command displays the current IP address configuration, including IPv4, IPv6, and IP addresses with which these addresses are associated.

The following command shows the IP configuration information for all configured network interfaces on a computer, including loopback interfaces, virtual interfaces, and disconnected interfaces:

```
Get-NetIPConfiguration -all
```

The following command gathers configuration information for specific network interface:

```
Get-NetIPConfiguration -InterfaceIndex 9
```

The `Get-NetIPInterface` command shows information about an IP interface, while the `Set-NetIPInterface` command can be used to modify an IP interface.

To configure a server with a static IP address, use the New-NetIPAddress command. This sets a static IP address, a subnet mask, and a default gateway to an interface with an index value of 7:

```
New-NetIPaddress -InterfaceIndex 7 -IPAddress 192.168.10.20 -PrefixLength
24 -DefaultGateway 192.168.10.1
```

To configure a DNS client server address with values of 192.168.10.2 and 192.168.10.3, type the following command:

```
Set-DNSClientServerAddress -InterfaceIndex 7 -ServerAddresses 192.168.10.2,
192.168.10.3
```

To join a computer to a workgroup or a domain, use the Add-Computer cmdlet:

```
Add-Computer -ComputerName "SRVCORE" -LocalCredential "SRVCORE\AdminLocal"
-DomainName "MCSACERTGUIDE.LOCAL" -Credential
MCSACERTGUIDE.LOCAL\AdminDomain -Restart -Force
```

This command adds the SRVCORE computer to the MCSACERTGUIDE.LOCAL domain and uses the LocalCredential parameter to supply a user account that has permission to connect to the SRVCORE computer. The -Credential parameter specifies a user account that has permission to join computers to the domain, while the -Restart parameter restarts a computer after a join operation completes. Finally, the -Force parameter suppresses any user confirmation messages.

To activate a server, simply use the slmgr.vbs -ipk <product_key> command, followed by the slmgr.vbs -ato command. If the activation is successful, no additional messages are displayed. The -ipk option installs the product key supplied in <product_key>, replacing any existing product keys. The -ato option performs operating system activation.

Instead of using PowerShell, Server Core and a server with a GUI can be managed via command-line commands.

The commands shown in the following tables are the most commonly used commands for specific task groups.

Configuration and installation commands are displayed in the following table:

Task	Command
Set the local administrative password	`net user administrator *`
Join a computer to a domain	`netdom join %computername% /domain:<domain> /userd:<domain\username> /passwordd:*`
Remove a computer from a domain	`netdom remove <computername>`
Add a user to the local administrators group	`net localgroup Administrators /add <domain\username>`
Remove a user from the local administrators group	`net localgroup Administrators /delete <domain\username>`
Add a user to the local computer	`net user <domain\username> * /add`
Add a group to the local computer	`net localgroup <group name> /add`
Change to a static IP address	`netsh interface ipv4 set address name <ID from interface list> source=static address=<preferred IP address> gateway=<gateway address>`
Set a static DNS address	`netsh interface ipv4 add dnsserver name=<name or ID of the network interface card> address=<IP address of the primary DNS server> index=1`
Enter a product key	`slmgr.vbs -ipk <product key>`
Activate the server	`slmgr.vbs -ato`

Frequent commands used to display and configure networking, addressing, and IPSEC configuration are listed in the next table:

Task	Command
Display or modify IPSEC configuration	`netsh ipsec`
Display or modify IP to physical address translation	`arp`
Display or configure the local routing table	`route`
View or configure DNS server settings	`nslookup`
Display protocol statistics and current TCP/IP network connections	`netstat`
Display protocol statistics and current TCP/IP connections using NetBIOS over TCP/IP (NBT)	`nbtstat`
Display hops for network connections	`pathping`
Trace hops for network connections	`tracert`

A table of useful and frequently used commands to manage services and processes can be found here:

Task	Command
List the running services	`sc query` or `net start`
Start a service	`sc start <service name>` or `net start <service name>`
Stop a service	`sc stop <service name>` or `net stop <service name>`
Retrieve a list of running applications and associated processes	`tasklist`
Start Task Manager	`taskmgr`

Essential disk and file system commands are listed in the next table:

Task	Command
Manage disk partitions	`diskpart`
Manage volume mount points	`mountvol`
Defragment a volume	`defrag`
Convert a volume to the NTFS file system	`convert <volume letter> /FS:NTFS`
Compact a file	`compact`
Take ownership of a file or folder	`icacls`

Windows Server Core and a server with a GUI can be managed using the Server Configuration Tool by typing in the `sconfig.cmd` command. The following screen shows the Server Configuration menu after executing the `sconfig.cmd` command:

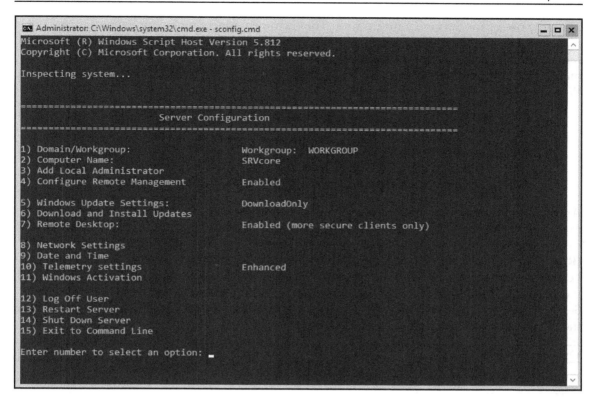

The Server Configuration Tool allows you to perform initial server configuration, such as setting the IP address of a network adapter and information about DNS servers, setting the date and time, activating Windows, and enabling a remote desktop or configuring remote management. Additionally, it allows you to join a server to a workgroup or a domain, change a computer's name, add local administrators, configure Windows update settings, and manage telemetry settings.

The purpose of the Server Configuration Tool is to provide a quick way to configure a server. Following this, a server will be managed using Server Manager, PowerShell remoting, or other scripting and remote management tools that offer more complex management functionality. It is also handy for administrators who are not well versed in Windows PowerShell.

 The Server Configuration Tool should not replace knowledge of Windows PowerShell. Windows PowerShell is a standard for task automation and configuration management and might be heavily tested, not only in exams in the *Microsoft Certified Solutions Associate: Windows Server 2016* track, but also in all exams in the *Microsoft Certified Professional* program.

Another common way to manage servers is to use the Server Manager. This is a management console that enables centralized management of both local and remote servers in a secure and a convenient way, without the need to configure **Remote Desktop Protocol (RDP)** ports. The Server Manager is already a functional part of Windows Server 2016. To be able to manage current and older server versions, certain software components are required. The following table shows Windows Server operating systems prior to Windows Server 2016 and corresponding software components that are required to be able to manage them through Server Manager:

Operating system	Required software components
Windows Server 2012 R2 or Windows Server 2012	• .NET Framework 4.6 • Windows Management Framework 5.0
Windows Server 2008 R2	• .NET Framework 4.5 • Windows Management Framework 4.0
Windows Server 2008	• .NET Framework 4 • Windows Management Framework 3.0

Server Manager is also a part of RSAT for Windows 10. The Windows Server operating system RSAT, supports depends on a server operating system the RSAT is installed on. Consult the following table to find out which version of Server Manager is compatible with which operating system:

Source operating system of the Server Manager that RSAT is installed on	Target operating system		
	Windows Server 2016	Windows Server 2012 R2	Windows Server 2012
Windows 10 or Windows Server 2016	Compatible	Compatible	Compatible
Windows 8.1 or Windows Server 2012 R2	Not Compatible	Compatible	Compatible
Windows 8 or Windows Server 2012	Not Compatible	Not Compatible	Compatible

To be able to manage remote servers using the Server Manager, you first need to add them to the list of managed servers. Under the **Manage** menu, select **Add Servers**:

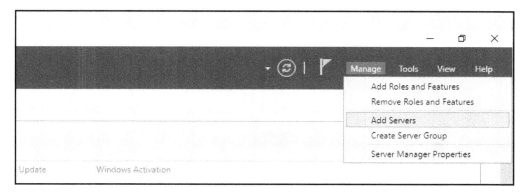

An **Add Servers** window will open. The left part of the window contains three tabs that will help you add new servers. If the computers you want to add to the list are members of a domain, choose the corresponding domain under **Location** to search for them. The **Operating System** option allows you to narrow the search to a particular operating system version, while **Name (CN)** allows you to enter a name or part of a name to filter the search even further:

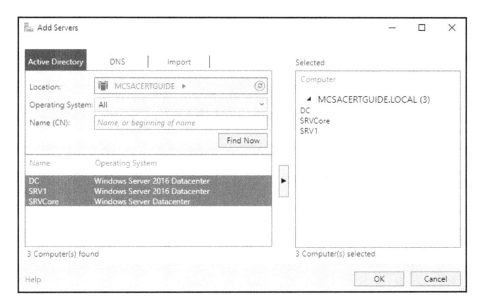

Clicking **Find Now** performs the search and the results pane will show the results. Selecting one or more computers and clicking on the arrow between the panes puts selected servers on a list of servers that will be added to the Server Manager:

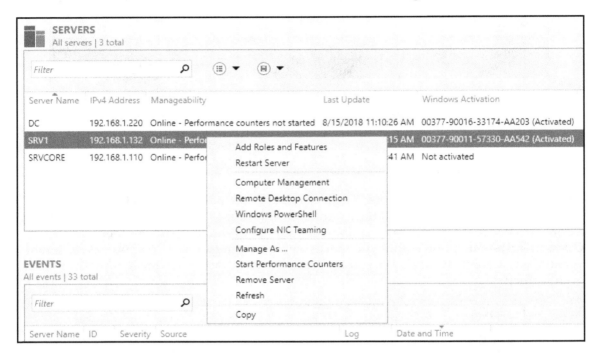

Once the servers are on the **All Servers** list, you can see basic information about them, including server name, IPv4 address, manageability status, time and date of the last update refresh, and activation information. Right-clicking on a server shows you the context menu available for that server. Configuring and managing multiple servers, as well as Server Core installations, is much easier from a centralized location. You can carry out several different actions, including monitoring server performance, establishing a remote desktop connection, rebooting a server, or starting the **Add Roles and Features Wizard**.

Installing and configuring Nano Server

Nano Server is a small footprint server designed for remote administration that targets data center and private cloud deployments. It was designed to have a significantly smaller installation than regular Windows Server operating systems, with a higher speed of deployment and a higher level of security and manageability.

Similar reasoning from a previous section, where we discussed Windows Server Core, can be applied to Nano Server. What if we could have an even smaller server that could be deployed faster and have even shorter servicing times? Nano Server was introduced in 2016, at the same time as Windows Server 2016. It seemed that it would be widely embraced, but the reality was quite different. Although Nano Server had a lot of potential, its small number of elements meant it was less popular than anticipated. The resemblance to Server Core was too close, and while developers needed a smaller server, administrators and IT professionals asked for better hardware and software support, which in turn defeated the purpose of Nano Server:

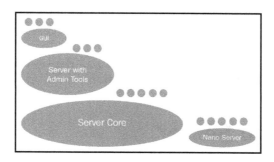

The graphic shows various Windows Server components and their relative sizes, such as the **GUI**, **Server Core**, and **Nano Server**, with its significantly smaller size compared to the Windows Server edition with a GUI.

Two years after Nano Server was introduced, the Windows Server engineering team revealed that support for some of the workloads would be removed from Nano Server and that it would now serve primarily as a container image, while Server Core would be the recommended server version for infrastructure deployment. Microsoft has since shifted their focus more to containers, and Nano Server is not going away anytime soon. The Nano Server is still on the list of topics that are tested in Windows Server 2016 exams, so we will cover the basics in this chapter.

You're most likely to use Nano Server as DNS server, a web or **Internet Information Services** (**IIS**) server, or as a host for a custom-built application. Nano Server supports only 64-bit workloads and does not support several services, which is no surprise due to its small size. There is no support for the following:

- Active Directory domain controller role
- Group Policy
- NIC teaming, except **Switch-Embedded Teaming** (**SET**)
- System Center Data Protection Manager or System Center Configuration Manager

- Local log on capability
- NIC Teaming
- Internet Proxy

This list is not definitive and we encourage you to check the Nano Server documentation for the most recent information.

Follow the link for the official Microsoft documentation on Nano Server in Windows Server 2016: `https://docs.microsoft.com/en-us/windows-server/get-started/getting-started-with-nano-server`.

Recently, Microsoft announced that from Windows Server version 1709, Nano Server will be available only as a container base OS image. This means that you will only be able to run Nano Server as a container in a container host. You will not be able to install it on a physical server, as many roles will be removed, such as Hyper-V support and driver support.

Deploying Nano Server

After downloading and extracting Windows Server 2016 ISO image, navigate to the folder containing the installation files. You will notice that the `NanoServer` folder contains several files, including the `NanoServer.wim` image; the `NanoServerImageGenerator` folder, which contains scripts that are used to build Nano Server images; and the `Packages` folder, which contains files that enhance the Nano Server installation with roles and features such as DNS, IIS, and failover clustering.

On the **Nano Server Image Builder Download** page, `https://www.microsoft.com/en-us/download/details.aspx?id=54065`, download **Nano Server Image Builder**, which will assist you in building the Nano Server image file. Nano Server Image Builder is a graphical interface tool for creating Nano Server images, bootable USB drives, and ISO files. Nano Server Image Builder can also automate your installation of Nano Server and create reusable PowerShell scripts. It is supported on Windows 10, Windows 8.1, Windows Server 2012 R2, and Windows Server 2016.

Nano Server Image Builder requires the Windows **Assessment and Deployment Kit (ADK)**, which can be installed and downloaded from the following page: `https://docs.microsoft.com/en-us/windows-hardware/get-started/adk-install`.

Before starting Nano Server Image Builder, you must install two components from the Windows ADK: **Deployment Tools** and **Windows Preinstallation Environment (Windows PE).**

To create a new Nano Server image, we will outline the procedure, along with additional explanation of the steps:

1. After starting **Nano Server Image Builder**, two scenario options are available to select, **Create a new Nano Server image** and **Create bootable USB media**. You will need to know the name of the server or servers to which you will be deploying an image. You will also need to have source installation files that will be used to create the Nano Server image and any required drivers ready. The **Select scenario** screen looks as follows:

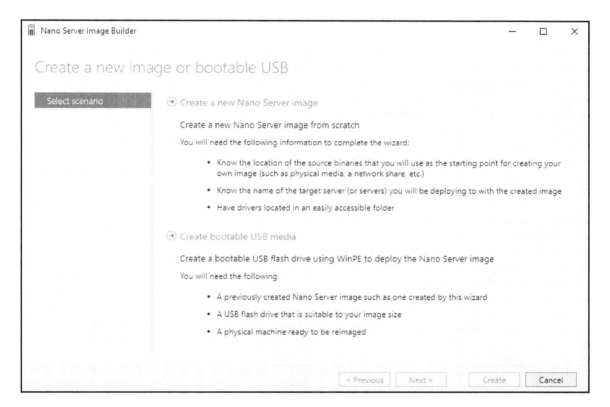

2. In the first steps of the wizard, select a location for the Windows Server media source, either in a local folder or on a shared network. Accept the license agreement and choose the deployment type, either to a virtual machine image or a physical machine image:

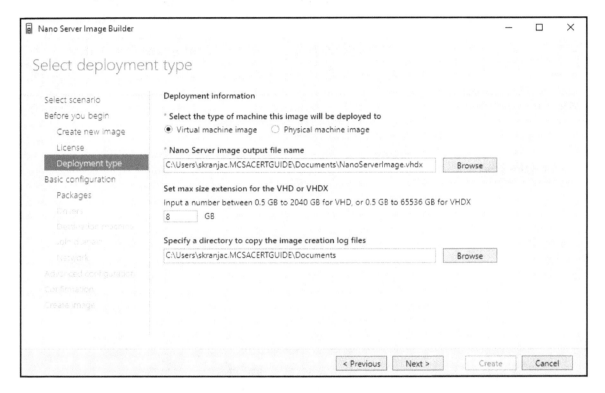

3. In the **Nano Server image output file name** option, ensure that you choose either VHD or VHDX, as this will determine the generation of a virtual machine that is created by the wizard, either **Generation one** or **Generation two**.

4. Next, you can choose whether the Nano Server edition is **Datacenter** or **Standard**. You can also add components that will be included in the image:

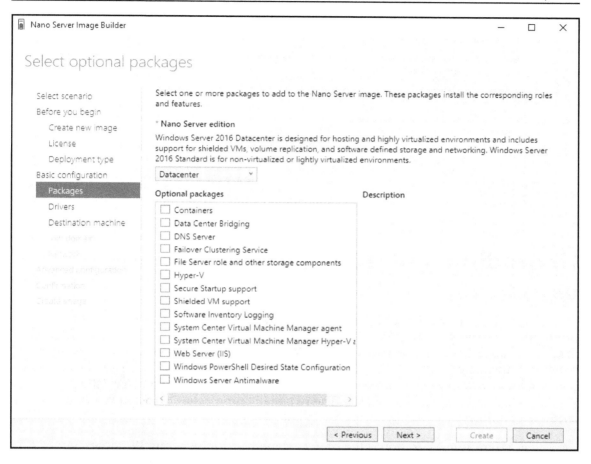

You can also add any drivers that you need to support planned workloads, join Nano Server to a domain, and set up network configurations such as PowerShell remoting, Window Remote Management, VLAN IDs, network address, subnet, gateway addresses, and more.

5. At the end, an advanced dialog prompts you either to create a Nano Server image or to choose advanced settings including debugging methods, remote options, servicing packages, or embedding additional files or scripts in the image.

Nano Server Image Builder is a graphical tool and wizard that creates a Nano Server image file. It is, however, limited with regard to automating tasks, speeding up deployments, and creating multiple images. This is why Microsoft included Nano Server Image Generator, a PowerShell module located in the `NanoServer` folder, in Windows Server 2016 ISO file.

Three PowerShell cmdlets are available:

- `New-NanoServerImage`: Creates a Nano Server installation image
- `Edit-NanoServerImage`: Modifies a Nano Server installation image
- `Get-NanoServerImage`: Gets available packages for a Nano Server installation image

Upgrading and migrating servers and workloads

In most cases, Windows Server 2016 will be deployed in environments that are already in production, meaning existing Windows Server editions prior to Windows Server 2016 will most likely already be on the hardware. Obviously, you will eventually need to perform a bare metal installation of Windows Server 2016 on some computers. It is also possible that you will need to change to a different Windows Server 2016 edition on an existing Windows Server 2016 installation, too. The two main approaches to install Windows Server 2016 are as follows:

- **Migration**: Migration is the preferred method for installing Windows Server 2016 and involves two computers. The first computer already runs a version of Windows Server, from which roles are moved. The second computer has a freshly installed Windows Server version, to which roles are moved.

    The term **migration** is not specific just to Windows Server 2016, but to any operating system version and it always involves two computers. Therefore, migration can be defined as moving one or more roles or features and their data from one computer to another computer, not upgrading that role or feature on a same computer. In this way, newly installed computer does not inherit bad configuration data, or old and unnecessary files from the old computers. This is the way that Microsoft recommends that you move existing workloads to a computer running the most recent Windows Server 2016 version.

- **Upgrade**: While migration involves two computers, upgrading only involves one computer. If you have a Windows Server machine configured and running but you want to keep the existing hardware, configuration, and installed applications, you should choose to do an upgrade instead of a migration. This process involves copying newer installation files to an existing, usually older, Windows Server installation version. This limits available upgrade options. Not every combination of older and newer Windows Server versions is supported, so you have to take supported upgrade paths into consideration.

The following table lists supported upgrade paths from older Windows Server versions to Windows Server 2016 version:

Upgrade from version	Upgrade to version
Windows Server 2012 Standard	Windows Server 2016 Standard or Datacenter
Windows Server 2012 Datacenter	Windows Server 2016 Datacenter
Windows Server 2012 R2 Standard	Windows Server 2016 Standard or Datacenter
Windows Server 2012 R2 Datacenter	Windows Server 2016 Datacenter
Hyper-V Server 2012 R2	Hyper-V Server 2016 (using the Cluster OS Rolling Upgrade feature)
Windows Server 2012 R2 Essentials	Windows Server 2016 Essentials
Windows Storage Server 2012 Standard	Windows Storage Server 2016 Standard
Windows Storage Server 2012 Workgroup	Windows Storage Server 2016 Workgroup
Windows Storage Server 2012 R2 Standard	Windows Storage Server 2016 Standard
Windows Storage Server 2012 R2 Workgroup	Windows Storage Server 2016 Workgroup

Transitioning to a newer Windows Server 2016 operating system is also not possible the following circumstances:

- Upgrading from Windows Server with a GUI to Windows Server Core edition. However, in prior versions, transitioning from Windows Server 2012 (or R2) Core edition to Windows Server 2012 (or R2) with a GUI is possible. After transitioning, you can proceed to upgrade.

- Upgrading from Windows Server Core edition to Windows Server with a GUI. Like in the previous scenario, prior to upgrading, transitioning from Windows Server 2012 (or R2) with a GUI to Windows Server 2012 (or R2) Core edition is possible, following which, upgrading is possible.

- Upgrading from one language to another, for example from an Italian edition of Windows Server 2012 to a Swedish version of Windows Server 2016.

- Upgrading from a licensed version of Windows Server to an evaluation version of an operating system.

- Upgrading from a 32-bit to a 64-bit architecture.

Converting from an evaluation version of a Windows Server operating system to a licensed Windows Server 2016 version is possible. To check whether the operating system is an evaluation version, open **System and Security** and then click on **System** in the **Control Panel**. **View Details** will show you the license information. Alternatively, from an Command Prompt, type `slmgr.vbs /dlv` or `DISM /online /Get-CurrentEdition` to check the edition information. After that, type `DISM /online /Set-Edition:<edition ID> /ProductKey:XXXXX-XXXXX-XXXXX-XXXXX-XXXXX /AcceptEula` to convert an evaluation version of an operating system to a retail version.

License conversion

Converting a release of an operating system to a different release of the same version is called a **license conversion**.

The following table shows license conversion paths:

Convert from	Convert to
Windows Server 2016 Standard	Windows Server 2016 Datacenter
Windows Server 2016 Essentials	Windows Server 2016 Standard
Windows Server 2016 Standard (evaluation)	Windows Server 2016 Standard (retail)Windows Server 2016 Datacenter (retail)

Automatic Virtual Machine Activation (AVMA)

AVMA has existed since Windows Server 2012. It is a feature that automatically activates virtual machines on Windows Server 2016 Hyper-V hosts if the host operating system is activated. The activation works even in disconnected systems. During activation, special AVMA activation keys must be used to activate virtual machines.

The following AVMA keys can be used for Windows Server 2016:

Edition	AVMA key
Datacenter	TMJ3Y-NTRTM-FJYXT-T22BY-CWG3J
Standard	C3RCX-M6NRP-6CXC9-TW2F2-4RHYD
Essentials	B4YNW-62DX9-W8V6M-82649-MHBKQ

Key Management Services (KMS) activation

KMS activation uses a client-server model for client or server operating system activation. The KMS service can reside on a client or operating system; it does not have to be a dedicated server. The KMS service can coexist with other services without operational issues.

A computer that has the KMS service installed is called the KMS server or the KMS host, while computers that connect to a KMS host to perform an activation are called KMS clients. Only KMS clients that reside on the same network as the KMS host can connect to that KMS host and perform an activation.

You can install the KMS host on a virtual or physical computer running any of the following operating systems: Windows 10, Windows Server 2016, Windows Server 2012 R2, Windows 8.1, or Windows Server 2012. If the KMS service is installed on a client operating system, only client operating systems can be activated, so a KMS host installed on Windows 10 or Windows 8.1 cannot activate Windows Server editions. A single KMS host can support an unlimited number of KMS clients and it is recommended that you have at least two KMS hosts in a larger environment in case one activation server becomes unavailable.

A KMS host activates KMS clients based on a minimum number of activation requests, or the threshold level. The KMS clients are activated in bulk. The threshold level for server operating systems and Microsoft Office volume editions is five, while the threshold level for client operating systems is 25. The threshold levels also apply to the period in which clients submit requests for activation. This period is 30 days and is applicable to the 50 most recent contacts.

Summary

In this chapter, we learned about the requirements for and installation methods of various different Windows Server 2016 editions. We then learned to how install Windows Server 2016 features and roles using Server Manager and Windows PowerShell. Next, we explored the install and configure of Windows Server Core and learned how to manage Windows Server installations using various tools. We have also seen how to install and configure Nano Server, a lightweight and compact Windows Server edition. Finally, we showed how to upgrade and migrate servers and workloads, and the differences between migration and upgrading, as well as operating system activation.

In the next chapter you will learn about creating, managing, and maintaining Windows images for deployment, planning for virtualization, and assessing hardware and software environment using Microsoft Assessment and Planning Toolkit.

Questions

To enhance your studies and to check your knowledge and understanding, please answer the following questions:

1. You purchased the following hardware:

Computer	Characteristics
SRV1	3 GHz 64-bit CPU, SLAT, DEP, 512 MB RAM
SRV2	5 GHz, 32-bit CPU, SLAT, DEP, 512 GB RAM
SRV3	6 GHz, 32-bit CPU, DEP, 512 GB RAM
SRV4	4 GHz, 64-bit CPU, SLAT, DEP, 128 GB RAM

Which computer or computers are capable of running the Hyper-V role? Choose all applicable answers.

   1. SRV1
   2. SRV2
   3. SRV3
   4. SRV4

2. Which of the following features are exclusive to Windows Server 2016 Datacenter Edition?
   1. Virtual machine disk and state encryption
   2. Software-Defined Networking
   3. Host Guardian Hyper-V Service
   4. Windows Server Containers
   5. Storage Spaces Direct

3. To which destinations does Server Manager support installing roles and fatures?
   1. WIM files
   2. VHD files
   3. Server pools
   4. ISO files

4. Which Windows PowerShell command installs a Windows Server 2016 role?
    1. `Set-WindowsFeature`
    2. `Get-WindowsFeature`
    3. `Install-WindowsFeature`
    4. `Get-MsolRole`

5. Which two commands do you need to use to activate Windows Server Core using a product key?
    1. `slmgr.vbs -dli`
    2. `slmgr.vbs -ato`
    3. `slmgr.vbs -dlv`
    4. `slmgr.vbs -dti`
    5. `slmgr.vbs -ipk`

6. Which two commands will join a server to a domain?
    1. `Set-MsolDomain`
    2. `netdom`
    3. `Join-Path`
    4. `Add-Computer`

7. You want to check whether the version of Windows Server is an evaluation version. If it is an evaluation version, you want to convert it to a retail version. Which commands should you use?
    1. `slmgr.vbs`
    2. `sc query`
    3. `sconfig.cmd`
    4. `dism.exe`

8. You need to install a server operating system that supports the following features:
    1. Active Directory Domain Controller
    2. DNS
    3. DHCP
    4. Group Policy

Which Windows Server 2016 Editions should you choose?

1. Windows Server 2016 Standard
2. Windows Server 2016 Datacenter
3. Windows Server Core
4. Nano Server

9. You have purchased 100 new servers. You plan to install and activate Windows Server 2016 Standard and Microsoft Office 2016 Volume Edition on a group of 20 servers, every week. You plan to use KMS for server activation. You notice that the servers fail to activate the Windows Server operating system and Microsoft Office. What should you do? Choose all the correct answers:
   1. Activate Microsoft Office 2016 using a product key
   2. Use Windows Server 2016 Datacenter instead of Windows Server 2016 Standard
   3. Activate servers in groups of 25
   4. Install Windows Server and activate servers every two weeks
   5. Activate computers in groups of 5

10. You want to change the existing Windows Server 2016 Standard installation to the Windows Server 2016 Datacenter Edition. What should you do?
    1. Migration
    2. Upgrading
    3. License conversion
    4. Bare metal installation

Further reading

To enhance your studies, consult these online resources for additional content:

- **Getting started with Windows Server 2016**: `https://docs.microsoft.com/en-us/windows-server/get-started/server-basics`
- **Windows Server Installation and Upgrade**: `https://docs.microsoft.com/en-us/windows-server/get-started/installation-and-upgrade`
- **Install Nano Server**: `https://docs.microsoft.com/en-us/windows-server/get-started/getting-started-with-nano-server`
- **Install Server Core**: `https://docs.microsoft.com/en-us/windows-server/get-started/getting-started-with-server-core`
- **Install Server with Desktop Experience**: `https://docs.microsoft.com/en-us/windows-server/get-started/getting-started-with-server-with-desktop-experience`

Windows Server Imaging and Deployment

2

In the second chapter of this book, we will look at Windows Server imaging tools, which can greatly reduce the time required to install Windows Server 2016 on multiple computers at once. We will take a look at what we need to deploy Windows Server in virtualized environments and examine the key points to consider when planning for Windows Server virtualization. We will then address how we can manage Windows Server 2016 images, apply updates, and install roles and features in offline images. Finally, we will learn how Windows PowerShell and the **Deployment Image Servicing and Management (DISM)** tool can help us manage Windows Server images.

In this chapter, we will cover the following topics:

- Assessment and planning
- Working with images
- Updating images

Technical requirements

In this chapter, we will use the following software:

- Windows Server 2016
- **Microsoft Assessment and Planning Toolkit** (**MAPT**)

Assessment and planning

When planning for virtualization, correctly assessing all infrastructure components is crucial for successfully completing migration projects. Only by having a complete and detailed picture of the entire infrastructure will we be able to get a stable virtual environment and workload operations.

Planning for Windows Server virtualization

Installing Windows Server 2016 is an easy process, and is far simpler than older editions. In a corporate environment, however, a server administrator or an IT professional is likely to have more than one server and, as simple as the installation process may be, it is time-consuming and inefficient to install one server at a time. Individuals and companies may also have different needs for installing a new operating system; there are decisions to be made regarding whether we want a client operating system or a server operating system, and whether we are in a corporate environment and require a massive deployment, or whether we are in a smaller company, office, or home for small, individual deployments. For this reason, Microsoft has developed multiple options for installing new operating systems.

Before getting into the details of the deployment and the various deployment programs and methods, let's take a look at virtualization. Today, we have more flexibility in the deployment of operating systems, as virtualization is more accessible and affordable than ever, not only for IT professionals and developers within large companies with huge data centers, but also for individuals. All you need is a credit card and, in less than a minute, you can have an operating system deployed.

But what is virtualization? Virtualization is essentially an abstraction. It refers to simply hiding or changing the reality of something from someone. Virtualization in the IT domain is the abstraction of physical hardware resources from a software program, which, in our case, is the operating system. In a nutshell, a hypervisor is fooling (or abstracting) the real hardware in such a way that the operating system thinks it is installed on real hardware.

There are many different types of virtualization, which we will take a brief look at here:

- **Server virtualization** is the most popular and well-known type of virtualization, and is the type that's often associated with the Windows Server operating system in the form of a software known as Windows Server Hyper-V. With this type of virtualization, you are able to run multiple servers and client operating systems on a physical machine, enabling you to achieve greater operating system density.

- **Desktop virtualization** is a very similar virtualization type that exists on Windows 10. It enables you to run multiple operating systems and applications on a client version of Hyper-V.

- **Application virtualization** is another type of virtualization that enables you to run multiple versions of the same application on an operating system. A practical example would be the need to run an older version of an application and the newest version of the same application concurrently, which are otherwise incompatible. Microsoft **Application Virtualization** (**App-V**) is an example of application virtualization.

- **Presentation virtualization** is a very common virtualization type that you might already be using without you having any knowledge of this. The best-known representative of it in Windows operating systems is **Remote Desktop Services** (**RDS**), where the applications run on a remote computer and the screen content is transported to the client computer.

There are other types of virtualization, such as network, storage, memory, and data virtualization, but these are beyond the scope of this book.

There are many advantages to virtualization, including the following:

- Provisioning or deploying virtual servers is much faster than provisioning physical servers.

- Adding hardware to virtual machines is easier and faster than adding hardware to physical servers.

- Consolidating multiple virtual machines onto a physical server increases server density, thereby leading to a more efficient server resource utilization, since multiple low-resource virtual machines can run simultaneously on a physical host.

- Lower operational costs.

- Virtual machines are easier and faster to back up and easier and faster to restore.

- It is easier to set up virtual machines to run in an isolated environment for development and testing purposes than it is to set up physical machines. Virtual machines can also be managed more efficiently.

- Virtual machines can be transferred to other physical servers in case of maintenance or hardware failures.

- Virtualized environments can be easier to back up or migrate to the cloud for increased redundancy or as a disaster recovery solution.

The main points to consider when planning for the virtualization of server workloads are as follows:

- **CPU usage**: Low processor usage machines are good virtualization candidates since a large number of these servers can be co-hosted, such as DHCP or DNS servers. High processor usage servers might not be good virtualization candidates because their high CPU operations might impact other co-hosted virtual machines. High-CPU virtual machines can be set up in a way that limits their CPU usage at certain levels to leave enough host CPU time for other workloads. This, however, impacts the performance of the CPU-limited virtual machine, which, in turn, impacts either the users it is servicing or the services it is running, because it is not receiving sufficient resources to process information in a timely manner.

- **Memory requirements**: Servers with lower memory usage are, of course, better virtualization candidates than servers with high memory usage, such as email servers (exchange servers, for example). Memory-demanding servers can be virtualized too, but require a different approach, such as limiting the maximum or upper memory limits or disabling the Dynamic Memory feature.

- **Input/output traffic**: *Chatty* servers, or servers that generate a large amount of traffic, such as file servers, can easily eat up all the bandwidth to the point where inbound and outbound traffic to co-hosted virtual machines is too slow and unreliable. Some solutions include installing multiple network interface cards, or even dedicated network cards, or enabling **Quality of Service (QoS)**.

- **Disk or storage usage**: Servers with lower disk I/O requirements are generally easier to virtualize, while servers with high disk I/O workloads require more disks that are faster and special for distributed storage with specific storage protocols.

- **Special server workloads**: Servers requiring special hardware or that have higher hardware resource demands require more detailed planning and investment.

- **Combined workloads**: Adequate planning and care is needed when planning for combined workloads to assess all aspects of the co-hosted servers' behavior to avoid resource depletion, poor performance and, consequently, a poor user experience.

- **Order of virtualization or virtualization priority**: Identifying the order in which servers should be virtualized is an important point in virtualization planning and assessment. One way to assess or identify the order of computers to be virtualized is by looking at the computers' impact on production. Depending on your environment, your priority for virtualizing your workloads might be based on something else, such as the company's departments or branches. The following are examples of prioritization based on the criticality or production impact:

    - **Non-critical** servers are the best candidates and should be virtualized first. These include development, sandbox, or testing environment servers, technician machines, and non-production servers.
    - **Low-risk** machines, such as servers that could be shut down for a few hours, should be the next in line for virtualization, such as duplicate server workloads that are often found in backup systems, web farms, or high-availability systems.
    - **Medium-risk** servers, such as RADIUS, proxy, or gateway servers, are good candidates for the next virtualization wave. These servers might be taken offline during the night or low peak periods, although they might already have some sort of redundancy in place and could be virtualized without downtime.
    - **High-risk** servers running critical line-of-business applications, database servers, email, or identity directory servers are usually virtualized last.

As you can see, some workloads are more suitable for virtualization than others. These servers are easier to virtualize because there are no special requirements or architectural designs to follow. Servers that have higher disk activity, require more memory, or run processor-intensive workloads, are generally harder to virtualize because more factors must be considered and they require more detailed and more careful planning. These considerations are valid, regardless of which type of hypervisor you choose. Hyper-V in Microsoft Windows Server 2016 supports several Windows Server and Windows client guest operating systems, as well as a large number of Linux and FreeBSD distributions to run in virtual machines.

An up-to-date list of supported Windows guest operating systems for Hyper-V on Windows Server is located at https://docs.microsoft.com/en-us/windows-server/virtualization/hyper-v/supported-windows-guest-operating-systems-for-hyper-v-on-windows, while a list of supported Linux and FreeBSD virtual machines for Hyper-V on Windows can be found at https://docs.microsoft.com/en-us/windows-server/virtualization/hyper-v/supported-linux-and-freebsd-virtual-machines-for-hyper-v-on-windows.

When planning for a Hyper-V virtualization, you need to consider several factors, such as the virtual machine generation and supported devices, the operating systems supported, the virtual hard disk types used, and the virtual network types. More on Hyper-V supported guest operating systems, settings, and features will be discussed in later chapters.

Assessing virtualization workloads

The MAPT, or MAP Toolkit, is a free utility that's used to gather detailed information about infrastructure, both software and hardware, and will help you discover and determine the status and inventory of the servers, workstations, and applications that are installed on your machines. It helps you plan for local deployment, readiness assessments, virtualization, and migration to Microsoft Azure virtual machines. The data the MAP Toolkit gathers can also help you to assess device driver availability, making hardware upgrade recommendations much easier. It is important to note that the MAP Toolkit does not need a software agent to collect the data and perform assessment; instead, it takes advantage of the available technologies to perform these tasks, such as Active Directory Domain Services, Computer Browser Service, SSH, the Remote Registry Service, and Windows Management.

MAP Toolkit can assist you in four main areas:

- Software usage tracking
- Private and public cloud migration and virtualization capacity planning
- Software and hardware migration readiness assessments
- Discovery and inventory of computers and applications

MAP Toolkit recognizes the following operating systems and technologies:

- Windows XP to Windows 10
- Windows 2000 Server to Windows Server 2016
- VMware: vSphere, vCenter, ESX, ESXi, Server

- SQL Server
- Oracle
- Hyper-V
- System Center Configuration Manager
- Exchange Server
- SharePoint Server
- BizTalk Server
- Lync/Skype for Business Server 2015
- Office 2016 and previous versions
- Internet Explorer
- Office 2016 and previous versions
- Visual Studio 2010 and 2012, Premium and Ultimate versions
- Linux distributions
- Software ID Tags

MAP Toolkit includes the following components:

- `MAPSetup.exe`: An installation package containing the tool and the SQL LocalDB
- `readme_en.htm`: An information page about installing the MAP Toolkit, including installation prerequisites and known issues
- `MAP_Sample_Documents.zip`: Contains sample reports and proposals
- `MAP_Training_Kit.zip`: Contains a sample database and instructions for completing various exercises

The operating systems that are supported are as follows:

- Windows 10
- Windows 7 Service Pack 1
- Windows 8
- Windows 8 Enterprise
- Windows 8.1
- Windows Server 2008 R2 SP1
- Windows Server 2012
- Windows Server 2012 R2
- Windows Server 2016

The following minimum hardware configurations are the absolute minimum that are required:

- A dual-core 1.5 GHz processor.
- 2 GB of RAM.
- 1 GB of available disk space.
- A network adapter card.
- A graphics adapter that supports a resolution of 1,024 x 768 or higher. At 1,024 x 768, using a DPI setting of more than 100% is not supported. At higher resolutions, DPI settings higher than 100% are supported.

 The inventory, assessment, and reporting performances are based primarily on the speed of the CPU and the amount of available RAM.

The software requirements are as follows:

- One of the following operating systems:
    - Windows 10 (Professional, Enterprise, and Ultimate)
    - Windows 8.1 (Professional and Enterprise)
    - Windows 8 (Professional and Enterprise)
    - Windows 7 with Service Pack 1 (Professional, Enterprise, and Ultimate)
    - Windows Server 2012 R2
    - Windows Server 2012
    - Windows Server 2016
    - Windows Server 2008 R2 with Service Pack 1
- .NET Framework 4.5 (download from `http://go.microsoft.com/fwlink/?LinkId=389161`).
- By default, the MAP Toolkit will install SQL Server 2012 Express LocalDB during setup. The following versions of SQL Server are also supported: SQL Server 2012, SQL Server 2014, and SQL Server 2016. Before running the MAP Toolkit installer, you will need to create an instance named `MAPS`. The MAP Toolkit requires the collation order of the database engine to be set to `SQL_Latin1_General_CP1_CI_AS`.

All of these components are also available as separate downloads.

To initiate MAPT setup, execute the `MAPsetup.exe` file. The installation is straightforward and, after starting the program, the first thing you need to do is choose the existing database or create a new database that will be used to store the assessment data collected.

Each time you perform scanning, that is, collect inventory data, the Microsoft Assessment and Planning Toolkit appends the data collected to the current database. This means that you are able to complete the scanning and assessment of your infrastructure using multiple available utilities over a few days, for example. That way, you will get the most complete overview of your existing environment.

Creating a new database or having separate reports and inventories is useful, as this allows you to perform an assessment of logical, legal, or otherwise separate environments or when you want to repeat an assessment to refresh the collected data with decommissioned or upgraded machines. Don't forget to include the database naming convention so that you're able to differentiate between different assessments and inventories.

Once MAP Toolkit has the working database defined, the **Overview** screen shows the available assessment scenarios, such as **Cloud**, **Desktop**, **Server**, virtualization scenarios, and a few others, as shown in the following screenshot:

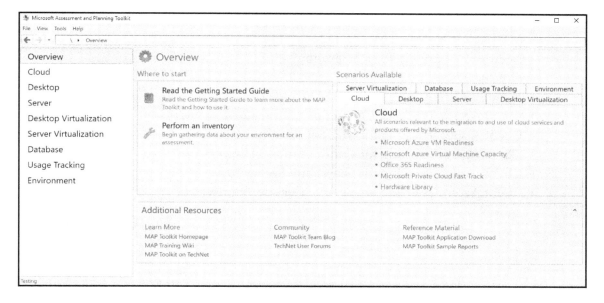

In the **Additional Resources** section, you can get help and additional information about MAPT. By going to the **MAP Toolkit Sample Reports** link, you can see how helpful and powerful MAP Toolkit is. The information that's gathered here is not just a mere list of computers found on a network, but a comprehensive report showing the client or server hardware configuration, the network configuration, possible reasons for not meeting the upgrade requirements, whether any hardware or software upgrades are required, device driver requirements, discovered applications, Volume License Agreement assessment details, SQL Server and database details, VMware migration details, and much more.

To perform a MAP scan, click on the **Perform an inventory** link on the **Overview** screen. The Inventory and Assessment Wizard will guide you through the assessment process and help you collect information using different inventory scenarios. The available setups are as follows:

- Windows computers
- Linux/UNIX computers
- VMware computers
- Active Devices and Users
- Exchange Server
- Endpoint Protection Server
- Lync Server
- **Software ID (SWID)** Tags
- SQL Server
- SQL Server with Database Details
- Microsoft Azure Platform Migration
- Oracle
- Windows Volume Licensing
- Client Access Tracking for Windows Server 2012 or later
- Client Access Tracking for SQL Server 2012 or later
- Client Access Tracking for Configuration Manager
- Client Access Tracking for SharePoint Server 2016
- Client Access Tracking for Remote Desktop Services

Each setup uses different methods to obtain information from network computers, including the **Lightweight Directory Access Protocol (LDAP)**, the **Simple Network Management Protocol (SNMP)**, and **Windows Management Instrumentation (WMI)**:

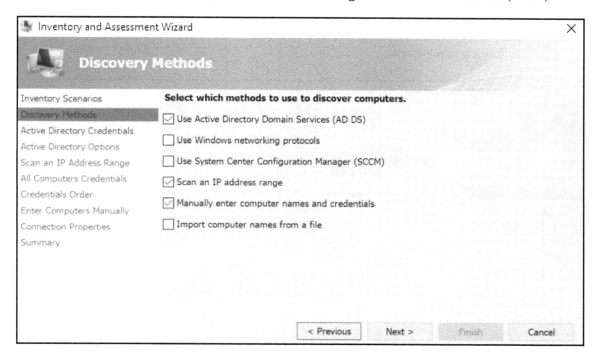

To discover the computers on the network, several methods are available:

- **Active Directory Domain Services (AD DS)**: This uses the LDAP to retrieve a list of computers from the domains, containers, and organizational units stored on the directory server. This requires the credentials of the domain account to be used to query the Active Directory Domain Services server, as shown in the following screenshot:

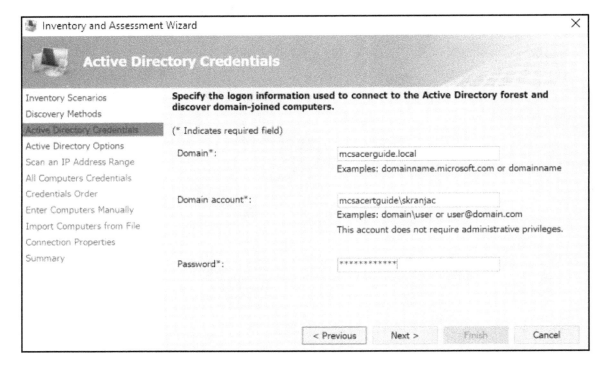

- **Windows Networking Protocols**: This helps to find computers in workgroups and in Windows NT 4.0-based domains using LAN Manager Application Programming Interfaces.
- **System Center Configuration Manager**: This enables you to discover computers that are managed by the System Center Configuration Manager and requires credentials of an account with access to the Configuration Manager WMI provider on the server you specify.

- **Scan an IP range**: This option allows you to define the start and end address of an IP address range that the Wizard will scan for computers. The Inventory and Assessment Wizard allows you to scan only 100,000 IP addresses at a time. If you want to scan IP ranges containing more IP addresses, you will need to perform multiple scans:

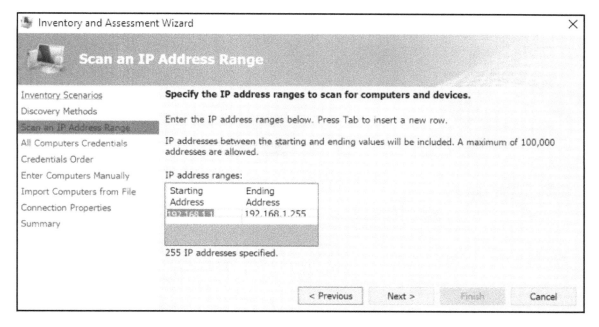

- **Manually enter computer names and credentials**: This is convenient when you have a few computers to discover. It requires you to enter your computer names or **fully qualified domain names** (**FQDN**) manually.
- **Import computer names from a file**: This method allows you to specify a list of up to 120,000 computer names to discover. The list can contain only computer names, NetBIOS names, IPv4 addresses, or FQDN, with each name on a new line without any special characters or delimiters, such as tabs, commas, or periods.

For all the technologies and platforms you have chosen in the previous steps, you need to supply the credentials that MAPT will use to connect to the specified computers.

The **Inventory and Assessment Wizard** that appears in the following screenshot shows all the credentials you have entered:

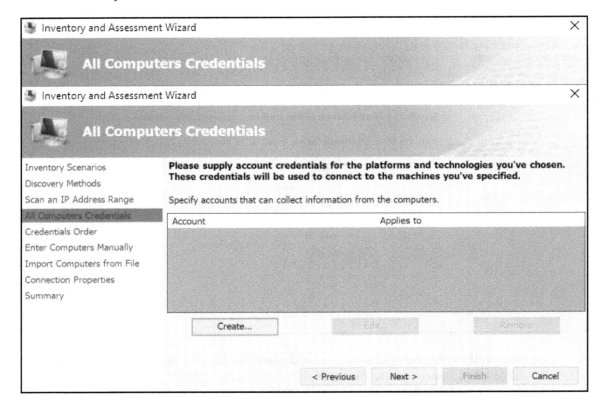

To create a credential entry, observe the following steps:

1. Click **Create...** and the **Account Entry** window will open, as shown in the following screenshot. Here, you specify the account name and the password to use, as well as one or more technologies MAPT will use to authenticate users in the scanning process:

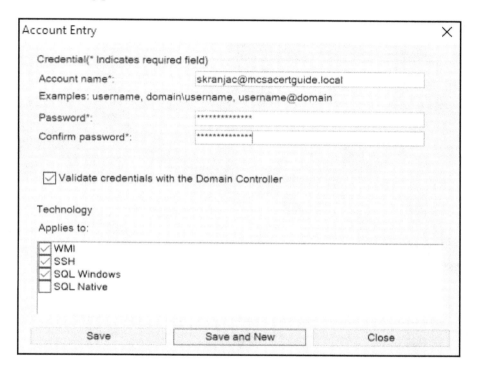

Some discovery methods do not require credentials for computer discovery and scanning. Others do, especially those that use WMI, SSH, or LDAP.

2. In the **All Computers Credentials Wizard** step, you create account entries that will be used to access each discovered computer.
3. The final step shows all configured wizard steps in one place so that you can review the configured settings, including possible configuration errors.

4. Click **Finish** and the computer scan will begin. The discovery progress is shown in a separate window. This includes information about discovered machines, currently inventoried and remaining machines, and the object count for the chosen collectors, as shown in the following screenshot:

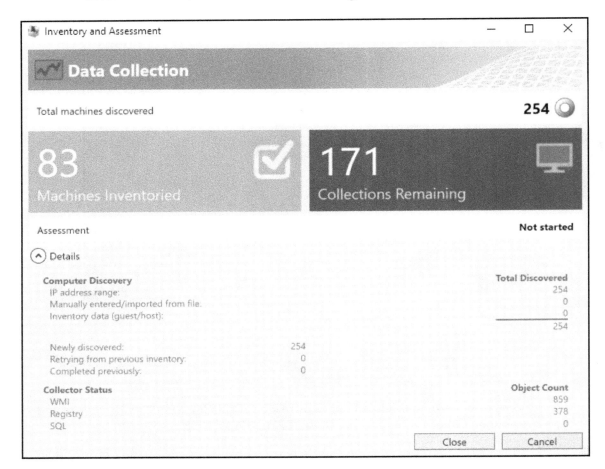

After data collection is complete, the assessment of the discovered machines begins. Once the assessment is finished, the **Overview** page presents the environment summary and information about the machines that have been found and inventoried.

5. To get an overview of specific scenarios, click on each scenario name in the left-hand pane to get additional details:

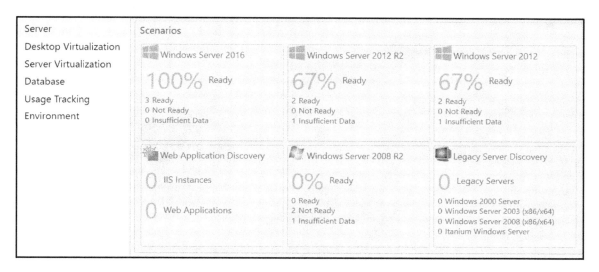

6. To get more details and to generate a scenario- or machine-specific assessment downloadable report in a Microsoft Excel worksheet, select the individual scenarios and choose the option to generate a report. You can also choose to repeat the process and initiate the inventory data collection again from the upper-left part of the screen:

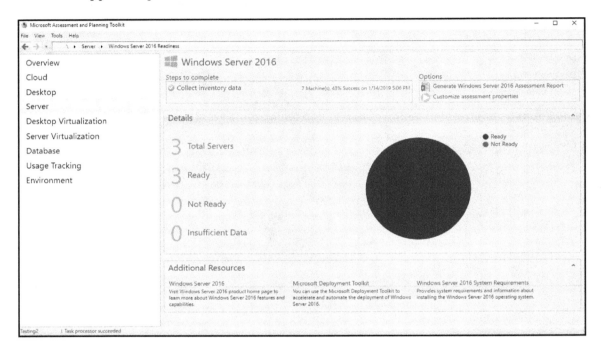

The following screenshot shows samples of the Microsoft Assessment and Planning Toolkit Report in Microsoft Excel format, the results of the discovery, the assessment of legacy Windows Server computers, and the Server Consolidation Report. Reports are exhaustive and detailed, allowing you to get a clear picture of a network environment. Each MAP Toolkit scenario report has its unique assessment details and information providing relevant information about the scanned machines' states:

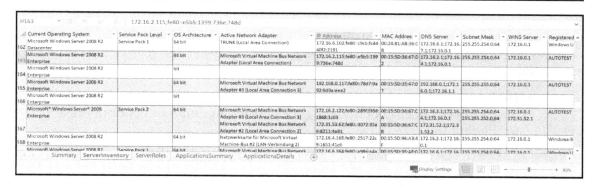

Some more samples of the Microsoft Assessment and Planning Toolkit Report are as follows:

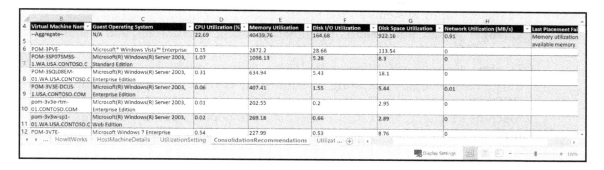

Working with images

A disk image is a file that contains the data and the same file structure as a physical disk or disk volume. As the image of a disk represents an exact copy of its physical sibling, disk images are used for various purposes, such as **disk cloning** (also known as **disk imaging**) and for backup. They are also used extensively in virtualization.

Disk imaging or disk cloning is the process of making a copy of a physical drive to a file (a disk image), and then using a disk image to create new disk images or physical drives, usually for the purpose of creating new physical or virtual computers. This enables the automation of computer deployments and saves significant amounts of time. The disk cloning process does not necessarily have to involve the disk image file, because cloning can be performed directly from disk to disk, but having an image has numerous advantages.

Windows uses its own image format, the **Windows Imaging File Format** (or **WIM**), which was introduced in Windows Vista. WIM images are compressed (using LZX or XPRESS compression) or uncompressed files containing operating system files, drivers, and applications. Using image files has the following advantages:

- **Update**: When operating system updates become available, you can update the image directly instead of updating the physical machine and performing an image capture.
- **Portable**: A disk image is a file that you can copy to and from any medium, making distribution, archiving, and backup easier. The WIM file format and its efficient compression methods allow you to store multiple versions of an operating system in the same file. For example, an image can contain Windows 10 Professional, Windows 10 Enterprise, and Windows 10 Education editions in a single file, with a file size that is significantly smaller than the individual sizes of all the operating systems added together.
- **Change**: You are able to add or remove operating system roles, and install or uninstall features or applications as needed.
- **Deploy**: A number of different deployment technologies or methods can use image files to deploy operating systems, such as **Windows Deployment Services** (**WDS**), System Center Configuration Manager, and System Center Virtual Machine Manager. You can also use images to deploy operating systems, even from portable media or from a shared network folder.

Preparing a machine for disk imaging

Before capturing a disk image using capturing or imaging software, you have to prepare a target computer for the capturing process. The preparation process, which involves generalizing a Windows operating system installation, removes the **Security Identifier** (**SID**) so that its installation can be captured as an image and deployed to different computers. An SID is a variable length value that's used to uniquely identify a Windows server or Windows Client installation (a computer), a user, a group, or the owner of an object. When joining a domain, each computer gets its own unique SIDs. When you clone a computer, the SID is cloned as well. This is where problems might occur if the installation is not prepared or generalized, because the domain controller needs to identify the computers uniquely. After a computer has been prepared, you can capture an image of the prepared computer and use it in deployment.

Using the System Preparation Tool or Sysprep

The most commonly used tool for preparing a computer is the System Preparation Tool, or **Sysprep** (sysprep.exe). This Microsoft tool is installed in the %WINDIR%\system32\sysprep directory and solves the problem of duplicate SID numbers. The Sysprep tool removes all computer-specific information from an image, including the SID numbers and computer-specific drivers. It also prepares the Windows installation for an **Out-of-Box Experience (OOBE)**, which involves setting a computer to boot to audit mode, allowing you to change the installation in more detail. Using Sysprep, you can prepare a generalized image that can be used to deploy computers with unique security identifiers.

Sysprep.exe is intended to prepare computers for imaging that are not joined to the domain but a member of a workgroup. If you run Sysprep on a computer joined to a domain, the computer will no longer be a domain member.

If you use Sysprep to capture an NTFS partition, any encrypted files or folders will be unusable and corrupt.

The Sysprep tool supports several switches that control its behavior and features:

Sysprep switch	Description
/generalize	Prepares a computer for imaging and deletes all unique system information. It also removes the SID and clears event logs and any system restore points.
/oobe	Restarts a computer in OOBE mode and shows the welcome screen after the computer restarts. You can then accept the end user license agreement, customize the installation by creating user accounts, and select the language, keyboard, and time zone.
/audit	Boots a computer to audit mode to customize the installation and add device drivers and applications.

/mode:vm	Prepares a **Virtual Hard Disk (VHD)**. You can then deploy the generalized VHD on the same hypervisor or virtual machine. The host on which you will deploy the prepared VHD needs to have the same hardware profile. Deploying a VHD to a virtual machine with a different hardware profile can cause unexpected behavior and issues. The only switches that work with the /mode:vm switch are /shutdown, /quit, and /reboot. You can only run the /mode:vm switch from inside a virtual machine. Running the VM switch from outside a virtual machine is not supported.
/shutdown	Shuts down the computer after the Sysprep tool finishes preparing the Windows installation.
/reboot	Restarts the computer after the Sysprep process finishes.
/quiet	Runs the Sysprep tool without displaying process messages.
/quit	Does not reboot or restart a computer after the Sysprep tool finishes.
/unattend:<answerfile>	Uses an answer file to apply settings to a Windows installation.

The high-level overview steps to prepare a Windows installation for imaging using Sysprep are as follows:

1. Install a Windows Server 2016 operating system.
2. Install all necessary applications, device drivers, services, features, and files that will be applied to cloned computers.
3. Run Sysprep.exe to prepare the computer for imaging. You can double-click on %WINDIR%\System32\Sysprep.exe or run Sysprep.exe from the command line with the following code: Sysprep.exe /generalize.
4. When the Sysprep command finishes, use an imaging tool to capture a prepared installation.

Using the Deployment Image Servicing and Management tool

The **Deployment Image Servicing and Management (DISM)** tool is a command-line tool that allows you to work with Windows image files, or service them in an offline state, while not in use. DISM can also be used to service a running or live Windows operating system. DISM is installed with Windows and you can also obtain it as part of the **Windows Assessment and Deployment Kit (Windows ADK)**, along with other deployment utilities. On Windows 10, DISM is located in the `%WINDIR%\System32\` folder, while in the Windows ADK, the DISM folder is `C:\Program Files (x86)\Windows Kits\<version>\Assessment and Deployment Kit\Deployment Tools\<arch>\DISM`, where the `<version>` is 8.0, 8.1, or 10, and the `<arch>` is x86 or amd64.

The DISM version in Windows Server 2016 supports servicing Windows 7, Windows Server 2008 SP2, WinPE 3.0, and later operating systems in x86 or x64 architectures. You can use DISM to perform a variety of tasks with both WIM files and Virtual Hard Disks (VHD and VHDX), including the following:

- Add, remove, and list packages
- Add, remove, and list drivers
- Add, remove, and list updates
- Add, remove, and list application packages
- Add or remove files and folders
- Add or remove languages
- Enable and disable Windows roles and features

After preparing and capturing a computer image, you are able to use it to deploy new computers. Computer hardware and software configuration changes over time. Microsoft publishes operating system updates and patches frequently, and new device driver versions are made available as well. These changes happen frequently, and applying them to a computer and capturing an image repeatedly makes the process time-consuming. DISM enables you to apply updates directly to images, thereby avoiding making unnecessarily laborious and lengthy changes to computers.

Modifying and servicing images involves doing the following:

- Mounting an image
- Editing or updating an image
- Saving changes and unmounting an image

To perform these tasks, you use the DISM tool, or its equivalent DISM PowerShell module commands. You can use these commands to maintain, manage, and update not only Windows Server and Windows client operating systems, but also Windows Server Core, Nano Server images, and Virtual Hard Disks as well. The most common commands are easily recalled by typing dism.exe in the Command Prompt window, which produces an output similar to the one that's shown in the following screenshot:

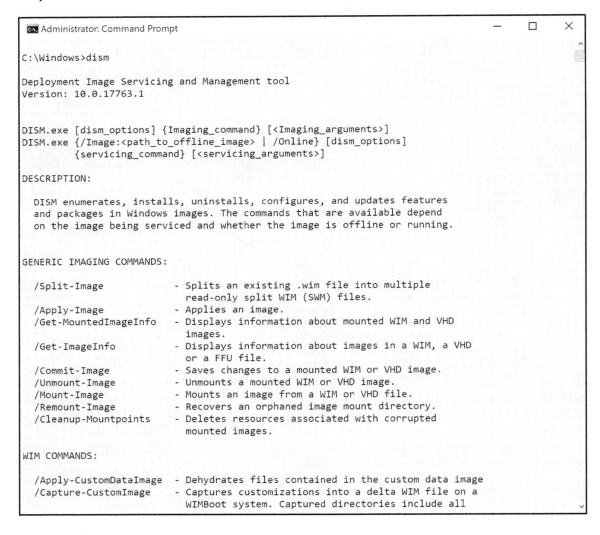

The most common switches that are used with DISM are listed in the following table. While this is not an exhaustive list, help with other supported switches, commands, and syntax can be reached by typing `dism.exe` (without switches) in an elevated command prompt:

DISM.exe Switch (DISM command)	Switch description
`/Append-Image`	Adds an additional image to a `.wim` file. This command-line switch does not apply to VHD files.
`/Apply-Image`	Applies a Windows image file (`.wim`) or a split Windows image (`.swm`) file to a specified partition.
`/Capture-CustomImage`	Captures incremental file changes based on the specific `install.wim` file to a new file.
`/Capture-Image`	Captures an image of a drive to a new `.wim` file. It captures all subdirectories and data except empty directories.
`/Cleanup-Mountpoints`	Deletes all resources associated with a corrupted, mounted image.
`/Commit-Image`	Saves the changes that you have made to a mounted image.
`/Delete-Image`	Deletes a volume image from a `.wim` file that has multiple volume images.
`/Export-Image`	Exports a copy of an image to another file.
`/Get-ImageInfo`	Displays information about the images that are contained in `.wim`, `.ffu`, `.vhd`, or `.vhdx` files.
`/Get-MountedImageInfo`	Returns a list of `.ffu`, `.vhd`, `.vhdx`, and `.wim` images that are currently mounted, as well as detailed information about the image.
`/List-Image`	Displays a list of the files and folders in an image. This command-line switch does not apply to VHD files.
`/Mount-Image`	Mounts an image from a `.ffu`, `.wim`, `.vhd`, or `.vhdx` file, to the specified directory.
`/Remount-Image`	Remounts a mounted image that has become inaccessible.
`/Split-Image`	Splits an existing `.wim` file into multiple read-only split `.swm` files. This command-line switch does not apply to VHD files.
`/Unmount-Image`	Unmounts the `.ffu`, `.wim`, `.vhd`, or `.vhdx` file and either saves or discards the changes.
`/Update-WIMBootEntry`	Updates the WIMBoot configuration entry.

The DISM tool has many equivalent DISM PowerShell module commands that are the same as the corresponding DISM switches. If you already know the DISM commands and have some PowerShell experience, you should have no problem working with DISM PowerShell commands. The following table lists the `dism.exe` command-line switches and their matching PowerShell cmdlets:

dism.exe command	DISM PowerShell cmdlet
/Add-Capability	Add-WindowsCapability
/Append-Image	Add-WindowsImage
/Apply-Image	Expand-WindowsImage
/Capture-Image	New-WindowsImage
/Cleanup-MountPoints	Clear-WindowsCorruptMountPoint
/Commit-Image	Save-WindowsImage
/Export-Image	Export-WindowsImage
/Get-Capabilities	Get-WindowsCapability
/Get-ImageInfo	Get-WindowsImage
/Get-MountedImageInfo	Get-WindowsImage -Mounted
/Get-WimBootEntry	Get-WIMBootEntry
/List-Image	Get-WindowsImageContent
/Mount-Image	Mount-WindowsImage
/Split-Image	Split-WindowsImage
/Remove-Capability	Remove-WindowsCapability
/Remove-Image	Remove-WindowsImage
/Remount-Image	Mount-WindowsImage -Remount
/Unmount-Image	Dismount-WindowsImage
/Update-WimBootEntry	Update-WIMBootEntry
/Image:<...> /Add-Driver	Add-WindowsDriver
/Image:<...> /Add-Package	Add-WindowsPackage
/Image:<...> /Add-ProvisionedAppxPackage	Add-AppxProvisionedPackage
/Image:<...> /Cleanup-Image /CheckHealth	Repair-WindowsImage -CheckHealth
/Image:<...> /Cleanup-Image /ScanHealth	Repair-WindowsImage -ScanHealth
/Image:<...> /Cleanup-Image /RestoreHealth	Repair-WindowsImage -RestoreHealth
/Image:<...> /Disable-Feature	Disable-WindowsOptionalFeature

/Image:<...> /Enable-Feature	Enable-WindowsOptionalFeature
/Image:<...> /Export-Driver	Export-WindowsDriver
/Image:<...> /Get-CurrentEdition	Get-WindowsEdition -Current
/Image:<...> /Get-Driverinfo	Get-WindowsDriver -Driver
/Image:<...> /Get-Drivers	Get-WindowsDriver
/Image:<...> /Get-Featureinfo	Get-WindowsOptionalFeature -FeatureName
/Image:<...> /Get-Features	Get-WindowsOptionalFeature
/Image:<...> /Get-Packageinfo	Get-WindowsPackage -PackagePath
/Image:<...> /Get-Packages	Get-WindowsPackage
/Image:<...> /Get-ProvisionedAppxPackages	Get-AppxProvisionedPackage
/Image:<...> /Get-TargetEditions	Get-WindowsEdition -Target
/Image:<...> /Optimize-Image	Optimize-WindowsImage
/Image:<...> /Remove-Driver	Remove-WindowsDriver
/Image:<...> /Remove-Package	Remove-WindowsPackage
/Image:<...> /Remove-ProvisionedAppxPackage	Remove-AppxProvisionedPackage
/Image:<...> /Set-Edition	Set-WindowsEdition
/Image:<...> /Set-ProductKey	Set-WindowsProductKey
/Image:<...> /Set-ProvisionedAppxDataFile	Set-AppXProvisionedDataFile

Mounting images

Before you can edit, change, or update an image, you have to mount an image first. Mounting an image connects it to a folder where, once the image is mounted, you can service the image, which means that you can add features or update drivers. A WIM file can contain multiple operating system images, but you can mount only one image in a file at a time. Each operating system image has its own identifier, which is a number that you refer to when mounting an image. If, for example, a Windows Server 2018 ISO file is extracted to a folder called c:\en_windows_server_2016_x64, the install.wim image is located in the \sources subfolder, and you can list the operating files it contains using one of the following commands:

```
DISM.exe /get-imageinfo
/imagefile:c:\en_windows_server_2016_x64\sources\install.wim
```

Or, alternatively, the following command:

```
DISM.exe /get-wiminfo
/wimfile:c:\en_windows_server_2016_x64\sources\install.wim
```

Alternatively, you can use PowerShell:

```
Get-WindowsImage -ImagePath
c:\en_windows_server_2016_x64\sources\install.wim
```

These three commands produce the same result. The following screenshot shows the output of the `dism.exe` command:

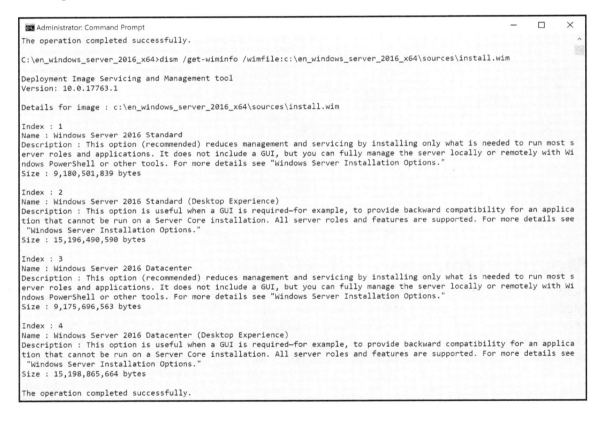

The following screenshot shows the output of the PowerShell command:

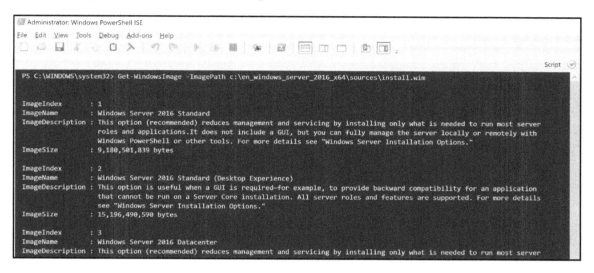

Note the `Index` field in the `dism.exe` output and the `ImageIndex` field in the PowerShell output and their values. Each operating system installation has it own unique identifier or index entry. The Windows Server 2016 Standard installation has index entry 1, the Windows Server 2016 Standard (Desktop Experience) installation has index entry 2, the Windows Server 2016 Datacenter installation has index entry 3, and the Windows Server 2016 Datacenter (Desktop Experience) installation has index entry 4.

Once you have identified the working Windows installation, mount it using the following commands:

```
DISM.exe /mount-image
/imagefile:c:\en_windows_server_2016_x64\sources\install.wim /index:4
/mountdir:c:\mount
```

Alternatively, you can use the PowerShell alternative:

```
Mount-WindowsImage -ImagePath
c:\en_windows_server_2016_x64\sources\install.wim -Index 4 -Path c:\mount
```

Updating images

After the image has been mounted, the most frequent image servicing tasks
are usually updating software and adding device drivers. DISM only supports device
drivers that are made up of .inf files. Drivers in executable (.exe) files and Microsoft
Windows Installer files (.msi) are not supported. When specified, the /Add-Driver switch
needs the location information of the driver's information (.inf) file and adds the driver to
the image. The /Recurse switch adds all the drivers that are found in a specified folder.
The following command adds all drivers in the c:\drivers folder to the image that's
mounted in the c:\mountedimage folder:

```
DISM.exe /image:c:\mountedimage /Add-Driver /driver:c:\drivers\ /recurse
```

If you prefer PowerShell, the equivalent command is as follows:

```
Add-WindowsDriver -Path c:\mountedimage -Driver c:\drivers -Recurse
```

Adding roles and features

You can use DISM to enable or disable Windows roles and features and also customize
Windows images. It is a very convenient feature that enables you to deploy computers with
pre-installed roles and features, thus avoiding the inconvenience of installing roles and
features and restarting a server after server deployment.

You have to identify which features are available in the mounted image and the exact name
of the feature or a role you want to add, using either /Get-Features or Enable-
WindowsOptionalFeature in DISM and PowerShell, respectively.

To identify which roles and features are available in the image mounted in c:\mount using
dism.exe, use the following command:

```
DISM.exe/image:c:\mount /Get-Features
```

This produces the following output:

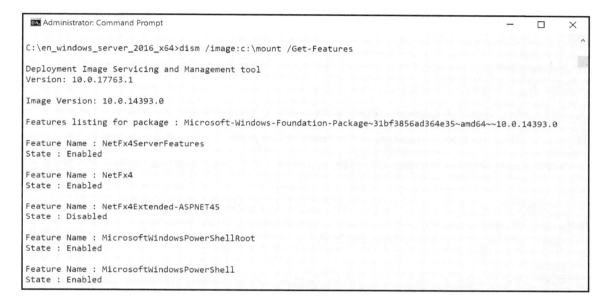

Alternatively, use the following PowerShell command:

```
Get-WindowsOptionalFeature -Path C:\mount
```

This produces exactly the same output, as shown in the following screenshot:

```
PS C:\WINDOWS\system32> Get-WindowsOptionalFeature -Path C:\mount


FeatureName : NetFx4ServerFeatures
State       : Enabled

FeatureName : NetFx4
State       : Enabled

FeatureName : NetFx4Extended-ASPNET45
State       : Disabled

FeatureName : MicrosoftWindowsPowerShellRoot
State       : Enabled

FeatureName : MicrosoftWindowsPowerShell
State       : Enabled
```

Some PowerShell command alternatives produce the same output as `dism.exe` commands and some PowerShell commands generate a more informative output. Both alternatives accomplish the same results; it is up to your personal preference as to which commands to use.

To enable a specific feature in the image, such as **IP Address Management (IPAM)**, use the following `dism.exe` command:

```
DISM.exe /image:c:\mount /Enable-Feature /FeatureName:IPAMServerFeature
```

To enable all of the parent features of the specified feature, use the `/all` option:

```
DISM.exe /image:c:\mount /Enable-Feature /all /FeatureName:Microsoft-Hyper-V
```

Sometimes, you want to disable a feature you no longer need or support. To disable a feature in an image, use the `Disable-Feature` option in DISM or the `Disable-WindowsOptionalFeature` command in PowerShell, as shown in the following example:

```
DISM
DISM.exe /image:c:\mount /Disable-Feature /FeatureName:RASRoutingProtocols

PowerShell
Disable-WindowsOptionalFeature -Path c:\mount -FeatureName
RASRoutingProtocols -Remove
```

When you are finished servicing an image, or you want to service a different image, you have to unmount the image. You have to specify whether you want to save or discard these changes using the `/commit` or `/discard` options.

To unmount an image that's mounted to the `c:\mount` folder and save your changes, use the following code:

```
DISM
DISM.exe /unmount-wim /mountdir:c:\mount /commit
or
DISM.exe /unmount-Image /mountdir:c:\mount /commit

PowerShell
Dismount-WindowsImage -Path C:\mount -Save
```

A list of the DISM command syntaxes we have discussed are shown as follows:

- The following command displays image information:

```
DISM.exe /Get-ImageInfo /ImageFile:<path_to_image.wim>
[{/Index:<Image_index> | /Name:<Image_name>}]
```

- The following command mounts an image:

```
DISM.exe /Mount-Image /ImageFile:<path_to_image_file>
{/Index:<image_index> | /Name:<image_name>}
/MountDir:<path_to_mount_directory> [/ReadOnly] [/Optimize]
[/CheckIntegrity]
```

- The following command services an image offline:

```
DISM.exe /image:<path_to_image_directory> [/Get-Drivers | /Get-
DriverInfo | /Add-Driver | /Remove-Driver | /Export-Driver]
```

- The following command services an image online:

```
DISM.exe /Online [/Get-Drivers | /Get-DriverInfo | /Export-Driver]
```

- The following command enables features in an image:

```
DISM.exe /Enable-Feature /FeatureName:<name_in_image>
[/PackageName:<name_in_image>] [/Source: <source>] [/LimitAccess]
[/All]
```

- The following command disables features in an image:

```
DISM.exe /Disable-Feature /FeatureName:<name_in_image>
[/PackageName:<name_in_image>] [/Remove]
```

- The following command unmounts an image:

```
DISM.exe /Unmount-Image /MountDir:<path_to_mount_directory>
{/Commit | /Discard} [/CheckIntegrity] [/Append]
```

The list of DISM command-line switches and their respective descriptions are shown in the following table:

DISM command option	Description
/mount-image	Mounts an image from a WIM or VHD file.
/imagefile:filename	Specifies the location and the name of the image file.
/index:#	Specifies the number of the image within the WIM file.
/name:imagename	Specifies the name of the image within the WIM file that you want to mount.
/mountdir:pathname	Specifies a folder on the local disk to mount an image to.
/image:foldername	Specifies the location of the mounted image.
/add-driver	Adds a driver to an image.
/driver:drivername	Specifies the location of the driver to add to an image.
/recurse	Adds all drivers in all subfolders.
/image:folder	Specifies the location of the image.
/enable-feature	Enables Windows features.
/featurename:feature	Specifies the name of the feature to enable.
/all	Enables all parent features for the specified feature.

Summary

In this chapter, we have discussed the different types of virtualization and the advantages that virtualization brings, along with the points to consider when planning and preparing an infrastructure for virtualization. We also had a look at how to perform hardware and software assessment and how to get an inventory of an infrastructure using the Microsoft Assessment and Planning Toolkit. After that, we explained how to speed up the deployment process using the System Preparation tool and the Deployment Image Servicing and Management tool. These two tools help us to prepare, manage, and service images that can later be used in bare-metal or virtualized environments.

In the next chapter, we will cover an important and fundamental topic – storage. You will learn how to configure disks and volumes, how to implement server storage for redundancy and resiliency, and how to implement storage space optimization technologies.

Questions

1. What are the benefits of virtualization? Choose all that apply.
   1. Faster server deployment
   2. Lower operational costs
   3. Slower and secure client deployment
   4. Running production workloads in a non-isolated environment
   5. Easier backup
   6. Server consolidation

2. What are the main considerations when planning for server virtualization? Choose all that apply.
   1. CPU usage
   2. Memory requirements
   3. Driver versions
   4. Disk usage
   5. Expansion ports compatibility

3. Which would you use to assess the infrastructure and gather details about the hardware and the software?
   1. WDS
   2. WAIK
   3. MAPT
   4. LAPS

4. True or False: The Microsoft Assessment and Planning Toolkit does not need any SQL Server version to run.
   1. True
   2. False

5. True or False: To perform an infrastructure assessment using the Microsoft Assessment and Planning Toolkit, you must be connected to the internet.
   1. True
   2. False

6. Which methods does the Microsoft Assessment and Planning Toolkit use to obtain information from network computers? Choose all that apply.
   1. NMAP
   2. IP address range scanning
   3. LDAP
   4. SNMP

     5. Fiddler

     6. WMI

7. What do you need to do before cloning a computer image?

     1. Defragment a drive and run `chkdsk.exe`

     2. Scan the drive for viruses

     3. Run `Sysprep.exe`

     4. Run `dism.exe`

8. You are preparing a computer for imaging. You want the computer to present a welcome screen after it restarts, and you want the user to select the language and keyboard layout. Which command should you run?

     1. `Add-WindowsCapability PowerShell cmdlet`

     2. `Dism.exe /enable-feature`

     3. `Sysprep.exe /generalize`

     4. `Sysprep.exe /oobe`

9. You are servicing an image. You want to add drivers from the `c:\drivers` folder to the image. You do not want to add drivers from the `c:\drivers\graphics` folder to the image. Which command should you run? Choose all that apply.

     1. `Add-WindowsDriver -Path c:\mountedimage -Driver c:\drivers -Recurse`

     2. `DISM.exe /image:c:\mountedimage /Add-Driver /driver:c:\drivers\ /recurse`

     3. `Add-WindowsDriver -Path c:\mountedimage -Driver c:\drivers`

     4. `DISM.exe /image:c:\mountedimage /Add-Driver /driver:c:\drivers\`

10. Which command do you need to run before servicing an image?

     1. `Get-WindowsOptionalFeature -Path C:\mount`

     2. `DISM.exe/image:c:\mount /Get-Features`

     3. `Get-WindowsImage -ImagePath c:\sources\install.wim`

     4. `DISM.exe /mount-image /imagefile:c:\sources\install.wim /mountdir:c:\mount`

Further reading

To further enhance your studies and prepare for the exam, or for future reference, you can visit the following online resources and articles:

- **Microsoft Assessment and Planning Toolkit – Getting Started Guide:** `https://social.technet.microsoft.com/wiki/contents/articles/17782.microsoft-assessment-and-planning-toolkit-getting-started-guide.aspx`
- **DISM Overview:** `https://docs.microsoft.com/en-us/windows-hardware/manufacture/desktop/what-is-dism`
- **DISM Reference:** `https://docs.microsoft.com/en-us/windows-hardware/manufacture/desktop/dism-reference--deployment-image-servicing-and-management`
- **DISM Best Practices:** `https://docs.microsoft.com/en-us/windows-hardware/manufacture/desktop/deployment-image-servicing-and-management--dism--best-practices`
- **Sysprep (System Preparation) Overview:** `https://docs.microsoft.com/en-us/windows-hardware/manufacture/desktop/sysprep--system-preparation--overview`
- **Sysprep Command-Line Options:** `https://docs.microsoft.com/en-us/windows-hardware/manufacture/desktop/sysprep-command-line-options`

3
Configuring and Implementing Storage

In this chapter, we will describe storage and storage-related technologies in Microsoft Windows Server 2016. Storage is one of the most important building blocks of every computer and operating system, including Microsoft operating systems. It is especially important in server operating systems as users depend on the servers' speed, efficiency, availability, and resilience. After all, our users' data is stored on disks. Having an efficient, reliable, and secure storage system needs to be on the top of our list of priorities.

In this chapter, we will cover the following topics:

- Configuring and managing disks and volumes
- Implementing and configuring server storage
- Implementing data deduplication

Technical requirements

In this chapter, we will use Windows Server 2016 Datacenter.

You can obtain evaluation versions of Windows Server 2016 Datacenter from the Microsoft Evaluation Center website (`https://www.microsoft.com/en-us/evalcenter/`) or directly from the product evaluation page (`https://www.microsoft.com/en-us/evalcenter/evaluate-windows-server-2016?filetype=ISO`), where you can choose how to try Windows Server 2016 – using the ISO file, in Azure, or in a virtual lab.

Configuring and managing disks and volumes

Before we look at the management and configuration of disk and volumes, it is important to be familiar with the building blocks of a Windows Server 2016 storage system.

A filesystem is a part of the operating system that controls how files are organized, named, and stored on a volume. A filesystem manages folders, files, and the information needed to locate and access these items by local users or remote users. Windows Server 2016 supports four file systems: **File Allocation Table (FAT)**, FAT32, NTFS, and **Resilient File System (ReFS)**.

FAT is sometimes referred to as FAT16 and has been present since MS-DOS. FAT32 was introduced with Windows 95 OSR2 and has been supported in Microsoft Windows operating systems since then. FAT uses a 16-bit file-allocation table entry while FAT32 has a 32-bit file-allocation entry.

The following table shows a comparison between the size limits of FAT and FAT32:

Description	FAT limits	FAT32 limits
Maximum file size	4 GB (minus 1 byte)	4 GB (minus 1 byte)
Maximum volume size	4 GB	32 GB
Files per volume	65,536	4,177,920
Maximum number of files and folders	512 files (within the root folder)	65,534 (within a single folder)

Windows Server 2016 supports FAT and FAT32 for backward-compatibility with older types of software and hardware, and as a support for removable or portable storage, such as flash (USB) drives. Flash drives can be formatted with NTFS, but FAT and FAT32 still remain the filesystems of choice for this type of storage.

The main filesystem in Windows Server 2016 is NTFS, as it was in the previous Windows Server versions. Microsoft's newest filesystem is ReFS. The NTFS filesystem addresses the weaknesses and limitations of FAT and FAT32, providing support for larger volumes and file sizes and an increase in security, which is essential not only for business use, but for personal use as well. It provides more advanced features, such as encryption, disk quotas, security descriptors, and Clustered Shared Volumes, in a failover cluster.

NT Filesystem (NTFS)

NTFS is the main filesystem on Windows Server and Windows client operating systems and it has many advantages.

Security

Filesystem security is greatly enhanced in NTFS with the following:

- **Encrypting Filesystem (EFS)**: An encryption technology that runs as an integrated system service providing transparent file encryption and decryption. File permissions and logon authentication protect files, folders, and network resources from unauthorized access. But what if a computer or disk is stolen? Without an access check, anyone that has physical access to disk or computer can access the data. When a user opens a file, EFS transparently decrypts the data. When a user saves the file, the data is encrypted without user intervention, in the background. EFS uses three encryption algorithms to encrypt and decrypt the data:
  - **DESX**: An enhanced version of **Data Encryption Standard** (DES).
  - **3DES** or **Triple-DES**: Uses a 128-bit or 168-bit key.
  - **AES** or **Advanced Encryption Standard**: The best alternative to DESX and 3DES. It uses a 256-bit key and a symmetric encryption algorithm, and it is equally fast in software and hardware implementations—significantly faster than DESX or 3DES—making it suitable to use as an encryption standard of choice in Windows OS.

- **Access Control Lists (ACL)**: Files and folders support Allow and Restrict permission types that can be applied at a granular level.
- **BitLocker Drive Encryption**: While EFS is a file-level encryption method that provides protection from users and processes, BitLocker is a volume-level encryption technology that provides additional data protection and security. It is integrated in the operating system and mitigates the threats of lost, stolen, or inadequately-decommissioned computers. It uses AES 265-bit encryption and supports the **Trusted Platform Module** (TPM) chip for increased security.

Support for large volumes

Depending on the cluster size, NTFS can support volumes as large as 256 terabytes. Consult the following table for NTFS cluster sizes and the respective volume sizes they support:

Cluster size	Largest volume size supported	Largest file size supported
4 KB	16 TB	16 TB
8 KB	32 TB	32 TB
16 KB	64 TB	64 TB
32 KB	128 TB	128 TB
64 KB	256 TB	265 TB

Reliability

Introduced in Windows Server 2008, **Self-Healing NTFS** increases the reliability of data and operating systems by continuously monitoring and correcting file-corruption problems. Before, a user had to use `chkdsk.exe` to repair corrupted files, which is a process that interrupts normal operating system operations. With Self-Healing NTFS, the system corrects and repairs most of the file-corruption issues without interrupting the user.

Clustered storage

Failover clusters take advantage of NTFS support for volumes that are continuously available and that can be accessed simultaneously by multiple cluster nodes.

Capacity enhancements

If the volume is low on free space, NTFS supports multiple ways to expand the free space:

- Allocating free space from the same disk or from a different disk
- Compressing the files using system-file compression
- Using disk quotas for controlling and tracking disk-space usage
- Using mounting points to mount a volume to an empty folder

Dynamic disks and volumes

NTFS adds the support for dynamic disks and volumes, which allow us to create volumes that span multiple disks and volumes that are fault-tolerant, such as mirrored, spanned, and striped volumes. Dynamic disks thus provide speed, reliability, and redundancy, characteristics very much appreciated in server environments.

Resilient Filesystem (ReFS)

Other than the filesystem of choice, NTFS, Windows Server 2016 supports the relatively new ReFS. It introduced new features that added numerous benefits, which are explained in the following sections.

Scalability

ReFS is designed to support significantly larger datasets than NTFS, without penalizing performance, which enables extremely large storage and file sizes. The following table shows the differences between the two filesystem limits:

Filesystem feature	NTFS	ReFS
Maximum file name length	255 *	255 *
Maximum path name length	32 K	32 K
Maximum file size	35 PB	256 TB
Maximum volume size	35 PB	256 TB

To better understand the preceding table, consult these points:

- * means Unicode characters
- TB = Terabytes = 1,000,000,000,000 B = 10^{12} bytes = 1,000 GB (Gigabytes)
- PB = Petabytes = 1,000,000,000,000,000 B = 10^{15} bytes = 1,000 TB (Terabytes)

Resiliency

ReFS is able to detect corruptions in a filesystem and repair the corruptions without taking storage offline or making the data unavailable, providing increased reliability and data integrity.

When used in Storage Spaces integration scenarios, ReFS detects and repairs data corruption automatically, with no downtime. Moreover, if a volume is corrupted and there is no alternative copy of the corrupted data, ReFS removes the corrupted data from the namespace.

During read and write operations, a process named **scrubber** occasionally scans the volume and automatically corrects the errors if the corrupt data is found.

Performance

For performance-demanding environments, such as virtualization scenarios, ReFS offers several advantages, such as **Mirror-Accelerated Parity**, a technology that brings mirroring and parity to Storage Spaces Direct and offers fast write performance paired with efficient fault-tolerance.

Block-cloning enables the operating system to perform fast and efficient copy operations, while **integrity streams** in ReFS maintain the data integrity and performs the validation using checksums, checking whether the data is corrupt, and performing the repairs accordingly.

NTFS is widely used as an all-purpose filesystem, while ReFS is used in specific workloads and scenarios where increased availability, scalability, and resilience is required.

Storage Spaces and Storage Spaces Direct take advantage of ReFS to achieve high-performance, mirror-accelerated storage, block cloning, and sparse VDL functionalities, which dramatically increase **virtual hard disk** (**VHD**) operations; alternate data copies, online corruption repair and integrity streams deal with data corruption.

The following table lists the feature or functional differences between NTFS and ReFS:

Feature or functionality	NTFS	ReFS
Offloaded Data Transfer (ODX)	Yes	No
Block clone	No	Yes
Sparse VDL	No	Yes
Mirror-accelerated Parity	No	Yes
File system compression	Yes	No
File system encryption	Yes	No
Transactions	Yes	No
Hard Links	Yes	No
Object IDs	Yes	No
Short names	Yes	No

Extended attributes	Yes	No
Disk quotas	Yes	No
Bootable	Yes	No
Page file support	Yes	No
Removable media support	Yes	No

Configuring sector sizes

In a computer storage system, the allocation unit or a cluster is a unit of disk space allocated to files. An allocation unit is the smallest unit, or disk space, that an operating system can assign to store the data, that is, a file. Allocation unit sizes vary, depending on the chosen filesystem. This diagram shows the physical structure of a disk system, illustrating the differences between **DISK SECTOR, TRACK SECTOR, CLUSTER OR ALLOCATION UNIT**, and **TRACK**:

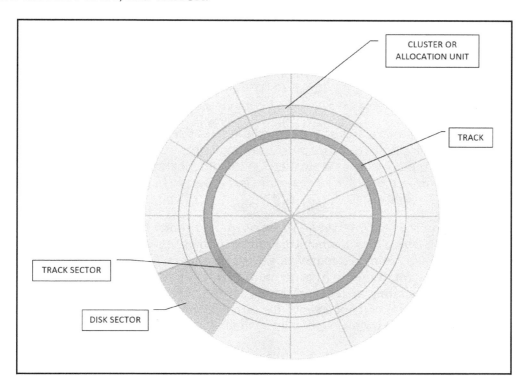

NTFS supports several allocation unit sizes, while ReFS has fewer choices, as shown here:

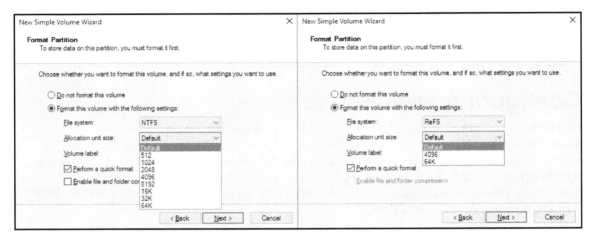

For example, if you store a 20-kilobyte file on a disk formatted with 16-kilobyte allocation units, the operating system allocates two allocation units for storing the file, or 32 kilobytes in total. That means the 20-kilobyte file uses 32 kilobytes of disk space. The difference, 12 kilobytes, is called **slack space**. The default NTFS allocation unit size is 4,096 bytes, although you can choose between 512 and 64 kilobyte sizes.

Depending on the sector size and on the typical file sizes you store on a volume, the slack space varies. For example, if you store mostly large files on a volume formatted with a smaller size sector, the slack space is smaller. On the other hand, if you store mostly small files on a volume formatted with a large sector size, expect to have a much larger slack space.

If you are running Hyper-V, the sector size choice has a direct impact on the storage I/O performance. From Windows Server 2012, VHD format has been optimized to have a 4,096-byte alignment with the host storage subsystem, resulting in better performance. If you used VHD files created with operating systems prior to Windows Server 2012, these VHDs are not aligned and will not achieve the same performance as VHDs created with the newer Windows operating systems.

To convert a VHD into a new format, use this PowerShell command:

```
Convert-VHD -Path E:\vms\testvhd\test.vhd -DestinationPath
E:\vms\testvhd\test-converted.vhd
```

To check whether the VHD is aligned, type the following PowerShell command:

```
Get-VHD -Path E:\vms\testvhd\test.vhd
```

Non-aligned VHDs will return the **Alignment** property as **0** (zero), while aligned VHDs will return the **Alignment** property as **1** (one).

VHD files use 512-byte logical sector sizes, while VHDX files use 4,096-byte logical sector sizes. Thus, choosing a default 4,096-byte disk sector size aligns perfectly with a VHDX logical sector size, avoiding any negative impact on the performance. Other major difference between the VHD and VHDX files is that the VHD maximum size is 2 TB, does not provide data protection, can't be resized live, and supports vendors other than Microsoft. On the other hand, VHDX files have a maximum size of 64 TB, provide data protection, can be resized live, handle snapshots better, and are only supported by Microsoft.

Configuring GUID Partition Tables (GPT disks)

Based on the type of a disk partition table, Windows Server 2016 supports two types of disks: **GUID Partition Tables** (**GPT**) and **Master Boot Record** (**MBR**) disks. In the following sections, we'll take a look at the difference between GPT and MBR disks.

MBR disks

MBR disks are a type of disk boot sector that contain information about how the disk partitions are organized. MBRs also contain information about the operating system boot procedure. MBR is an old system, introduced in March 1983, and it originally supported FAT12 on DOS 2.0. Later, with the introduction of DOS 3.0, it was upgraded to support FAT16 filesystems as well. It has several limitations, one of which is that the maximum addressable storage space is 2 TB.

An MBR disk supports a maximum of four primary partitions. Alternatively, you can create up to three primary partitions, an extended partition, and up to 128 logical drives within the extended partition.

On an MBR disk, the partition and boot data is stored in an entry saved in one place only. If this data is corrupted or erased, even partially, you could lose all the data stored on a disk.

The following screenshot shows **Disk 1**, which is initialized as an MBR disk. It has three primary partitions (assigned drive letters **E**, **F**, and **G**) and one logical drive (drive letter **H**) within an extended partition. **Disk 2** is initialized as a GPT disk, with five primary partitions:

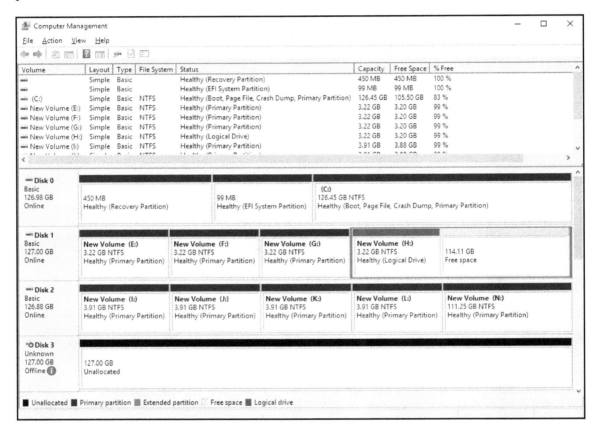

GPT disks

GPT disks were introduced as a part of the **Extensible Firmware Interface** (**EFI**) initiative. GPT disks support disk sizes up to 18 **Exabytes** (**EB**), greatly surpassing the 2-TB limit of MBR disks. GUID partition tables use error-checking (CRC32) and primary and backup partition tables. This means that the data is more secure, redundant, and has increased integrity compared to MBR partition tables. If one entry is corrupted, GPT can attempt recovery using backup tables or checksum data.

Theoretically, GUID partition tables can have an unlimited number of partitions. However, GPT disks support up to 128 partitions, in contrast to MBR disks, which support only four partitions. The limit is imposed by the amount of space that is reserved for storing partition entries.

To support booting from GPT disks, a computer needs to support the **Unified Extensible Firmware Interface (UEFI)** standard. In addition, the Windows operating system needs to be a 64-bit edition that is newer than Windows Server 2003 or Windows XP.

For more information about GUID Partition Tables and UEFI support in Windows, consult the following pages:

- **Frequently asked questions about Windows and GPT**: `https://docs.microsoft.com/en-us/previous-versions/windows/hardware/design/dn640535(v=vs.85)`
- **Frequently asked questions about UEFI firmware**: `https://docs.microsoft.com/en-us/previous-versions/windows/it-pro/windows-8.1-and-8/hh824898(v=win.10)`

Initializing disks

To initialize a disk as an MBR or GPT disk, perform the following steps:

1. Open the Start menu.
2. Scroll down the program list to the letter W and expand **Windows Administration Tools**.
3. Open **Computer Management**.
4. Alternatively, to skip steps 1-3, right-click on Start and choose **Computer Management**. If the Server Manager is opened, you can start the Computer Manager from the **Tools** menu.
5. Under **Storage**, click **Disk Management**

6. If the disk is **Offline**, right-click and bring the disk **Online**, as shown in the following screenshot:

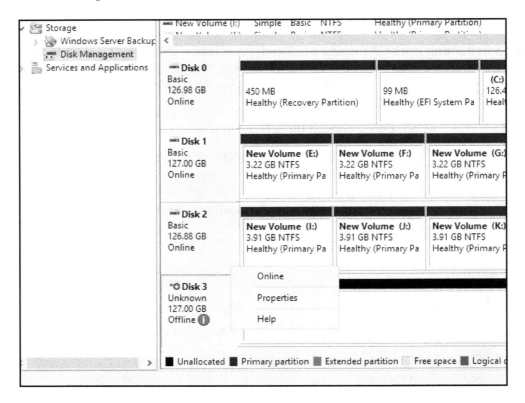

7. Right-click again and click **Initialize Disk**. An **Initialize Disk** dialog box opens:

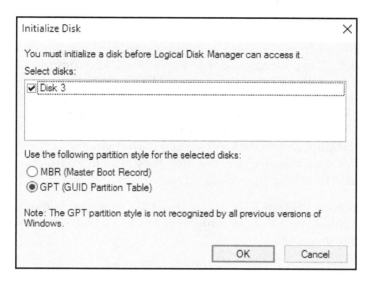

8. From the list of available (online) disks, select all the disks that you want to initialize, use the appropriate partition style, and click **OK**.

9. To convert between GPT and MBR disks, right-click on a disk name and, depending on the current disk partition style, choose to convert either to GPT or MBR:

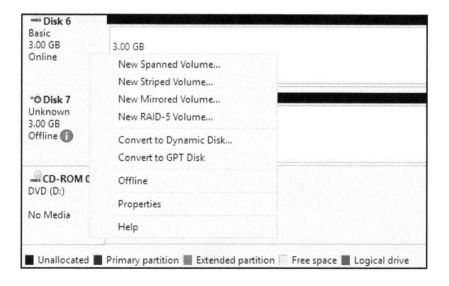

Creating VHD and VHDX files using Disk Management or Windows PowerShell

Windows Server 2016 supports creating, mounting, and unmounting **Virtual Hard Disks** (**VHD** or **VHDX**) using Disk Management or PowerShell. The computer does not have to have a Hyper-V role installed to create and mount VHDs. What's more, you can perform these actions in Windows 10, Windows 8.1, Windows Server 2012, and Windows Server 2012 R2. Although VHDs and VHDXs are most commonly used in Hyper-V environments, they are convenient to use as ordinary, physical hard disks that offer the additional convenience of portability. Once mounted, virtual hard disks appear in the operating system like any other disk. Because they are files, they offer extra functionalities, including portability, duplication, backing up, and archiving.

 To create a VHD or VHDX, either in Disk Management or using PowerShell, you must be a member of the **Administrators** or the **Backup Operators** group.

Creating VHD and VHDX files using Disk Management

Follow these steps to create a VHD or VHDX:

1. You can open Disk Management either by using the Server Manager, right-clicking on the Start menu, or running the `diskmgmt.msc` file.
2. From the **Action** menu, select **Create VHD**. The **Create and Attach Virtual Disk** dialog box opens:

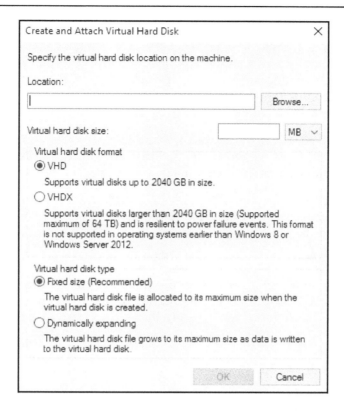

3. In **Location**, specify the location in which to store the virtual hard disk. You cannot specify a \Windows folder as a location to save a VHD or VHDX.

4. Specify the virtual hard disk size. The size cannot be smaller than 3 MB.

5. Specify the virtual hard disk format. A VHD supports virtual disks up to 2 TB in size, while VHDX offers the possibility to create a resilient virtual disk that is larger than 2 TB in size.

6. Choose a virtual hard disk type. Creating a fixed size virtual hard disk reserves the disk space in advance and the VHD (or VHDX) file size equals the size specified in step 4. Even if you do not have any files stored on the virtual hard disk, if you choose to create a 100 GB disk, the VHD occupies 100 GB of hard disk space. In contrast, dynamically expanding virtual hard disks initially allocates as little as possible of the hard disk space and expands as you add content to the VHD.

7. Click **OK** to create the virtual hard disk. If you selected to create a fixed disk, the bigger the virtual hard disk size is, the more time it takes to allocate disk space.

In Windows operating systems prior to Windows Server 2016, there were a lot of discussions about which format is better, fixed or dynamically expanding. Generally, fixed virtual disks are potentially less fragmented than dynamically-expanding disk, allowing for a better read/write performance. Dynamically expanding virtual hard disks could make them more fragmented due to the expansion to non-contiguous disk space, which negatively affects performance.

If you choose VHD, fixed-size disks are recommended, whereas if you choose VHDX, dynamically-expanding disks are recommended instead. This has to do with virtual hard disks and the operating-system optimizations that we discussed previously in this chapter.

To find out more about Hyper-V and VHD performance related to dynamically-expanding versus fixed disks, visit the following page:

`https://blogs.technet.microsoft.com/winserverperformance/2008/09/19/hyper-v-and-vhd-performance-dynamic-vs-fixed/`

The Hyper-V VHD Performance White Paper has additional information about VHD performance. Although it applies to older server operating systems, it offers valuable insight into virtual hard disk operations:

`https://blogs.msdn.microsoft.com/taylorb/2010/02/26/hyper-v-virtual-hard-disk-vhd-performance-white-paper/`

Creating VHD and VHDX files using Windows PowerShell

As always, to automate tasks and save time, you can use PowerShell to create VHD and VHDX files.

If you have already installed the Hyper-V module as a part of the Hyper-Management Tools feature, the cmdlets for creating virtual disks are already available to use. To check whether the Hyper-V tools and features are installed, type this simple PowerShell command:

```
Get-WindowsFeature -Name *hyper*
```

The following screenshot shows the output of this command, with the features installed and their names:

```
PS C:\Users\Administrator> Get-WindowsFeature -Name *hyper*

Display Name                                    Name                    Install State
------------                                    ----                    -------------
[ ] Hyper-V                                     Hyper-V                     Available
    [X] Hyper-V Management Tools                RSAT-Hyper-V-Tools          Installed
        [ ] Hyper-V GUI Management Tools        Hyper-V-Tools               Available
        [X] Hyper-V Module for Windows PowerShell  Hyper-V-PowerShell       Installed
```

Even if you don't have the Hyper-V module installed, you can add the Hyper-V PowerShell module in a few ways:

- To install just the Hyper-V PowerShell Module, but not the Hyper-V role itself, type the following:

   ```
   Install-WindowsFeature -Name Hyper-V-PowerShell
   ```

- To install Hyper-V hypervisor and all tools, type one of these two commands:

   ```
   Install-WindowsFeature -Name Hyper-V, RSAT-Hyper-V-Tools
   Install-WindowsFeature -Name Hyper-V -IncludeManagementTools
   ```

- Once the Hyper-V PowerShell module is installed, you can list the available Hyper-V PowerShell commands with the following:

   ```
   Get-Command -Module hyper-v
   ```

- Alternatively, you can use the following command to pop out the window with a searchable list of available commands:

   ```
   Get-Command -Module hyper-v | Out-GridView
   ```

- To create a VHD or VHDX disk using the New-VHD PowerShell command, type the following:

   ```
   New-VHD -Path c:\newdisk.vhdx -Dynamic -SizeBytes 100GB
   ```

The command creates a new, 100 GB, dynamically-expanding virtual disk in a VHDX format. The following command creates a 20-GB differencing VHD disk, with a parent disk called Basedisk.vhd located in the c:\VHDs folder:

```
New-VHD -ParentPath c:\VHDs\Basedisk.vhd -Path c:\DiffDisk.vhd -
Differencing -SizeBytes 20GB
```

This PowerShell example is a convenient way to create and prepare a virtual disk for production:

```
$diskpath = "C:\VHDs\Disk1.vhdx"
$disksize = 200GB
New-VHD -Path $diskpath -Dynamic -SizeBytes $disksize | Mount-VHD -Passthru
|Initialize-Disk -Passthru |New-Partition -AssignDriveLetter -
UseMaximumSize |Format-Volume -FileSystem NTFS -Confirm:$false -Force
```

The `New-VHD` command in this example uses the pipe (|) character to concatenate commands into one and creates the 200-GB VHDX-type dynamically-expanding virtual hard disk. It also mounts, initializes, and formats the disk. There is no special parameter to create a VHD or VHDX; the extension you specify in the commands determines which format will be created. To specify additional options when using the `New-VHD` command, you can take advantage of the following required and optional command parameters.

The required parameters are as follows:

- `Dynamic`: Creates a dynamic disk
- `Fixed`: Creates a fixed-size disk
- `ParentPath`: Specifies a path to a parent disk
- `Path`: Specifies a path where a disk is created
- `SizeBytes`: Specifies the size of a disk in bytes
- `SourceDisk`: Specifies the source disk of a disk to create

The optional parameters are as follows:

- `AsJob`: Runs the command as a background job
- `BlockSizeBytes`: Specifies the disk block size in bytes
- `CimSession`: Runs a command on a remote computer or in a remote session
- `ComputerName`: Specifies the Hyper-V host or hosts on which the disk is created
- `Confirm`: Prompts for confirmation before running the command
- `Credential`: Supplies the credentials to run the command
- `Differencing`: Creates the differencing disk
- `LogicalSectorSizeBytes`: Specifies the virtual disk's logical sector size in bytes, between 512 and 4,096 bytes
- `PhysicalSectorSizeBytes`: Specifies the physical sector size in bytes, between 512 and 4,096 bytes
- `SizeBytes`: Specifies the virtual hard disk size
- `WhatIf`: Simulates the execution of the command

Mounting virtual hard disks

The virtual hard disk is mounted automatically, as the part of the creating process. Obviously, you can mount or dismount a virtual hard disk regardless of its origin, as long as is it in the VHD or VHDX format. To mount a disk, or rather, attach a disk, use Disk Management. To attach a VHD or VHDX, do the following:

1. From the Server Manager, open **Computer Management**.
2. Click **Disk Management**.
3. On the **Action** menu, click **Attach VHD**. The **Attach Virtual Hard Disk** menu dialog box will open.
4. Choose a VHD or VHDX file to attach.
5. Optionally, you can select the **Read-only** check box to ensure that you cannot modify the attached disk.
6. Click **OK** and the disk will be attached.

When a VHD or VHDX is attached, it behaves as any other hard disk attached to the computer and is distinguishable from the other disks by its blue icon. In the following screenshot, the attached VHDX disk is **Disk 8**:

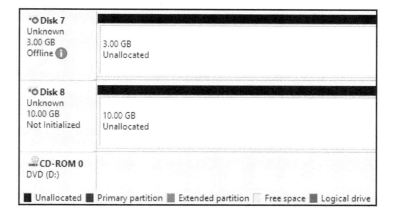

Before it can be used, it must be initialized; one or more partitions need to be created and formatted and it needs to have a letter assigned.

When you no longer need a disk, right-click on it in **Disk Management** and click **Detach** or select a disk and select the same command from the **Action** menu. You must have administrative privileges to attach and detach virtual hard disks.

Mounting virtual hard disks using PowerShell

The GUI actions of attaching and detaching disks have their equivalents in PowerShell. You can use cmdlets from the Hyper-V module and the Storage module to mount and dismount virtual hard disks. To use the Hyper-V cmdlet to mount a VHD or VHDX disk, type the following commands:

```
Mount-VHD -Path C:\VHDs\Disk1.vhdx
Mount-VHD -Path C:\VHDs\Disk1.vhdx -ReadOnly
```

To mount the disk in the read-only state, use the `-ReadOnly` parameter. To use the Storage module cmdlets to mount the VHD or VHDX disks, use the following:

```
Mount-DiskImage -ImagePath C:\VHDs\Disk1.vhdx
```

To detach or dismount an attached disk, you can use either `Dismount-VHD` or `Dismount-DiskImage` with the same parameters that specify the disk path.

Configuring NFS and SMB shared folders

Once you have attached the drives and assigned them a letter, you are able to create folders and store data in them. To give users access to folders and data over the network, you must configure the folder to be shared, and define user-access control over the shared resources.

Windows Server 2016 supports **Server Message Block** (**SMB**), a network file-sharing protocol that enables applications to communicate on top of the TCP/IP protocol, in a client-server scenario. It allows a user or an application to access remote resources on a server. Windows Server 2012 introduced SMB 3.0, while Windows Server 2016 and Windows 10 support version 3.1.1. Newer versions of Microsoft operating systems support the latest SMB version, which introduced significant performance and security improvements over the older protocol versions. Operating systems older than Windows Vista and Windows Server 2008 support only SMB version 1, which has a significant security vulnerability.

Microsoft addressed the SMB v.1 vulnerability in Microsoft Security Bulletin MS17-010, explaining Security Updates for the Microsoft Windows SMB Server (4013389). Using SMB v.1 communication should be avoided, and operating systems should be patched to avoid possible remote code execution. See `https://docs.microsoft.com/en-us/security-updates/securitybulletins/2017/ms17-010` for more information.

The Storage Service role service in Windows Server 2016 provides a storage management functionality. It is installed by default and cannot be removed. The File Server role service manages shared folders and if it is not installed, the operating system installs it automatically when you create a shared folder.

There are several ways to configure sharing. The easiest and quickest way is to right-click on the folder you want to share, hover over **Share with**, and click **Specific people...**:

A **File Sharing** dialog box opens, where you can add a user to the list of people who have access to the folder. Here, you can only add or remove a user and assign read or read/write sharing permissions.

To configure sharing permissions and a few more options, right-click on a folder, then select **Properties** to open the folder's properties window. In the **Sharing** tab, two options are available: **Network File and Folder Sharing** and **Advanced Sharing**. **Network File and Folder Sharing** opens the same window as in the previous example, while **Advanced Sharing** allows you to configure sharing with more control over the sharing process, as well as configuring more sharing options. To configure **Advanced Sharing**, click on the **Advanced Sharing** button. The following window will open:

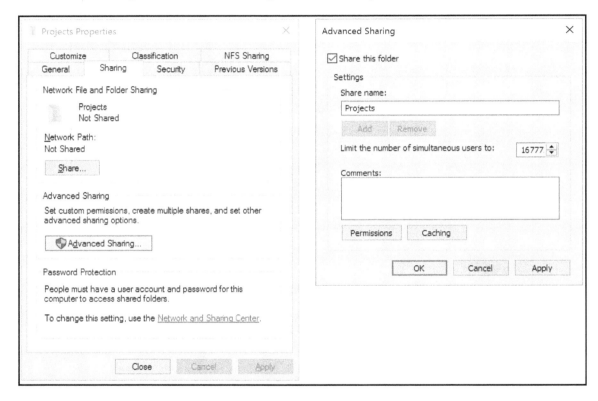

To turn sharing on and enable advanced options, click the **Share this folder** check box. You can limit the number of simultaneous users who can access the shared folder over the network at the same time. To configure shared folder permissions more granularly, click on the **Permissions** button to open the **Permissions** window. Here, you can add or remove users and groups and set **Allow** or **Deny** shared permissions for users and groups in the list. **Advanced Sharing** also allows you to configure file-caching, to choose which files are available to users who are offline.

Besides the SMB protocol, Windows Server 2016 supports **Network File Protocol** (**NFS**), which allows file transfers between computers using Windows and non-Windows operating systems, such as Linux or UNIX. The server for the NFS role service enables a computer to act as a file server for other non-Windows computers. The client for the NFS feature enables the Windows Server computer to access UNIX-based NFS servers:

1. To configure folder-sharing using the NFS protocol, the Server for NFS role service must be installed. Right-click on a folder and choose **Properties**, then click on the **NFS Sharing** tab:

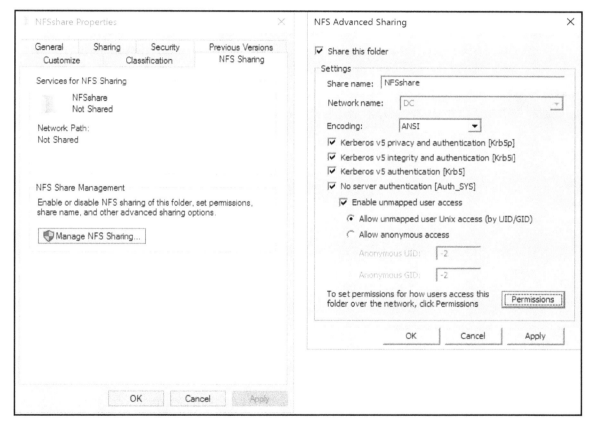

2. To enable or disable NFS sharing, set sharing permissions, and configure other advanced sharing options, click on the **Manage NFS Sharing...** button. Advanced options include choices of encoding, authentication methods, and anonymous client access configuration.

Configuring shares using the Server Manager

The Server Manager allows you to perform advanced configuration and management of shared folders on a single server or on multiple servers. Both SMB and NFS shared folders are supported.

Creating SMB shared folders

To create a folder share using the Server Manager, use the following steps:

1. Open the **Server Manager** from the Start menu.
2. On the menu on the left, click **File and Storage Services**. A submenu will appear.
3. Click **Shares** and the **Shares** page will open with two additional tiles: **VOLUME** and **QUOTA**, as shown in the following screenshot:

4. From the **TASKS** menu on top of the **Shares** tile, select **New Share** and the **New Share Wizard** will appear. Five options are available, three for creating SMB shares and two for creating NFS shares.
   - **SMB Share - Quick**: This offers options for a quick configuration of the basic sharing options.
   - **SMB Share - Advanced**: This offers advanced configuration options, such as **Management Properties** and **Quota** options.

- **SMB Share - Applications**: This offers configuration options suitable for specific workloads, such as Hyper-V.
- **NFS Share - Quick**: This provides the quickest way to configure NFS shares, displaying the basic options.
- **NFS Share - Advanced**: This provides advanced configuration options, such as **Management Properties** and **Quota** options:

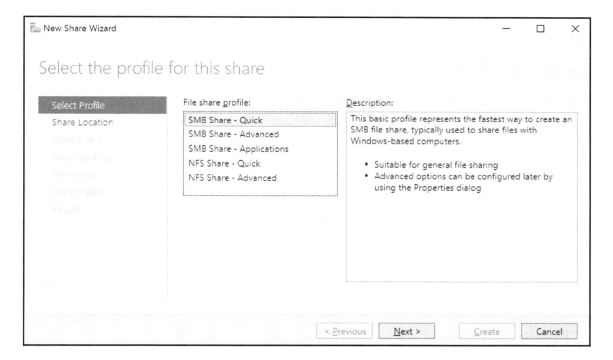

5. Select the **SMB Share – Advanced** file share profile and click **Next**. You can navigate through the **New Share Wizard** either by clicking on the **Next** and **Previous** buttons, or by selecting the step name from the list on the left side of the wizard.

6. In the **Share Location** step, select the server and a volume on which you will configure the shared folder. For a server to appear in the **Server** list, the **File Server Resource Manager** role service must be installed:

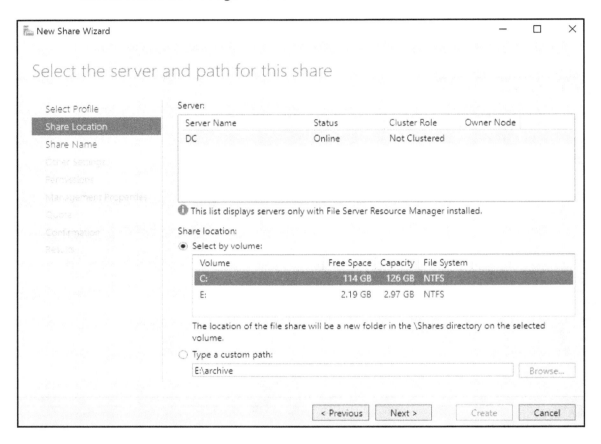

7. To select the **Share** location, either select the volume where the shared folder will be created, or type a custom path to the shared folder. Alternatively, you can click on the **Browse** button and point to the location of shared folder. Click **Next**.

8. On the **Share Name** page, type in the shared name of the shared folder and enter the share description if you like, to describe the contents or the purpose of the shared folder. The local path and the remote path are populated automatically. If the specified folder does not exist, a folder is created. Click **Next**:

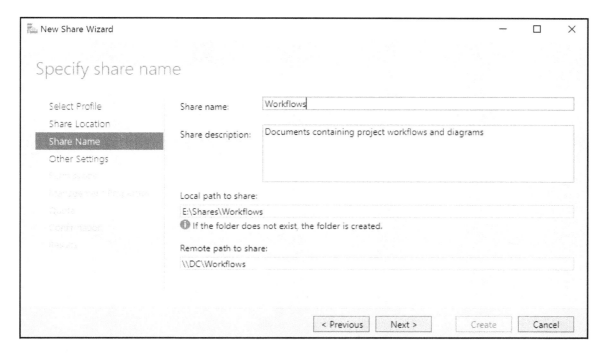

9. The **Other Settings** page contains various configuration options:
   - **Enable access-based enumeration**: When enabled, only the files and folders that a user has permission to access are displayed. For files and folders that a user does not have permission to access, Windows Server hides them from the user's view. The filtering of the files and folders happens on the file server at the time of the request. It is very important to keep in mind that access-based enumeration is neither a security feature nor an access-control feature.

- **Allow caching of share**: Enable this feature to make the content of the folder available if users are offline. If a user marks the folder or a file as **Always Available Offline**, a client computer stores a local copy of the data. If a user is offline, a local copy is used until a folder share is online and available again, when the synchronization of the data occurs.
- **Enable BranchCache on the file share**: Enable this option to take advantage of BranchCache, a feature that allows remote computers to share locally-cached shared-folder data.
- **Encrypt data access**: Check this option to enable secure data transfer between a shared folder and a user:

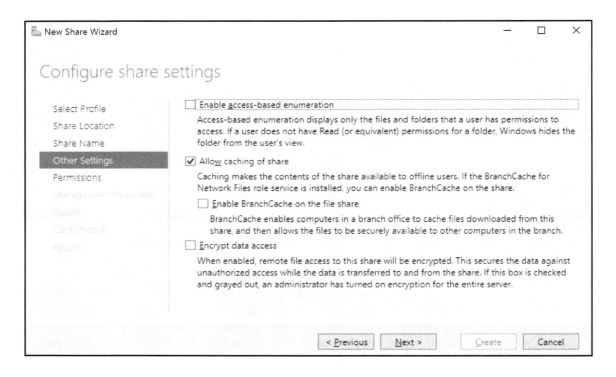

10. The **Permission** option page will open. It allows you to configure and customize access-control permissions of the shared folder and its content. When you click on the **Customize permissions...** button, the **Advanced Security Settings** for the current folder open. Here, you can configure permission entries, share permissions, auditing settings, and check the effective access permissions of a user for the shared folder you are configuring:

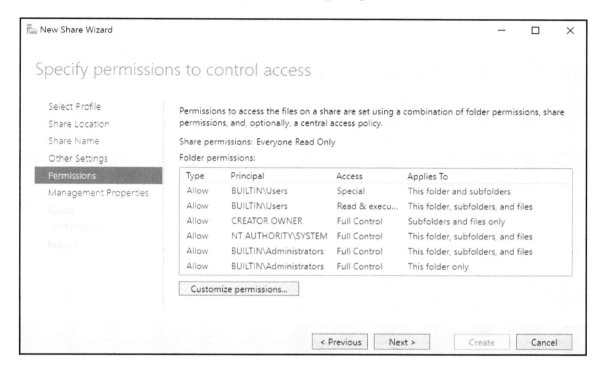

In the **Share** tab, you can assign **Allow** or **Deny** share settings for the current folder that will be applied to a chosen security principal. Three share permissions are available and the abilities they allow or deny are cumulative, from the most restrictive (**Read**), to the most permissive (**Full control**). The share permissions control the following behavior:

- **Read**: The user can access folders within the shared folder; execute files; and display file data, attributes, filenames, and folder names.
- **Change**: The user can delete folders and files, change file attributes, modify data, add files, and create folders.
- **Full Control**: The user can take ownership of files, change file permissions. File and folder permissions are explained in more detail later in this chapter. When you are done configuring permissions, click **OK**:

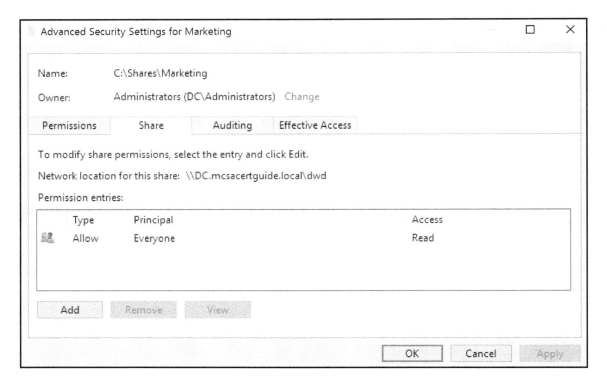

11. The **Management Properties** page is the first of the two advanced configuration pages. Here, you can specify the **Folder Usage** value of the folder, which refers to the values used in the classification rules. The classification rules and classification properties are defined in the **File Server Resource Manager**. You can also specify the **Folder Owner Email** addresses – used for contacting the person responsible for assistance if you are unable to connect to the shared resources, usually an administrator or a user with a delegated role. Click **Next**:

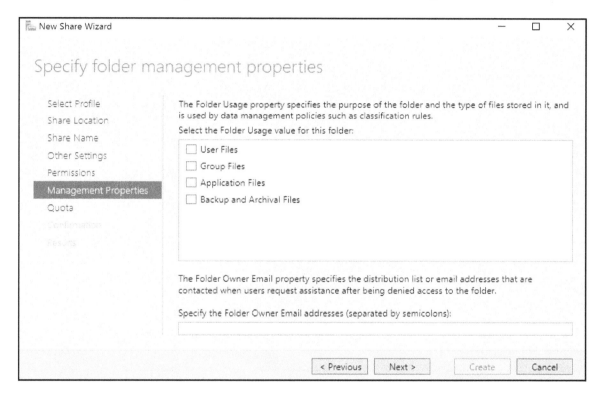

12. In the second of the two advanced configuration pages, you can turn on quota-monitoring for a shared folder. You can configure folder-storage usage monitoring and apply limits to the amount of data users can store in a shared folder. Several templates are available, but you can make changes later if you don't specify the quota settings now:

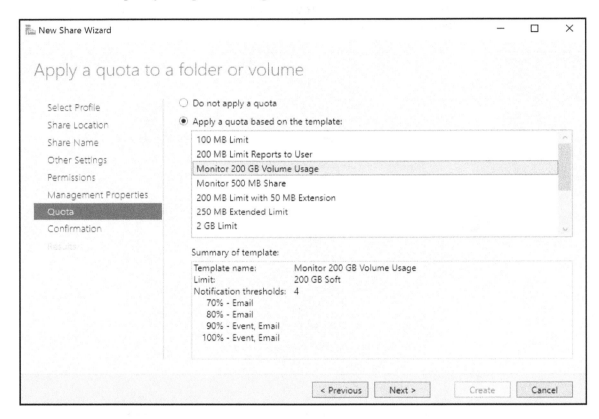

13. Configure the quota options, then click **Next** and a **Confirmation** page will appear with a summary of the selected wizard options. After confirming that the settings are correct, click **Create**:

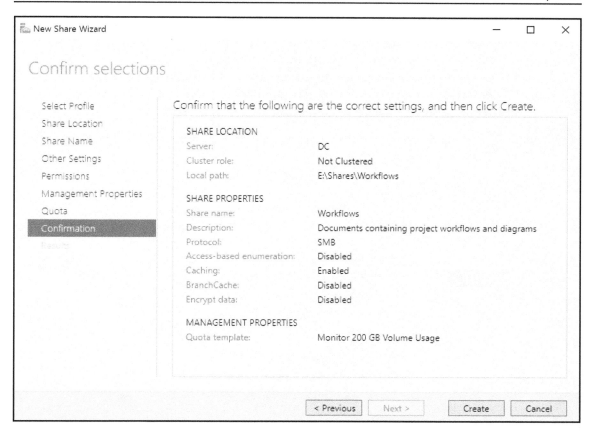

14. A **Results** page appears with information about the status of the individual steps. Click **Close** to close the **New Share Wizard** window.

Creating NFS shared folders

The procedure to create an NFS folder share using the Server Manager involves using the same New Share Wizard introduced in the previous section. We will skip the steps that are the same as when creating SMB shared folders. Instead, we will show the steps specific to creating NFS folder shares:

1. Open the **Server Manager** from the Start menu and navigate to **File and Storage Services**.
2. On the **Shares** page, select **New Share**, and start the **New Share Wizard**.

3. Select the **NFS Share – Advanced Profile** and proceed with the configuration steps. The **Share Location** and **Share Name** steps are identical to the steps in the SMB shared folder wizard and are not shown here.

4. On the **Authentication** page, choose the authentication methods used for the folder share you are configuring. The available methods are **Kerberos v5 authentication** and **No server authentication**. Click **Next**:

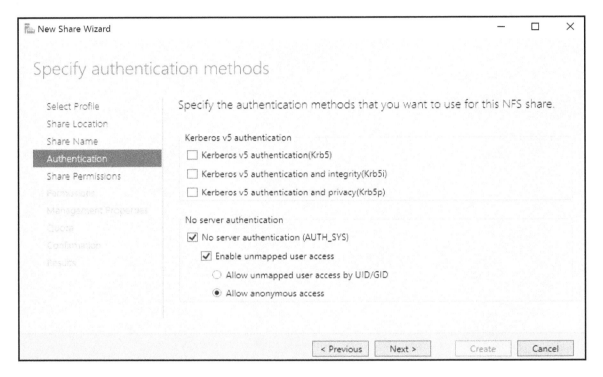

5. The **Share Permissions** screen will open with a list of the currently-configured share permissions. To add, edit, or delete a permission, choose the respective buttons.

6. The rest of the options are identical to the SMB sharing wizard steps.

Configuring sharing using PowerShell

Managing shares and sessions is possible using PowerShell as well. Windows Server 2016 support for SMB sharing operations is provided via the SmbShare PowerShell module and its cmdlets. The following examples show how you can use the SmbShare cmdlet to get information about the shares.

- To display the SmbShare commands, type the following commands:

  Get-Command –Module SmbShare –name *smbs*

  The output of the preceding command is seen in the following screenshot:

```
PS C:\Users\Administrator> Get-Command -Module SmbShare -name *smbs*

CommandType     Name                                    Version    Source
-----------     ----                                    -------    ------
Alias           cssmbse -> Close-SmbSession             2.0.0.0    SmbShare
Alias           gsmbs -> Get-SmbShare                   2.0.0.0    SmbShare
Alias           gsmbsc -> Get-SmbServerConfiguration    2.0.0.0    SmbShare
Alias           gsmbse -> Get-SmbSession                2.0.0.0    SmbShare
Alias           gsmbsn -> Get-SmbServerNetworkInterface 2.0.0.0    SmbShare
Alias           nsmbs -> New-SmbShare                   2.0.0.0    SmbShare
Alias           rsmbs -> Remove-SmbShare                2.0.0.0    SmbShare
Alias           ssmbs -> Set-SmbShare                   2.0.0.0    SmbShare
Alias           ssmbsc -> Set-SmbServerConfiguration    2.0.0.0    SmbShare
Function        Block-SmbShareAccess                    2.0.0.0    SmbShare
Function        Close-SmbSession                        2.0.0.0    SmbShare
Function        Get-SmbServerConfiguration              2.0.0.0    SmbShare
Function        Get-SmbServerNetworkInterface           2.0.0.0    SmbShare
Function        Get-SmbSession                          2.0.0.0    SmbShare
Function        Get-SmbShare                            2.0.0.0    SmbShare
Function        Get-SmbShareAccess                      2.0.0.0    SmbShare
Function        Grant-SmbShareAccess                    2.0.0.0    SmbShare
Function        New-SmbShare                            2.0.0.0    SmbShare
Function        Remove-SmbShare                         2.0.0.0    SmbShare
Function        Revoke-SmbShareAccess                   2.0.0.0    SmbShare
Function        Set-SmbServerConfiguration              2.0.0.0    SmbShare
Function        Set-SmbShare                            2.0.0.0    SmbShare
Function        Unblock-SmbShareAccess                  2.0.0.0    SmbShare
```

- To list all available shares, you could use Server Manager, but the Get-SmbShare PowerShell command will display all shares on a computer, including hidden shares and additional share information. Type Get-SMbShare without parameters to list all the available shares:

  Get-SmbShare

The output of the preceding command can be seen in the following screenshot:

```
PS C:\Users\Administrator> Get-SmbShare

Name              ScopeName Path                  Description
----              --------- ----                  -----------
ADMIN$            *         C:\Windows            Remote Admin
C$                *         C:\                   Default share
E$                *         E:\                   Default share
IPC$              *                               Remote IPC
Legal Documents   *         E:\Legal Documents
Projects          *         E:\Projects
Workflows         *         E:\Shares\Workflows   Documents containing project workflows and diagrams
```

- To get more information about a folder, you will still use `Get-SmbShare`, but to list all properties of a shared folder, you can use the `Format-List` or `Select-Object` properties:

```
Get-SmbShare -Name "Legal Documents" | Format-List -Property *
Get-SmbShare -Name "Legal documents" | Select-Object *
Get-SmbShare -Name "Legal documents" | Select *
```

All three of these examples will list the properties of the `Legal Documents` shared folder:

```
PS C:\Users\Administrator> Get-SmbShare -Name "Legal documents" | Format-List -Property *

PresetPathAcl         : System.Security.AccessControl.DirectorySecurity
ShareState            : Online
AvailabilityType      : NonClustered
ShareType             : FileSystemDirectory
FolderEnumerationMode : AccessBased
CachingMode           : Manual
SmbInstance           : Default
CATimeout             : 0
ConcurrentUserLimit   : 0
ContinuouslyAvailable : False
CurrentUsers          : 0
Description           :
EncryptData           : False
Name                  : Legal Documents
Path                  : E:\Legal Documents
Scoped                : False
ScopeName             : *
SecurityDescriptor    : O:LAG:S-1-5-21-2591145696-2776910881-2959176607-513D:(A;OICI;FA;;;BA)(A;OICI;FA;;;WD
                        )
ShadowCopy            : False
Special               : False
Temporary             : False
Volume                : \\?\Volume{3a5deb9d-02ab-4462-89f0-4b9871d9576f}\
PSComputerName        :
CimClass              : ROOT/Microsoft/Windows/SMB:MSFT_SmbShare
CimInstanceProperties : {AvailabilityType, CachingMode, CATimeout, ConcurrentUserLimit...}
CimSystemProperties   : Microsoft.Management.Infrastructure.CimSystemProperties
```

- To create a new folder share, use the `New-SmbShare` command. The syntax for this is as follows:

```
New-SmbShare -Name sharedname -Path pathname
```

The `Name` parameter specifies the name of the SMB share and accepts 80 or less characters, while a `Path` parameter specifies the location of the folder that you want to share.

While the `Name` and `Path` parameters are required, other parameters are optional:

- `AsJob`: Runs the command as a background job
- `CATimeout`: Specifies the length of time after which the shared folder will time out
- `CachingMode`: Specifies one of the five caching modes for the share: `None`, `Manual`, `Documents`, `Programs`, or `BranchCache`
- `ChangeAccess`: Specifies the users that will have permission to change the share
- `CimSession`: Runs the command on a remote computer or in a remote session
- `ConcurrentUserLimit`: Specifies the maximum number of simultaneous connections
- `Confirm`: Prompts the user for confirmation before running
- `ContinuouslyAvailable`: Specifies that the share is continuously available
- `Description`: Specify the description of a share—a maximum of 256 characters is accepted
- `EncryptData`: Specifies that the share is encrypted
- `FolderEnumerationMode`: Specifies the visibility of a folder to users
- `FullAccess`: Specifies accounts that will have full share access
- `NoAccess`: Specifies accounts that will be denied access to the share
- `ReadAccess`: Specifies accounts that will have read permission
- `ScopeName`: Defines the scope name of the share
- `SecurityDescriptor`: Specifies the security descriptor for the share

- Temporary: Specifies whether the share will be temporary, which means that it will be available until the computer next restarts
- ThrottleLimit: Specifies the maximum number of simultaneous operations to run the cmdlet
- WhatIf: Shows what would happen if the command is run

- To change the existing share and modify its properties, use the Set-SmbShare cmdlet. For example, the first command line encrypts the Marketing share, and the second command adds the description for the Production share:

```
Set-SmbShare -Name "Marketing" -EncryptData $True
Set-SmbShare -Name "Production" -Description "Production
Documentation" -Force
```

When you have set up the folder shares and the user starts connecting to them, you might want to manage share sessions. This includes monitoring share sessions, closing sessions, and adding or removing shares and permissions.

- To get information about currently-established sessions between the SMB server and the SMB clients, use the Get-SmbSession cmdlet:

```
Get-SmbSession
```

The output of the preceding command can be seen in the following screenshot:

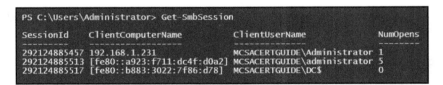

- To display information about a connection established with a specific SMB client, or to display session information about the specific session, use the following:

```
# Connection information about a client whose IP address is
192.168.1.231
Get-SmbSession -ClientComputerName "192.168.1.231"

# Connection information about a client with a provided ID
Get-SmbSession -SessionId 292124885513
```

The output of the preceding command can be seen in the following screenshot:

```
PS C:\Users\Administrator> Get-SmbSession -ClientComputerName "192.168.1.231"

SessionId      ClientComputerName  ClientUserName            NumOpens
---------      ------------------  --------------            --------
292124885457   192.168.1.231       MCSACERTGUIDE\Administrator 1


PS C:\Users\Administrator> Get-SmbSession -SessionId 292124885513

SessionId      ClientComputerName        ClientUserName            NumOpens
---------      ------------------        --------------            --------
292124885513   [fe80::a923:f711:dc4f:d0a2] MCSACERTGUIDE\administrator 3
```

Of course, you would use your own values for the `-SessionId` and `-ClientComputerName` parameters in the previous examples, as in any subsequent examples.

- A session has additional information that can be displayed using the `-Property` parameter:

```
Get-SmbSession -SessionId 292124885457 | Select-Object -Property *
```

The output of the preceding command can be seen in the following screenshot:

```
PS C:\Users\Administrator> Get-SmbSession -SessionId 292124885457 | Select-Object -Property *

SmbInstance          : Default
ClientComputerName   : 192.168.1.231
ClientUserName       : MCSACERTGUIDE\Administrator
ClusterNodeName      :
Dialect              : 3.1.1
NumOpens             : 1
ScopeName            : *
SecondsExists        : 10042
SecondsIdle          : 197
SessionId            : 292124885457
TransportName        :
PSComputerName       :
CimClass             : ROOT/Microsoft/Windows/SMB:MSFT_SmbSession
CimInstanceProperties : {ClientComputerName, ClientUserName, ClusterNodeName, Dialect...}
CimSystemProperties  : Microsoft.Management.Infrastructure.CimSystemProperties
```

- Any open session can be closed using the `Close-SmbSession` command by providing the session parameters:

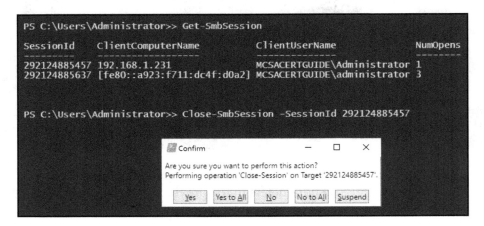

Before terminating the session, the confirmation dialog prompts you to decide whether you are sure you want to complete the command. Terminating a session closes any open files and ceases session communication with the client. The client can always establish a new session with the server, but the changes to the files opened during the session that was terminated might not be saved. A client does not receive any notifications about the session being terminated, so this operation should be performed with caution. These examples show how the session can be terminated in three different ways: specifying the connected SMB client user name, the client computer name, or the session ID number:

```
# Close session specifying user credentials
Close-SmbSession -ClientUsername MCSACERTGUIDE\Administrator

# Close session specifying SMB client computer name
Close-SmbSession -ClientComputerName "192.168.1.231"

# Close session specifying a specific session ID
Close-SmbSession -SessionId 292124885457
```

Terminating a session closes all files that were opened during that session. If you want to close just one file, you would use the `Get-SmbOpenFile` cmdlet to list all the open files first, and then `Close-SmbOpenFile` to close a specific file:

```
PS C:\Users\Administrator>> Get-SmbOpenFile

FileId          SessionId       Path                          ShareRelativePath ClientComputerName            ClientUserNam
                                                                                                              e
------          ---------       ----                          ----------------- ------------------            -------------
292057777485 292124885457 E:\Legal Documents\                                   192.168.1.231                 MCSACERTGU...
292057778465 292124885637 E:\Projects\                                          [fe80::a923:f711:dc4f:d0a2]   MCSACERTGU...
292057778553 292124885457 E:\Legal Documents\                                   192.168.1.231                 MCSACERTGU...
292057778573 292124885457 E:\Projects\New folder New folder                     192.168.1.231                 MCSACERTGU...
292057778589 292124885457 E:\Projects\                                          192.168.1.231                 MCSACERTGU...


PS C:\Users\Administrator>> Get-SmbOpenFile -FileId 292057777485 | Select-Object -Property *

SmbInstance          : Default
ClientComputerName   : 192.168.1.231
ClientUserName       : MCSACERTGUIDE\Administrator
ClusterNodeName      :
ContinuouslyAvailable : False
Encrypted            : False
FileId               : 292057777485
Locks                : 0
Path                 : E:\Legal Documents\
Permissions          : 1048705
ScopeName            : *
SessionId            : 292124885457
ShareRelativePath    :
Signed               : True
PSComputerName       :
CimClass             : ROOT/Microsoft/Windows/SMB:MSFT_SmbOpenFile
CimInstanceProperties : {ClientComputerName, ClientUserName, ClusterNodeName, ContinuouslyAvailable...}
CimSystemProperties  : Microsoft.Management.Infrastructure.CimSystemProperties
```

As displayed in the screenshot, the commands to display a list of open files, to display information about a file, and to close a specific file are the following:

```
# Display a list of open files on a SMB server computer
Get-SmbOpenFile

# Display detailed information about opened file
Get-SmbOpenFile -FileId 292057777485 | Select-Object -Property *

# Close specified file
Close-SmbOpenFile -FileId 292057777485
```

Configuring file and folder permissions

To control who has access to files and folders, alongside share permissions, Windows Server 2016 also uses file and folder access permissions. Permissions are a vital part of the Windows security architecture and are used for authorizing computers, groups, and users to access files and folders or objects on a network.

Sometimes, users identify permissions with user rights. Permissions and rights are two different things; permissions are attached to objects, while user rights are attached to user accounts. User rights are also identified as privileges, such as the right to log on remotely or locally, while permissions define which actions are allowed by a subject on an object, such as modifying the content of a file or listing a folder.

Permissions are defined in **Access Control Entries** or **ACEs**, which are elements of the **Access Control List**, or **ACL**. There are two types of ACLs: a **Discretionary ACL (DACL)** and a **System ACL (SACL)**. The DACL specifies who has access to an object while the SACL controls the generation of audit messages.

In the authorization and access-control model, a subject has an Access Token, which contains a list of privileges. The operating system performs access checks and compares the list of privileges to the ACE entry in the object's DACL security descriptor. It examines and compares each ACE until a match is found. Then, a decision is made as to whether to allow or deny access.

As you can see, the information about who has access to a folder or a file is contained within a file or a folder itself. For this reason, moving a file or a folder also moves their respective ACLs. Both share permissions and access permissions combined have an influence if a security principal (a user, a group or a computer) is allowed to access an object. The access permissions are defined on an object itself:

1. To define an object's permissions, right-click on an object, open the **Properties** window, and click on the **Security** tab. In the following screenshot, the folder properties are on the left, while the file properties are on the right:

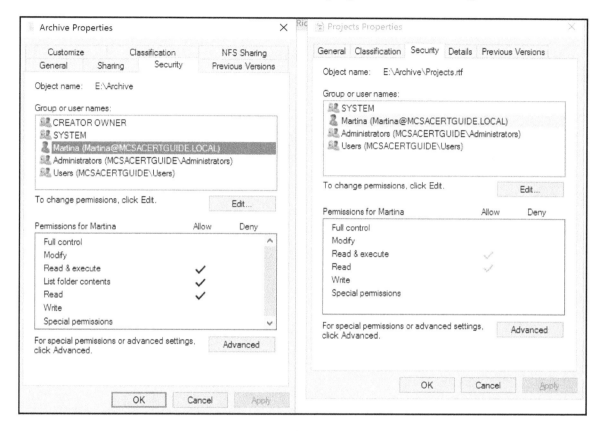

The **Security** tab has two parts: **Group or user names**, where you manage security objects on the object, in this case a file or a folder, and **Permissions**, where you define the permissions or ACL entries for the selected security objects. The security objects that can be defined are built-in security principals, service accounts, computers, groups, and users.

2. To edit the list of security objects, click the **Edit...** button, and a similar window to the **Security** tab opens. In the following screenshot, the security properties of the folder are on the left and the security properties of the file are on the right:

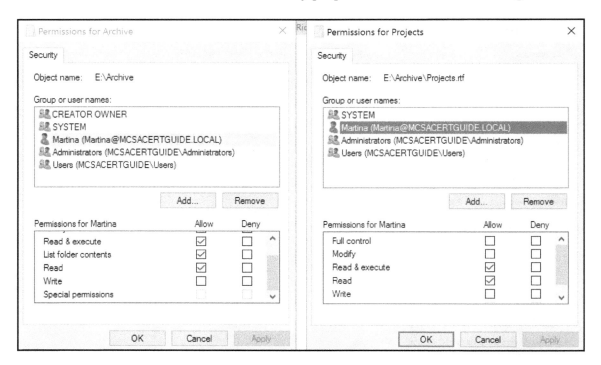

The object's **Security** properties window contains a list of security objects list and their respective permissions. These permissions are **Basic** permissions and allow you to quickly define the most common access rights. Each type of security object has its own specific rights, as do file and folder permissions. The basic permissions are **Write**, **Read**, **Read & execute**, **Modify**, and **Full control**. The **Advanced** permissions are configurable from the previous window.

The following table shows which special permissions are allowed in each basic permission option:

Special Permissions	Full Control	Modify	Read & Execute	List Folder Contents (folders only)	Read	Write
Read Permissions	●	●	●	●	●	●
Change Permissions	●					
Create Files/ Write Data	●	●				●
List Folder/ Read Data	●	●	●	●	●	
Traverse Folder/ Execute File	●	●	●	●		
Create Folders/ Append Data	●	●				●
Delete Subfolders and Files	●					
Delete	●	●				
Read Attributes	●	●	●	●	●	
Read Extended Attributes	●	●	●	●	●	
Write Attributes	●	●				●
Write Extended Attributes	●	●				●
Take Ownership	●					
Synchronize	●	●	●	●	●	●

The special permissions for files and folders are as follows:

- **Read Permissions**: Indicates whether files can be read.
- **Change Permissions**: Indicates whether files can be changed.
- **Create Files/Write Data**: The Create Files permission indicates whether files can be created in the folder. The Write Data permission indicates whether changes can be made and existing content can be overwritten. This permission applies to files only.
- **List Folder/Read Data**: The List Folder permission indicates whether file names and subfolder names in the folder can be viewed. List Folder only affects the contents of that folder; it does not affect whether the folder you are setting the permission on will be listed. List Folder applies to folders only. The Read Data permission indicates whether the data in the files can be viewed and applies to files only.

- **Traverse Folder/Execute File**: The Traverse Folder permission indicates whether moving through folders to reach other files or folders is allowed, even if the user has no permissions on the traversed folders. It applies to folders only. The Traverse folder takes effect only when the group or user is not granted the Bypass traverse-checking user right in the Group Policy snap-in. By default, the Everyone group is given the Bypass traverse-checking user right. The Execute File permission indicates whether program files can be run. Setting the Traverse Folder permission on a folder does not automatically set the Execute File permission on all files in that folder.

- **Create Folders/Append Data**: The Create Folders permission indicates whether folders in the folder can be created. The Append Data permission indicates whether changes appended to a file, that is, to the end of the file, can be made, without changing, deleting, or overwriting existing data in the file.

- **Delete Subfolders and Files**: Indicates whether subfolders and files can be deleted, even if the Delete permission has not been set on the subfolder or file.

- **Delete**: Indicates whether the file or folder can be deleted. You can delete a file or folder if you have been granted the Delete Subfolders and Files permission on the parent folder, even if you do not have the Delete permission on a file or folder.

- **Read Attributes**: Indicates whether the NTFS attributes of a file or folder can be viewed.

- **Read Extended Attributes**: Indicates whether the extended attributes of a file or folder can be viewed. Extended attributes are specific to programs and may be different for each program.

- **Write Attributes**: Indicates whether the attributes of a file or folder can be changed. The Write Attributes permission does not imply creating or deleting files or folders, it only includes the permission to make changes to the attributes of a file or folder.

- **Write Extended Attributes**: Indicates whether the extended attributes of a file or folder can be changed.

- **Take Ownership**: Indicates whether taking ownership of the file or folder is allowed. The owner of a file or folder always has the right to change permissions on it, irrespective of any existing permissions that protect the file or folder.

- **Synchronize**: Applies only to multithreaded, multiprocess programs, and indicates whether threads to synchronize the file or folder are allowed.

Two types of permissions exist: **explicit permissions** and **inherited permissions**. You may hear of a third type of a permission, called implicit permission, but some disagree with this being called a permission because implicit permissions do not have ACL entries:

- Explicit permissions are the permissions that are set on an object.
- Inherited permissions are propagated or inherited from a parent object to a child object. Inherited permissions ease the process of administration and give the permissions consistency between objects in a folder, or in a container.
- Implicit permissions are permissions that are implied on an object rather than explicitly defined. For example, not giving explicit read and write permissions to a user implicitly denies that user the permission to read and write to the given object.

The best way to deny a user access to an object is with implicit permission. As a rule, if you do not want a user to have rights on an object or to perform specific actions on an object, do not configure a deny permission, simply don't configure a permission at all. Because a deny explicit permission has a priority over any allow permissions, explicitly denying permissions is not recommended unless you know exactly what you want to accomplish and unless you know the consequences of explicit denial. You must know which effective permissions will be defined on this kind of object.

Modifying Advanced Security Settings

To modify or make advanced changes to the permissions of a security object, do the following:

1. Open the object's properties.
2. Select the **Security** tab.
3. Click on the advanced button, which opens the **Advanced Security Settings** for the given object.

4. On the **Permissions** tab, select a user, group, or other security object:

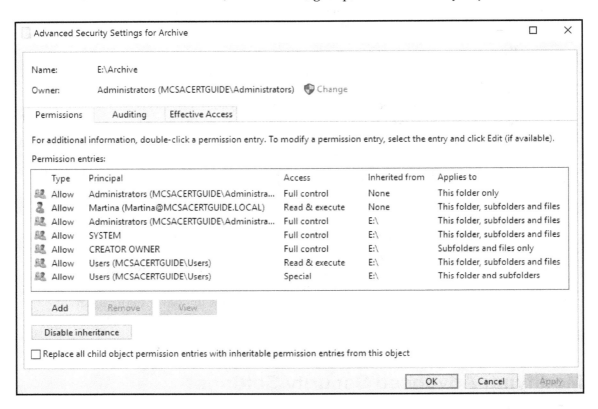

5. Click **Edit**, and the **Permission Entry** window will open.

6. Click **Advanced Permissions** on the right to expand the permissions and show the advanced permissions. Set up the necessary permissions and click **OK** multiple times to close all open dialog boxes:

When you create a folder, all objects created in that folder inherit the permissions of their parent container. You can break the inheritance by clicking on the **Disable inheritance** button:

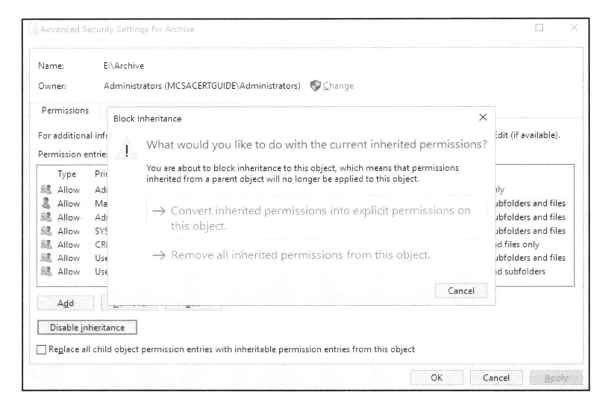

Before disabling the inheritance, the operating system asks you if you want to convert the inherited permissions into explicit permissions or remove all inherited permissions from the object, which sets the **Read** and **Read & execute** permissions on the object. After that, you can set your own permissions or set inheritance from this folder onward by selecting the **Replace all child object permission entries with inheritable permission entries from this object** checkbox.

The best practice for setting permissions to objects is to set permissions on groups. This way, you can add or remove permissions by group membership, that is, by adding or removing objects from a group. Files can be moved out of folders and placed in other folders, and if you set permissions on objects instead (for example, files), managing, modifying, adding or removing permissions from files becomes virtually impossible. This makes it difficult to ensure that every file has the right set of permissions.

Implementing and configuring server storage

Windows Server 2016 uses Storage Spaces, a storage technology that helps protect your data in case of a drive failure. It combines the capacity of multiple disks to create a storage pool, and then uses this increased, combined storage capacity to create Storage Spaces. A Storage Space is a software-defined storage: a pool, a volume, a disk, or a virtual hard disk that is resilient, flexible, and expandable. Storage Spaces are also supported on Windows 10. They can be used in the following ways in Windows Server 2016:

- With all storage in a single, standalone server
- In a cluster, with a storage attached locally to each node, using Storage Spaces Direct
- In a cluster, with SAS drives placed in one or more enclosures

Configuring storage pools

To be able to use a storage space within Storage Spaces, you must create a storage pool. A storage pool, which is a collection of physical disks combined from multiple sources, can be created using one disk only. Doing this, however, defies its primary purpose, which is resiliency.

To create a storage pool using Server Manager, follow these steps:

1. Open **Server Manager** and select **File and Storage Services**.
2. In the menu on the left, choose **Storage Pools**:

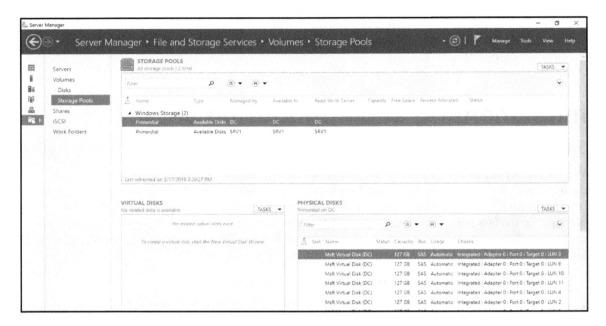

3. If you have added servers to the Server Manager, they appear on the **Storage Pools** server list. You notice that two storage pools are available, one on each server: DC and SRV1. A **Primordial** pool is a default pool of available disks on a server. This is not a Storage Space pool, and selecting a primordial pool on a server shows the available storage that can be used to create storage pools.

4. Right-click on the **Storage Pools** pane or click **Tasks** and select a **New Storage Pool**. A **New Storage Pool Wizard** window opens:

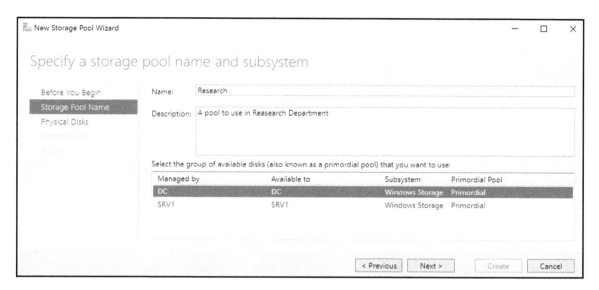

5. You will see the introductory first step, then click **Next**. In the **Storage Pool Name**, enter the name of the storage pool and its description. Select a **Primordial** pool of disks from which the storage pool will be created and click **Next**.

6. On the **Physical Disks** page, select the disks that will be used to create the storage pool. In the **Allocation** column, choose **Hot Spare**, **Manual**, or **Automatic**. Disks marked as a **Hot Spare** are not used until a disk in the pool fails. Then, the Hot Spare disk replaces the failed disk:

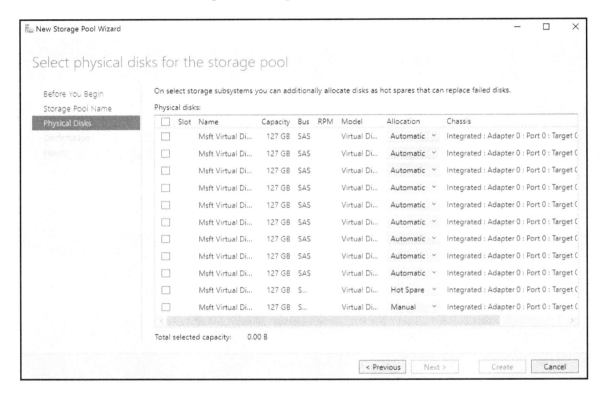

After the storage pool is created, to be able to take advantage of the features that Storage Spaces provide, you must create a virtual disk.

Be careful, virtual disks in Storage Spaces are not the same disks as those used in Hyper-V; you cannot use the storage that is defined by the abstraction layer in Storage Spaces. Windows, particularly PowerShell cmdlets, uses the term **VirtualDisk** to refer to disks created in Storage Spaces and **VHD** as the files used in Hyper-V.

To create a virtual disk in a storage space pool, perform the following steps:

1. Open the **Server Manager** and select **File and Storage Services**.
2. In the menu on the left, choose **Storage Pools**.
3. In the **Virtual Disk** pane in the bottom left, select **Tasks**, then select **New Virtual Disk**.
4. The **Select the storage pool** dialog box opens, displaying a list of available storage pools. Select an available storage pool and click **OK** to open a **New Virtual Disk Wizard**.
5. Enter a name, choose a description for the virtual disk, and then click **Next**.
6. Enclosure awareness automatically protects data by storing copies in separate enclosures. Click **Next**.
7. The **Storage Layout** step allows you to choose the physical layout of the virtual disk:
   - **Simple**: Data is spread over physical disks to increase performance at the expense of resiliency. If a single disk fails, the data is lost.
   - **Mirror**: Data is spread across the disks in multiple copies. This decreases the pool's capacity but increases reliability. To be able to recover from a disk failure, use at least two disks, or three if in a cluster. To protect against two disks failing, you must use at least five disks.

- **Parity**: Both data and parity are spread across physical disks. The pool space is also reduced, because of parity, but the reliability is increased. This setup protects against disk failures as well; to recover from a disk failure, you must use at least three disks, and to recover from two disk failures, you will need at least seven disks.

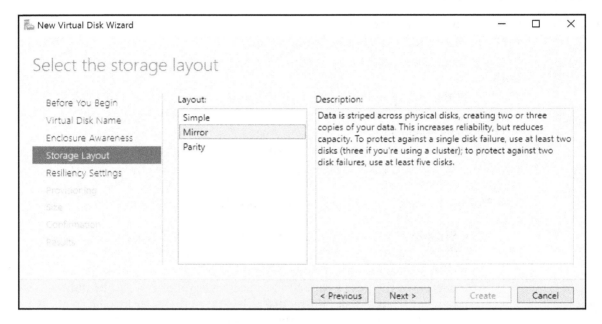

8. If you select **Mirror**, in the next step, you have the possibility to choose the resiliency type, which can be either a **Two-way mirror** or a **Three-way mirror**. Two-way mirror resiliency uses two disks to protect data from a single disk failure, while a Three-way mirror needs at least five disks to protect from two disk failures:

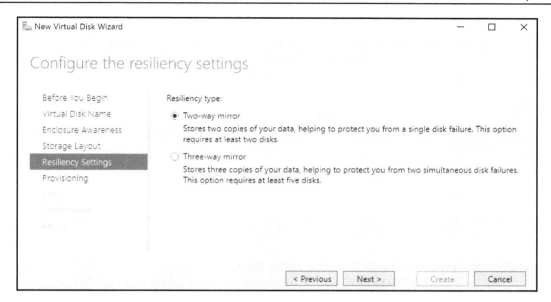

9. If you select **Parity**, you have the option to choose between **Single parity** or **Dual parity**. Single parity stores two copies of the data, uses at least three disks, and protects you from single-disk failure. Dual parity stores three copies of the data to protect you against two-disk failures, but requires at least seven disks:

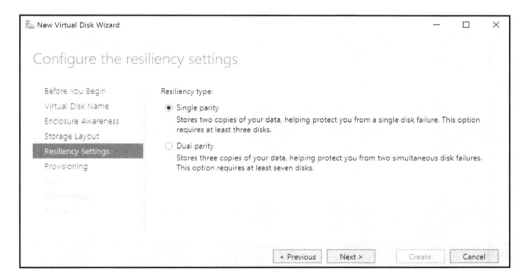

10. Configure the resiliency settings for either **Mirror** or **Parity**, then click **Next**.
11. Under the **Provisioning** type, you need to choose either the **Thin** or **Fixed** provisioning method. Thin provisioning increases the virtual disk space as the data is populated. Fixed provisioning creates the virtual disk space from the pool that is equal to the virtual disk size. Click **Next**.
12. Specify the size of the virtual disk and click **Next**.
13. On the **Confirmation** page, the wizard displays a summary of the selections. Click **Create** and the results of the wizard actions are displayed.

The final step is to create one or more volumes on the virtual disks that you have created. As with the disks, you do not have to use the whole disk space to create a volume.

To create a volume, complete the following steps:

1. Open the **Server Manager** and select **File and Storage Services**.
2. In the menu on the left, choose either **Disks** or **Storage Pools**:
   - For **Disks**, right-click on a disk or a virtual disk in the **Disks** pane and select **New volume**.
   - For **Storage Pools**, right-click on a virtual disk in the **Virtual Disks** pane and select **New volume**.
3. A **New Volume Wizard** opens. On the **Server and Disk** window, choose a server and then choose a disk where the volume will be created. Click **Next**:

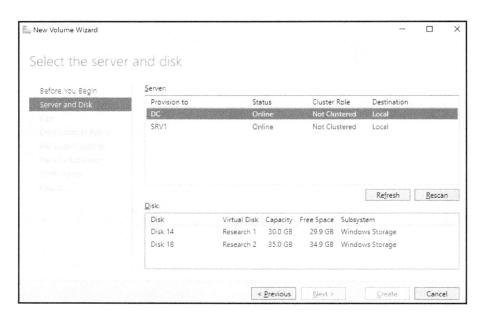

4. Specify the size of the volume and click **Next**.

5. In the **Drive Letter or Folder** step, you can assign a drive letter to a volume, assign a folder to a volume, or not assign anything to a volume. When you assign a folder, the volume appears as a folder within a drive.

6. Configure a filesystem to use, the allocation unit, and a volume label. There is also an option to generate short file names in an 8.3 format for better compatibility with some 16-bit applications, accessing the volume from client computers. If turned on, this option reduces the file operation performance. Click **Next**.

7. Turn on data deduplication and perform the initial steps. We will address data deduplication later in the chapter.

8. After confirming the selections, click **Create** and the volume is created.

Configuring the Internet Small Computer Systems Interface

Internet Small Computer Systems Interface (**iSCSI**) is an IP-based networking standard for connecting data-storage components over a network, usually in storage-area networks or SANs. It enables physically-separate components to communicate over an IP protocol, using TCP port 3260.

iSCSI resolves the problem of connecting remote storage components as well as enabling applications that do not work with mapped drives to use them.

There are two components involved in iSCSI communication: the **iSCSI initiator**, which resides on a server, and the **iSCSI target**, which resides on a storage device. The iSCSI protocol works by transmitting block-level storage data between the iSCSI initiator and the iSCSI target by encapsulating SCSI commands and data in packets that are suitable for transporting via a network, such as WAN, LAN, or the internet. After arrival, the packets are disassembled, and the operating system and applications see the storage as locally-attached storage.

In a Windows Server, the **iSCSI Target Server** role provides the support for storage available via the iSCSI protocol. As the operating system performs the calculations of encapsulating and disassembling the packets, the iSCSI protocol operations can cause significant stress on the CPU, negatively impacting the server operations. The overall processor utilization depends on the number of targets, disks, and sessions, as well as on the speed of the processor.

Additionally, you can install the **iSCSI Host Bus Adapter** (**iSCSI HBA**), a hardware component that offloads iSCSI operations using a dedicated processor. The downside is that iSCSI HBA adapters can be expensive, and the free version that comes with Windows Server might be a better choice if the cost is a decisive factor.

Windows Server takes advantage of iSCSI in several ways:

- Support for block-level storage makes remote storage accessible and available for consolidation at the remote locations.
- Using network and diskless boot, diskless server deployment is easy and very fast, making it ideal for cluster storage or for virtual machines running on Hyper-V.
- iSCSI is a standard, which means products of different vendors are able to communicate easily.
- Runs Windows Server as a network block-storage device for testing in development, demonstration, and lab environments, before deployment in a storage area network.

To configure iSCSI connections, use the iSCSI Initiator in the Control Panel:

1. Right-click on Start and open the **Control Panel**. Navigate to **Administrative Tools** and double-click on the **iSCSI Initiator**.
2. If prompted, start the service.
3. To discover the iSCSI Target, click on the **Discovery** tab and then click on **Discover Portal...**.

4. In the **Discover Target Portal** dialog box, enter an IP address or the DNS name of a target server. Click **OK**:

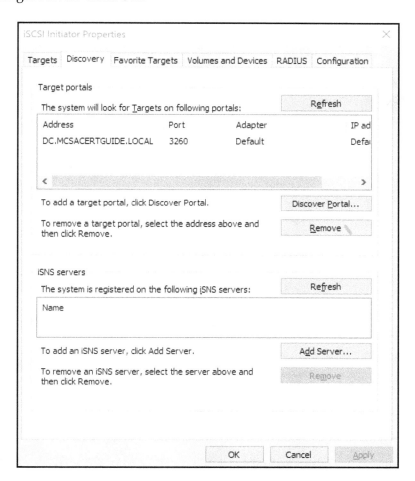

Creating and configuring iSCSI disks, target servers, and iSCSI initiators can be done through a wizard in the Server Manager as well:

1. Open the **Server Manager** and select **File and Storage Services**.
2. In the menu on the left, choose **iSCSI**.
3. In the **iSCSI Virtual Disks** pane, either click anywhere in the pane, or click **Tasks** and select **New iSCSI Virtual Disk**.

4. The **New iSCSI Virtual Disk Wizard** starts and the **Select iSCSI virtual disk location** window opens. Here, you choose the storage location volume:

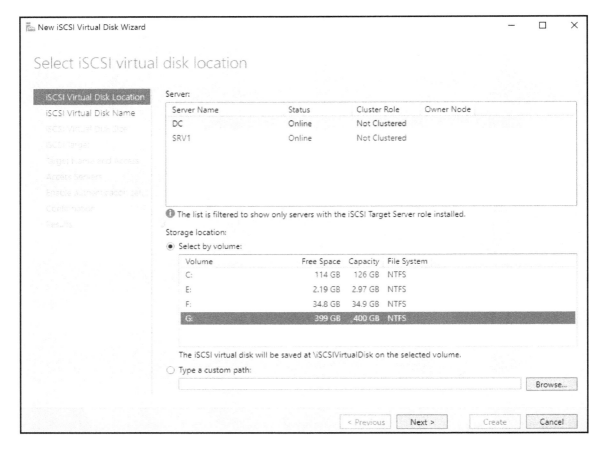

5. Type the name of the virtual hard disk (VHDX file) and an optional description. Click **Next**.

6. Choose the virtual disk size and the type: fixed, dynamically-expanding, or differencing. Click **Next**.

7. Choose an existing iSCSI target or create a new target and proceed to the next step.

8. Choose a name for the target and click **Next**.

9. At this point, click the **Add** button to add an iSCSI initiator or the initiators that will access this iSCSI virtual disk:

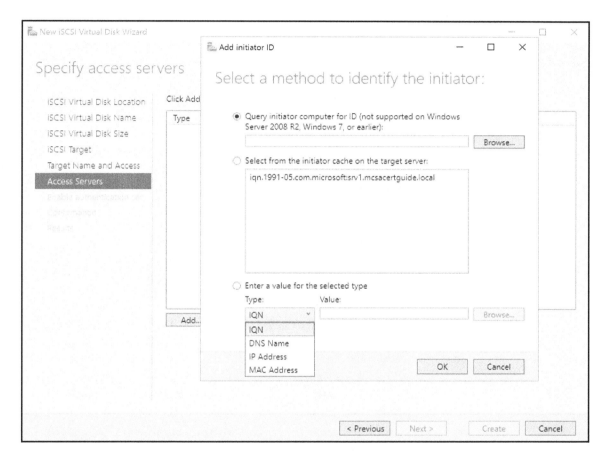

10. Select an initiator from a list of clients in an Active Directory from the initiator cache (if you have connected previously) or provide an IQN, DNS name, IP address, or MAC address to specify a target. Click **OK** and click **Next**.
11. You can also choose to enable connection authentication. Click **Next** to proceed to the summary and click **Create**.

Implementing data deduplication

Data deduplication is a feature of Windows Server that helps to reduce redundant data, increase the available storage space, and reduce storage costs. The deduplication service scans the storage, examines data, and finds redundant or duplicate portions of data. Redundant data is removed and stored only once, or compressed to save space.

To configure deduplication, you must first enable it on a volume:

1. Open the **Server Manager** and select **File and Storage Services**.
2. Do one of the following:
    - In the menu on the left, select **Volumes**, then in the **Volumes** pane, right-click on a volume and select **Configure Data Deduplication**.
    - In the menu on the left, select **Disks**, then in the **Volumes** pane, right-click on a volume and select **Configure Data Deduplication**.
3. In the **Duplication Settings** for the selected folder, click on the drop-down menu and select one of the following three options to turn data deduplication on:
    - **General-purpose file server**: Users' files may have many duplicate files or similar files. Typical shared folders that might benefit from data deduplication are user home folders, software-development shares, and work folders.
    - **Virtual Desktop Infrastructure (VDI) server**: Virtualization guests are very similar to one another in that virtual hard disks in a VDI share common, identical data.
    - **Virtualized Backup Server**: Data between snapshots might not change or changes might not be that big, making backup servers ideal data deduplication candidates.
4. Once you select an option for data deduplication, other options on the page are available to set up. The default time before files are deduplicated is three days, but you can change this to whatever works best for you.
5. If you want to exclude specific folders and types of documents from the deduplication process, enter their file extensions and choose the folders to exclude.

6. Click on the **Set Deduplication Schedule** button to configure the deduplication process' working schedule:

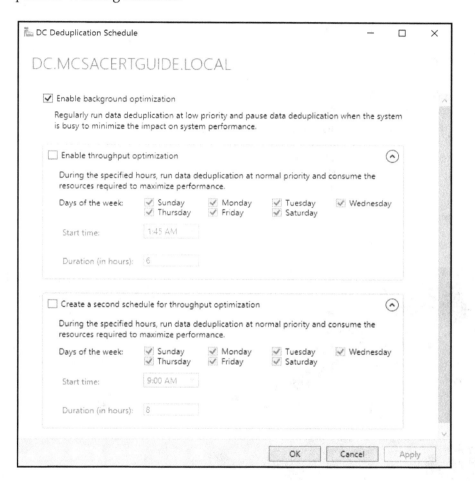

7. Background optimization is turned on by default and I recommend you leave it like this in order to throttle the deduplication process while the server is idle or low on utilization. This way, data deduplication won't disrupt normal server operations with a high disk I/O or a high processor utilization. The two **throughput optimization** settings allow data deduplication to be carried out at a normal priority level during the specified period. For example, you can schedule data-deduplication optimization to run during the night and during the weekends—which is usually when users are not working—to minimize the impact on user operations.

8. Click **OK** twice to close all data-deduplication windows.

Microsoft PowerShell has commands for command-line administration of data deduplication as well. To get the list of supported PowerShell cmdlets within the `Deduplication` module, type the following:

```
Get-Command -Module Deduplication
```

The output of the preceding command can be seen in the following screenshot:

```
PS C:\Users\Administrator> Get-Command -Module Deduplication

CommandType     Name                          Version      Source
-----------     ----                          -------      ------
Function        Disable-DedupVolume           2.0.0.0      Deduplication
Function        Enable-DedupVolume            2.0.0.0      Deduplication
Function        Expand-DedupFile              2.0.0.0      Deduplication
Function        Get-DedupJob                  2.0.0.0      Deduplication
Function        Get-DedupMetadata             2.0.0.0      Deduplication
Function        Get-DedupSchedule             2.0.0.0      Deduplication
Function        Get-DedupStatus               2.0.0.0      Deduplication
Function        Get-DedupVolume               2.0.0.0      Deduplication
Function        Measure-DedupFileMetadata     2.0.0.0      Deduplication
Function        New-DedupSchedule             2.0.0.0      Deduplication
Function        Remove-DedupSchedule          2.0.0.0      Deduplication
Function        Set-DedupSchedule             2.0.0.0      Deduplication
Function        Set-DedupVolume               2.0.0.0      Deduplication
Function        Start-DedupJob                2.0.0.0      Deduplication
Function        Stop-DedupJob                 2.0.0.0      Deduplication
Function        Update-DedupStatus            2.0.0.0      Deduplication
```

Enabling data deduplication using PowerShell is straightforward using the `Enable-DedupVolume` cmdlet:

```
Enable-DedupVolume -Volume "g:" -UsageType Backup
```

This command enables the data deduplication on a `G:` volume and specifies a volume that will be treated and optimized for a virtualized backup server workload.

If you do not want to wait for three days (depending on the settings) to start the deduplication process, you can start the process manually by typing the following:

```
Start-DedupJob -Volume "g:" -Type Optimization -Memory 20
```

To get the status of a deduplication job, type the following:

```
# Lists the status of all volumes with enabled data deduplication
Get-DedupStatus

# Lists the data deduplication status formatted for better readability
Get-DedupStatus | Format-List
```

Summary

The building block of every Windows Server installation, either physical or virtual, is the storage. In this chapter, we looked at configuration and storage management, and introduced more advanced topics, such as Storage Replica and deduplication.

In the next chapter, we will cover the Hyper-V installation and configuration, and the installation of management tools. We will explore how to perform remotely manage Hyper-V hosts and implement nested virtualization, as well as introduce relevant PowerShell commands for Hyper-V administration and the automation of other Hyper-V-related tasks.

Questions

1. What are the advantages of NTFS over FAT and FAT32? Choose all that apply.
    1. Security
    2. Support for smaller file sizes
    3. Fewer fragmented files
    4. Self-healing
    5. Support for larger file sizes
2. Which virtual disk types and formats can be created using Disk Management?
    1. Fixed size
    2. VHD
    3. Differencing
    4. Dynamically expanding
    5. Pass-through

      6. VHDX

      7. VHD Set

3. You are configuring a folder share. You want to enable Linux users to access files in a shared folder. What should you do?

      1. Install the Active Directory Directory Services (AD DS) server role

      2. Install the Network Controller server role

      3. Install the client for the NFS feature

      4. Install Server for NFS

      5. Install Work Folders

4. You are configuring a new shared folder using **New Folder Wizard**. You want to be able to specify storage usage limits for the folder. Which two options should you choose? Each answer represents a complete solution.

      1. SMB Share – Quick

      2. SMB Share – Advanced

      3. SMB Share – Applications

      4. NFS Share – Quick

      5. NFS Share – Advanced

5. Your company has its main office in New York and a subsidiary in Washington. The New York office has a Windows Server 2016 file server named SRV1. The Washington subsidiary has a Windows Server 2016 file server named SRV2. You want to enable the Washington users to work on their file even in the case of loss of network connectivity, and to enable users to save time and download costs you should make a downloaded file available to other users in the Washington office. Which two options should you configure? Each answer is part of the solution.

      1. Enable access-based enumeration for folders on SRV1

      2. Enable access-based enumeration for folders on SRV2

      3. Enable caching of shares on SRV1

      4. Enable caching of shares on SRV2

      5. Enable BranchCache on the file share on SRV1

      6. Enable BranchCache on the file share on SRV2

6. You want to create a volume using Storage Spaces and assign it a drive letter. What should you do? Choose all that apply.
    1. Create a virtual disk
    2. Initialize disks as MBR disks
    3. Create a VHD
    4. Create a storage pool
    5. Initialize disks as GPT disks
    6. Create a VHDX

7. You are creating a virtual hard disk using Storage Spaces. You have six physical hard disks. Which resiliency types are you able to choose? Choose all that apply.
    1. Single parity
    2. Dual parity
    3. Two-way mirror
    4. Three-way mirror

8. You are configuring an iSCSI initiator. Which is NOT a valid type to identify an initiator?
    1. DNS name
    2. URL address
    3. IP address
    4. MAC address
    5. IQN

9. Which is a default port number for the iSCSI target server?
    1. 3620
    2. 3260
    3. 3026
    4. 3062

10. You are configuring a data-deduplication feature on a Windows Server 2016 file server to comply with your company's data-storage savings policy. You enable the deduplication feature. Users complain that file-operation performance on a file server has degraded significantly. Which two actions should you take?
    1. Configure BranchCache
    2. Enable throughput optimization
    3. Set processor affinity
    4. Enable background optimization
    5. Instruct users to mark folders as Always Available Offline

Further reading

If you want to learn more about the topics covered in this chapter, check out the following resources:

- **Storage Spaces overview**: `https://docs.microsoft.com/en-us/windows-server/storage/storage-spaces/overview`
- **Overview of the FAT, HPFS, and NTFS filesystems**: `https://support.microsoft.com/en-my/help/100108/overview-of-fat-hpfs-and-ntfs-file-systems`
- **Resilient Filesystem (ReFS) overview**: `https://docs.microsoft.com/en-us/windows-server/storage/refs/refs-overview`
- **Managing Disks**: `https://docs.microsoft.com/en-us/windows-server/storage/disk-management/manage-disks`
- **iSCSI Target Server overview**: `https://docs.microsoft.com/en-us/windows-server/storage/iscsi/iscsi-target-server`

4

Getting to Know Hyper-V

The Hyper-V role in Windows Server enables you to virtualize operating systems and to create a dynamic and efficient computing environment. In this chapter, we will be determining the hardware and software requirements for Hyper-V, before looking at how to install, configure, and manage it. We will configure the **virtual machine** (**VM**) memory and Integration Services, determine the appropriate usage scenarios of Generation 1 and Generation 2 VMs, perform remote management of remote Hyper-V hosts, and implement nested virtualization.

We will then create a VM, configure VM memory, and export and import virtual machines. Finally, we will configure the Hyper-V storage, create VHD and VHDX virtual hard disks, and configure Hyper-V networking by configuring Hyper-V virtual switches.

In this chapter, we will cover the following topics:

- Installing and configuring Hyper-V
- Configuring and maintaining virtual machines
- Configuring Hyper-V storage
- Configuring Hyper-V networking

Technical requirements

In this chapter, you will need one of the following:

- Windows Server 2016 Datacenter edition
- Windows Server 2016 Standard edition

You will also need hardware that meets or exceeds the hardware requirements for running a Hyper-V server role. The Hyper-V hardware requirements are explained in the *Determining the hardware and compatibility requirements for installing Hyper-V* section.

Installing and configuring Hyper-V

Hyper-V is a role in Windows Server 2016 that allows you to run multiple guest operating systems within a host operating system. The guest and host operating systems share hardware resources but act independently. This is possible using **virtualization**, a technology that enables the abstraction of hardware resources – including the processor, the memory, and the network – and provides isolation for the guest operating systems.

A Windows Server 2016 that runs Hyper-V is called a **host**, while a guest operating system is called a **virtual machine** or a **guest**. Each virtual machine runs in an isolated environment and a Hyper-V host can run multiple virtual machines simultaneously. There are many benefits of virtualization, including the following:

- Provisioning virtual machines is much faster than provisioning physical machines. This leads to a more efficient and agile environment.
- A virtualized environment provides increased business continuity.
- Increased server density allows significant monetary savings as multiple virtualized workloads can run on a single server.

The **Virtual Machine Manager** (**VMM**) or the **Hypervisor** is the software layer that sits on top of the hardware. Its task is to provide isolated environments, also called **partitions**, where each environment has its own isolated, virtualized hardware resources, including memory, processor, network, and storage subsystems. Hypervisor controls one or more of the guest operating systems that sit on top of a hypervisor.

The following diagram shows the schematic overview of a VMM Type 1 Hypervisor:

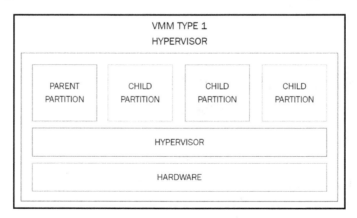

Three major types of hypervisors exist today: VMM Type 2, VMM Hybrid, and VMM Type 1. Hyper-V runs a VMM Type 1 hypervisor, which provides the best performance, security, and control compared to other types of hypervisors.

On a system without a hypervisor, an operating system sits directly on top of the hardware. After you install a Hyper-V role, the operating system changes fundamentally: the hypervisor replaces an operating system and sits on top of the hardware, and then a parent or root partition is created. The parent partition hosts the virtualization stack and owns the resources that are not owned by the hypervisor, such as the memory and some of the devices. Multiple partitions are possible, and every other partition created is called a **child partition**, in which guest operating systems or virtual machines are installed.

Determining the hardware and compatibility requirements for installing Hyper-V

Hyper-V is supported on the following Windows Server 2016 operating system versions:

- Windows Server 2016 Standard edition
- Windows Server 2016 Datacenter edition
- Windows Server 2016 Hyper-V edition
- Microsoft Hyper-V Server 2016 edition

Along with the software requirements, Hyper-V has some general hardware requirements. Some Hyper-V features require additional hardware requirements. The general Hyper-V hardware requirements include the following:

- A 64-bit processor with **Second Level Address Translation (SLAT)**. SLAT is required to install virtualization components, but is not required to install Hyper-V management tools, such as Hyper-V cmdlets for PowerShell, Hyper-V manager, or others.
- A CPU that supports hardware-assisted virtualization. Intel processors have **Intel Virtualization Technology (Intel VT)** and AMD processors have **AMD Virtualization (AMD-V)**.
- **Data Execution Prevention (DEP)** must be hardware-enforced and enabled. Intel systems have **Execute Disable Bit (XD bit)** and AMD systems have **No-Execute Bit (NX bit)**.

- VM Monitor Mode Extension.
- A minimum of 1 GB of RAM, and a recommended 2 GB of RAM. This does not include the memory requirements for virtual machines installed in guest partitions.

Each specific Hyper-V feature has its own special hardware requirements.

Shielded virtual machines

Shielded virtual machines rely on virtualization-based security features. The host requirements include the following:

- UEFI 2.3.1c for secure boot
- **Trusted Platform Module (TPM)** v2.0
- IOMMU (Intel VT-d) for **direct memory access (DMA)** protection

The virtual machine requirements include the following:

- Generation 2 virtual machine
- Windows Server 2012 or newer as the guest operating system

Discrete device assignment

The host requirements for discrete device assignment include the following:

- Processor support for Intel **Extended Page Table (EPT)** or AMD **Nested Page Table (NPT)**.
- Intel's VT-d with the Interrupt Remapping capability (VT-d2) or any version of AMD **I/O Memory Management Unit (I/O MMU)**.
- DMA remapping – Intel VT-d with Queued Invalidations or any AMD I/O MMU.
- **Access Control Services (ACS)** on PCI Express root ports.
- The firmware tables must expose the I/O MMU to the Windows hypervisor.
- Devices are required to have GPU or non-volatile memory express (NVMe). Be sure to check for device characteristics because not every device supports discrete device assignment.

Supported Windows guest operating systems for Hyper-V

The following table lists the supported server operating systems that can be installed as guests on Hyper-V in Windows Server 2016. It also shows the number of supported virtual processors:

Supported Windows Server operating systems	Maximum number of virtual processors supported
Windows Server 2016	240 for generation 2 64 for generation 1
Windows Server 2012 R2	64
Windows Server 2012	64
Windows Server 2008 R2 with Service Pack 1	64
Windows Server 2008 with Service Pack 2	8

The following table lists the supported client operating systems:

Supported Windows client operating systems	Maximum number of virtual processors supported
Windows 10	32
Windows 8.1	32
Windows 7 with Service Pack 1 (Ultimate, Enterprise, and Professional editions)	4

In Windows Server 2016, Microsoft licensing is based on Operating System Environments (OSEs). Windows Server 2016 Standard edition has two OSEs, and Windows Server 2016 Datacenter has unlimited OSEs. If you have Windows Server 2016 Standard edition and are running a Hyper-V server role only, you are allowed to apply both OSEs to virtual machines. If you are running one or more roles besides the Hyper-V role on Windows Server 2016 Standard edition, one OSE applies to the host, leaving you with just one OSE for the virtual machines. Note that the Windows Server 2016 Enterprise Edition price is roughly six times greater than Windows Server 2016 Standard edition.

Supported non-Windows client operating systems

For detailed information about the supported OS versions and features, consult the following resources:

- **CentOS and Red Hat Enterprise Linux**: https://docs.microsoft.com/en-us/windows-server/virtualization/hyper-v/supported-centos-and-red-hat-enterprise-linux-virtual-machines-on-hyper-v
- **Debian**: https://docs.microsoft.com/en-us/windows-server/virtualization/hyper-v/supported-debian-virtual-machines-on-hyper-v
- **Oracle Linux**: https://docs.microsoft.com/en-us/windows-server/virtualization/hyper-v/supported-oracle-linux-virtual-machines-on-hyper-v
- **SUSE Linux**: https://docs.microsoft.com/en-us/windows-server/virtualization/hyper-v/supported-suse-virtual-machines-on-hyper-v
- **Ubuntu**: https://docs.microsoft.com/en-us/windows-server/virtualization/hyper-v/supported-ubuntu-virtual-machines-on-hyper-v
- **FreeBSD**: https://docs.microsoft.com/en-us/windows-server/virtualization/hyper-v/supported-freebsd-virtual-machines-on-hyper-v

Installing Hyper-V

When you install a Hyper-V role, along with the hypervisor, the following virtualization components are also installed: the Hyper-V Virtual Machine Management Service, the virtualization WMI provider, the **Virtualization Service Provider** (**VSP**), the **Virtual Machine Bus** (**VMBus**), and the **virtual infrastructure driver** (**VDI**).

Various connectivity and management tools are also available, and although these components are not part of the virtualization stack, they are vital for the correct functioning of Hyper-V. These tools include the following:

- The Hyper-V Manager console
- The Hyper-V module for PowerShell
- The Virtual Machine Connection or VMConnect
- Windows PowerShell Direct

VMConnect is used to interact with virtual machines so you can perform various tasks with a virtual machine, such as the following:

- Installing an operating system in a virtual machine
- Modifying the settings of a virtual machine

- Creating a checkpoint
- Connecting to an image (an `.iso` file) or a USB drive
- Starting and shutting down a virtual machine
- Pausing or resetting a virtual machine

To install the Hyper-V role on Windows Server 2016 using the Server Manager, follow these steps:

1. Open the **Server Manager**.
2. Click **Manage**, then select **Add Roles and Features**.
3. Choose **Role-based or feature-based installation** and click **Next**.
4. On the **Select destination server** screen, click **Select server from the server pool**, choose the server from the server pool on which you will install the Hyper-V role, and click **Next**.
5. On the **Select server role** screen, select the checkbox next to **Hyper-V**. The **Add features that are required for Hyper-V** dialog box shows, asking you to confirm the installation of Remote Server Administration Tools for Hyper-V. Review the screen and click **Add Features**. Click **Next**:

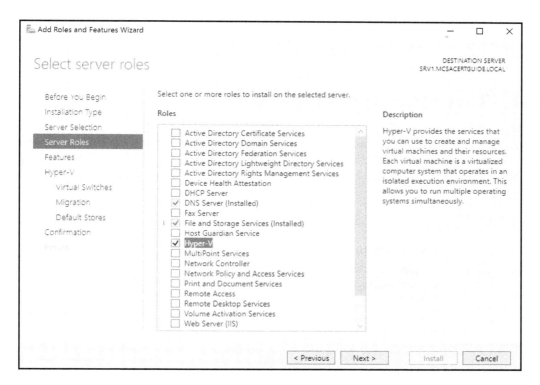

6. The **Select features** screen appears. You can verify that the Hyper-V Management Tools were automatically selected. Click **Next**.

7. The Hyper-V information screen appears. Click **Next** again.

8. On the **Create Virtual Switches** screen, select a network adapter that will be used with Hyper-V to create a virtual switch. At least one virtual switch is required to provide network connectivity to virtual machines. A recommended practice is to have a network adapter dedicated for remote administration. Click **Next**.

9. On the **Virtual Machine Migration** screen, specify whether you want to configure this server for migration, if you have multiple Hyper-V servers. Click **Next**.

10. The **Default Stores** screen defines the default locations to store virtual hard disk files and virtual machine configuration files. Click **Next**.

11. The **Confirmation** screen is the final screen, on which you can choose whether the server will be restarted automatically if required. Click **Install**.

You are then prompted to restart the server. It will restart multiple times before the installation finishes. Once the installation is complete, open **Server Manager** and notice the Hyper-V menu available, along with multiple new Start menu shortcuts.

To install Hyper-V using PowerShell, use the following command:

```
Install-WindowsFeature -Name Hyper-V -IncludeManagementTools -Restart
```

Installing management tools

As you already know, you are prompted to install management tools during the Hyper-V role installation procedure, which are responsible for installing the tools to manage the Hyper-V host and guest virtual machines. In order to manage the Hyper-V server remotely, you can install Hyper-V Remote Server Administration Tools on a server that does not have the Hyper-V role installed.

To install the Hyper-V Remote Server Administration Tools, follow these steps:

1. Open the **Server Manager**.
2. Click **Manage**, then select **Add Roles and Features**.
3. Choose **Role-based or feature-based installation** and click **Next**.

4. On the **Select destination server** screen, click **Select server from the server pool**, choose the server from the server pool on which you will install the Hyper-V role, and click **Next**.

5. On the **Select server role** screen, click **Next**.

6. The **Select features** screen appears. Expand **Remote Server Administration Tools** and then expand **Hyper-V Management Tools**.

7. Select the checkbox next to **Hyper-V GUI Management Tools**.

8. Select the checkbox next to **Hyper-V Module for Windows PowerShell**. Click **Next** and then click **Install**.

To perform the same procedure in PowerShell, use the following commands:

```
# Installs complete Hyper-V Management Tools which includes Hyper-V GUI
Management Tools and Hyper-V Module for Windows PowerShell
Install-WindowsFeature -Name RSAT-Hyper-V-Tools

# Installs Hyper-V GUI Management Tools
Install-WindowsFeature -Name Hyper-V-Tools

# Installs Hyper-V Module for Windows PowerShell
Install-WindowsFeature -Name Hyper-V-PowerShell
```

You can now manage Hyper-V servers remotely using Hyper-V Manager and PowerShell.

Performing remote management of Hyper-V hosts

Whether or not a computer has the Hyper-V role installed, you can use **Remote Server Administration Tools** (RSAT) to manage Hyper-V hosts and, consequently, guest virtual machines on these hosts as well. There are some restrictions, however, on which versions of Hyper-V can be managed on these computers. Consult the following table to understand the management compatibility:

Hyper-V Manager version	Hyper-V Host version
Windows 2016Windows 10	Windows Server 2016 Windows Server 2012 R2 Windows Server 2012 Windows 10 Windows 8.1
Windows Server 2012 R2Windows 8.1	Windows Server 2012 R2 Windows Server 2012 Windows 8.1

Windows Server 2012	Windows Server 2012
Windows Server 2008 R2 Service Pack 1 Windows 7 Service Pack 1	Windows Server 2008 R2
Windows Server 2008 Windows Vista Service Pack 2	Windows Server 2008

Remote management of Hyper-V hosts can be achieved using the Hyper-V Manager console. To manage a remote Hyper-V server, follow these steps:

1. Open the Start menu and navigate to the **Windows Administrative Tools** menu.
2. Click **Hyper-V Manager**.
3. Do one of the following:
   - Right-click on **Hyper-V Manager** in the Console Tree (in the left pane) and select **Connect to Server...**.
   - In the **Actions** pane (in the right pane), click **Connect to Server...**:

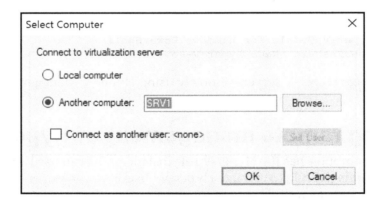

4. The **Select Computer** dialog box opens. Select **Another computer** and type the name of the Hyper-V server you want to manage, or click **Browse...** and select a Hyper-V server from the **Select Computer** dialog box. Once you have typed the computer name or selected a computer, click **OK**:

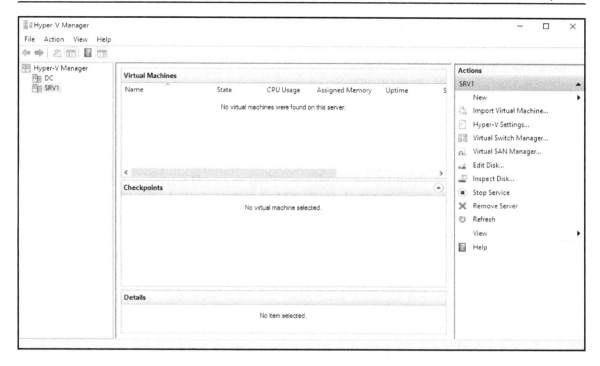

5. The selected Hyper-V server is now listed in the Console Tree.

To be able to remotely manage Hyper-V hosts that are not in your domain, or with no domain, you will have to use PowerShell because there is no Active Directory Domain Controller to perform the required authentication.

On a Hyper-V computer you want to manage, type the following PowerShell commands:

```
Enable-PSRemoting
Enable-WSManCredSSP -Role server
```

The Enable-PSRemoting cmdlet configures the computer to receive Windows PowerShell remote commands, and the Enable-WSManCredSSP cmdlet enables **Credential Security Support Provider** (**CredSSP**) authentication on a client or a server computer to pass the user credentials to a remote computer to be authenticated.

On a computer that will be used to manage remote Hyper-V host, type the following commands:

```
Set-Item WSMan:\localhost\Client\TrustedHosts -Value
"here_type_fqdn_of_hyperv_host"
Enable-WSManCredSSP -Role client -DelegateComputer "
here_type_fqdn_of_hyperv_host "
```

Then, follow these steps:

1. Configure the following group policy by clicking on **Computer Configuration** | **Administrative Templates** | **System** | **Credentials Delegation** | **Allow delegating Fresh Credentials with NTLM-only Server Authentication**.
2. Click **Enable** and type in `wsman/ here_type_fqdn_of_hyperv_host`.
3. Open the **Hyper-V Manager**.
4. In the left pane, click **Hyper-V Manager** and then click on **Connect to Server....** Alternatively, you can click click **Connect to Server...** in the pane on the right.

Using Windows PowerShell Direct

Using PowerShell Direct, you can remotely manage Windows Server 2016 or Windows 10 virtual machines from a Windows Server 2016 or Windows 10 host. This feature greatly reduces the complexity and the extra steps involved in managing virtual machines. Instead of opening a VM connection window, connecting to a VM, opening a PowerShell console, and typing commands, you can enter commands directly in the PowerShell console on the host itself.

To be able to use PowerShell Direct, you must meet the following prerequisites:

- The virtual machine must run Windows Server 2016 or Windows 10
- The host operating system must run Windows Server 2016 or Windows 10
- You must be logged on to a host as a Hyper-V administrator
- The virtual machine must be running locally on the host and booted
- You must supply valid credentials for the virtual machine you want to manage

You can run PowerShell Direct either by running a PowerShell Direct session using `PSSession` cmdlets or using the `Invoke-Command` cmdlet:

- To run a PowerShell Direct session using `PSSession` cmdlets, do the following:

```
# To create a session
Enter-PSSession -VMName <VMName>

# or
Enter-PSSession -VMGUID <VMGUID>

# To close a session
Exit-PSSession
```

- To run a PowerShell Direct session using the `Invoke-Command` cmdlet, do the following:

```
# This command runs C:\scripts\script1.ps1 script
Invoke-Command -VMName PSTest -FilePath C:\scripts\script1.ps1
# This commands runs a single command
Invoke-Command -VMName PSTest -ScriptBlock { cmdlet }
```

Implementing nested virtualization

Nested virtualization is a feature that allows a client operating system to act as a virtualization host. This means running Hyper-V in a virtual machine that is running on a Hyper-V host. While this configuration is not intended for production workloads because of various limitations and reduced performance, it is an excellent feature for testing, development, or learning purposes.

In order to enable nested virtualization, a client virtual machine needs to run a Windows Server 2016 or Windows 10 operating system. Moreover, you will need to enable nested virtualization with this simple PowerShell command:

```
Set-VMProcessor -ExposeVirtualizationExtensions 1 -VMName
"type_the_VM_name"
```

If you need to disable the nested virtualization feature, type the following:

```
Set-VMProcessor -ExposeVirtualizationExtensions 0 -VMName
"type_the_VM_name"
```

Configuring virtual machine settings

Now that you have installed the Hyper-V role, it is time to create a virtual machine. When you create a virtual machine, its configuration settings are stored in a **virtual machine configuration** (`.vmc`) file in XML format. A VM also uses one or more virtual disks, which are `.vhd` or `.vhdx` files, and a `.vsv` file that contains a VM's saved state, if you saved a VM instead of shutting it down.

Creating a VM

To create a VM in Hyper-V manager, perform the following steps:

    1. Open **Hyper-V Manager**:

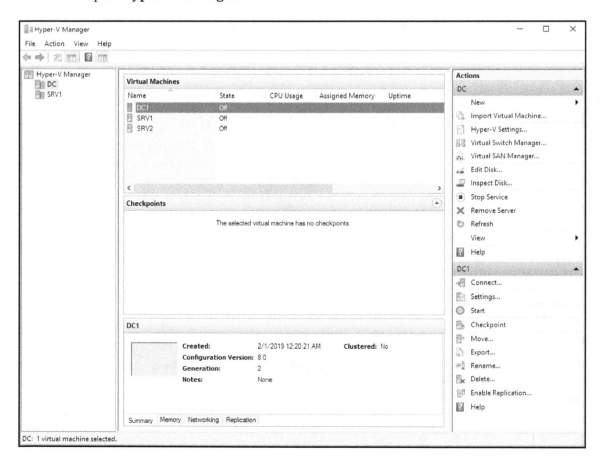

2. In the Console Tree (in the pane on the left), select the server you want to manage and create a virtual machine on.

3. In the **Actions** pane (in the pane on the right), click **New** and then click **Virtual Machine...**.

4. The **New Virtual Machine Wizard** starts and the **Before You Begin** information page appears. Inspect the information on the screen and, if you wish, click on **Do not show this page again**. Click **Next**.

5. On the **Specify Name and Location** page, type the VM name. You can choose to store the VM in a different location to the default setup location, as specified in the Hyper-V settings. Click **Next**:

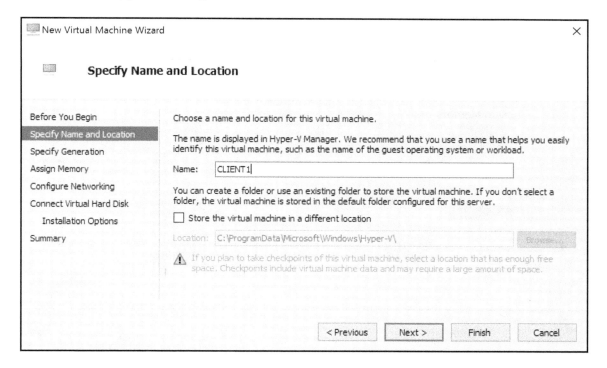

6. On the **Specify Generation** screen, specify whether you want to create a Generation 1 VM or Generation 2 VM. Generation 2 VMs only support 64-bit operating systems and provide enhanced security and the newest virtualization features. Choose carefully, because once a VM has been created, the generation type cannot be changed. To change the generation type, you will have to delete the VM and create it again. Click **Next**.

7. In the **Assign Memory** screen, choose the amount of **Startup memory** that is available to the VM. This is not the minimum memory that will be available to a VM, but instead the initial amount of RAM that will be allocated for a VM to start. The memory commitment can change as the VM workload changes and it may be less than the start-up memory amount. You also have the option to choose whether the VM will use Dynamic Memory, a feature that uses the **ballooning** process to dynamically adjust memory for a VM. Click **Next**:

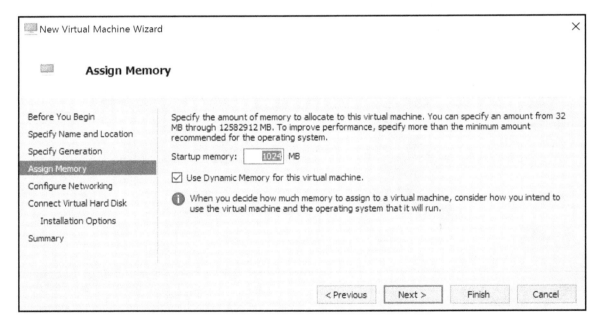

8. On the **Configure Networking** screen, choose the virtual switch that the VM will use to connect to the network resources. Click **Next**.

9. On the **Connect Virtual Hard Disk** screen, you can create a virtual disk and specify its size and location, use an existing virtual hard disk, or choose to attach a virtual hard disk later. Click **Next**:

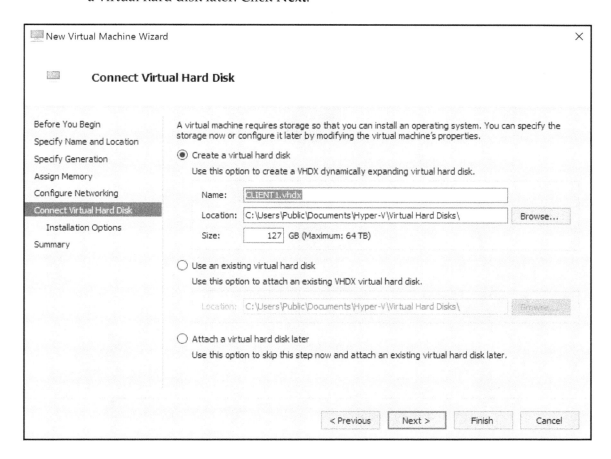

10. The **Installation Options** screen appears. You can choose how the operating system will be installed onto a VM. One of the options is to install an operating system later or to install an operating system from physical media, specifying a drive letter, or from an `.iso` file. Alternatively, if you selected to create a Generation 1 VM, you can install an operating system from a bootable floppy disk. If you selected a Generation 2 VM, the floppy disk installation option will not be present. Finally, you will have the option to install from a network-based installation server. Click **Next**:

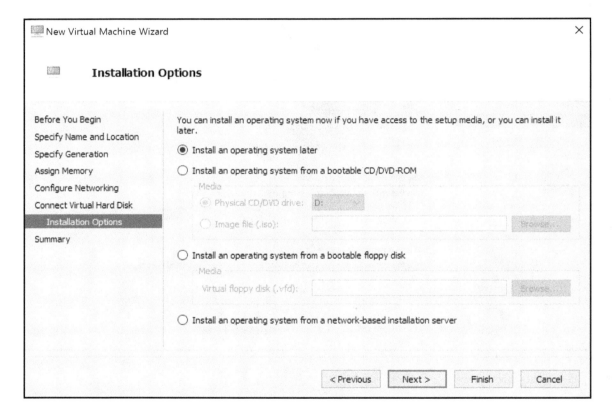

11. The last screen is the **Summary** screen. Review the selections and choose **Finish** to create a VM with the chosen parameters.

Once you have created a virtual machine, you can edit its settings to install additional components and fine-tune the VM's hardware configuration. Some virtual machine settings will not be present in both Generation 1 and Generation 2 VMs. The generation type impacts how a VM boots and which operating system it supports. Generally, a Generation 2 type VM has some advantages over a Generation type 1 VM, including the following features:

- Secure Boot
- Support for larger boot volumes
- Faster booting using the SCSI boot instead of IDE booting
- PXE booting with a synthetic adapter
- Hot network adapters
- Shielded VMs
- Storage Spaces Direct

 For a complete overview of VM generation types, and the features and operating systems supported, visit `https://docs.microsoft.com/en-us/windows-server/virtualization/hyper-v/plan/should-i-create-a-generation-1-or-2-virtual-machine-in-hyper-v`.

To configure and manage the VM settings, open the Hyper-V Manager and do one of the following:

- Right-click on a VM in the middle pane and choose **Settings**.
- In the middle pane, select a VM and click on **Settings** in the **Actions** pane (on the right).

The **Settings** window opens. The following screenshots show the high-level differences between the settings of the Generation 1 and Generation 2 virtual machines. Virtual machine settings might differ, obviously, as a result of different hardware installed. The settings for a Generation 1 virtual machine are as follows:

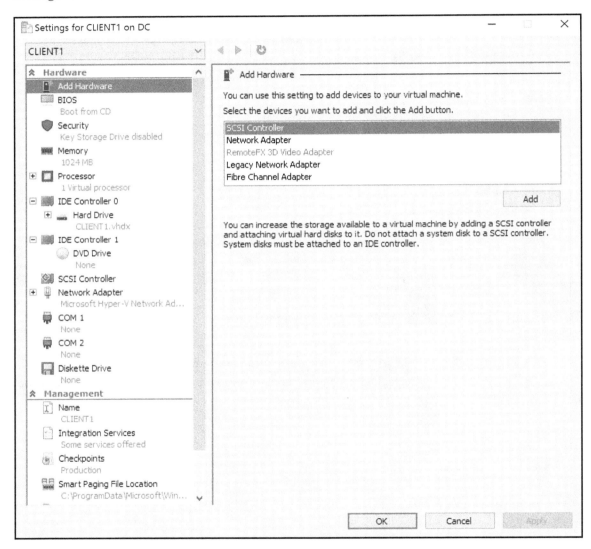

The settings for a Generation 2 virtual machine are as follows:

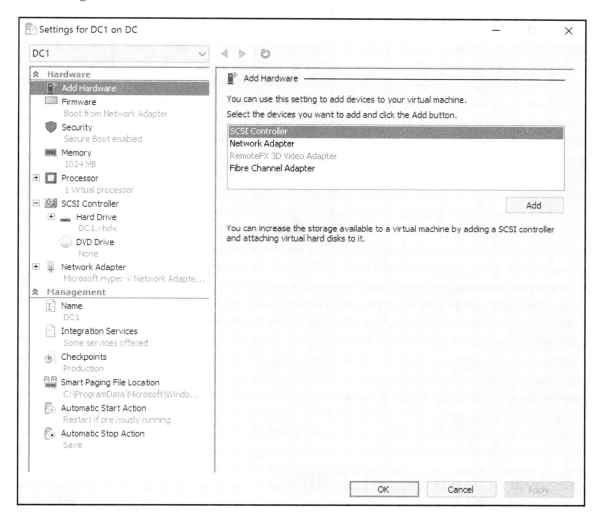

A very convenient feature is the drop-down menu, which allows you to switch from one VM to another without repeatedly closing and opening the **Settings** window.

The **Settings** pane in the VM Settings window has two sections: **Hardware** and **Management**. The first setting is the **Add Hardware** setting. Generation 1 and Generation 2 VMs support different hardware. The following screenshot shows the hardware supported by Generation 1 VMs:

The following screenshot shows the hardware supported by Generation 2 VMs:

To add a controller or an adapter, simply select the hardware and click **Add**. The **RemoteFX 3D Video Adapter** is grayed out, and the official message says it is no longer supported. If you have configured it previously, then you can keep using it on existing VMs, but you can't apply it to any new VMs.

If you do require the excellent GPU acceleration and video performance of the RemoteFX 3D Video Adapter, PowerShell might be able to help you. Enter the following command to enable the RemoteFX 3D Video Adapter for a specific VM:

```
Add-VMRemoteFx3dVideoAdapter -VMName Type_a_VM_Name
```

Configuring the VM memory

In the **Settings** window, click on **Memory** to define the amount of memory that a VM can use. If Dynamic Memory is not enabled, the minimum and maximum RAM options will not be enabled either, meaning the VM will allocate the amount of RAM specified previously. If Dynamic Memory is enabled, however, this is the amount of memory that is reserved during the boot process. After the VM has started, the amount of memory a VM uses is defined by the **Minimum RAM** and **Maximum RAM**. A VM's memory allocation changes as the requirements change. Thanks to a **balloon** driver, responsible for the process of *ballooning*, which is reclaiming allocated memory from a host, the allocated memory is returned to the system.

To change the amount of memory a VM uses, open the settings and type a new value. When you close the settings window or click the **Apply** button, the VM automatically adjusts to the new values. If the **RAM** setting is grayed out and unavailable, check whether the VM has saved properly.

A memory buffer is a soft-reserved amount of memory for possible memory expansion, represented as a percentage of the currently allocated memory. The memory weight slider is used to prioritize a VM in the memory allocation process over other VMs:

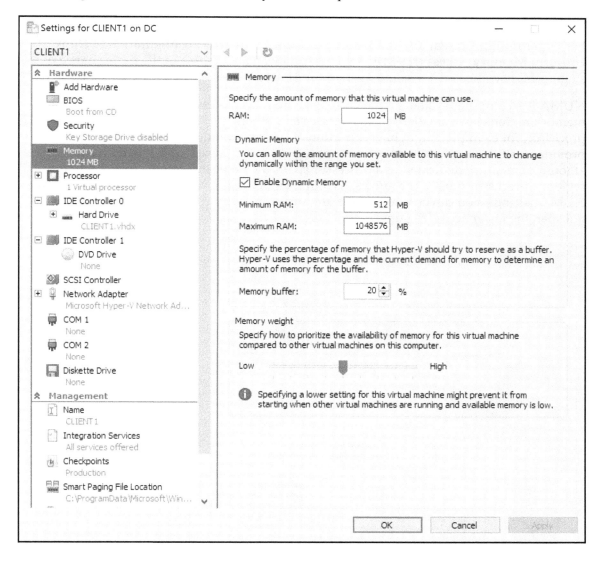

Hyper-V uses Smart Paging to enable a reliable start-up process for the virtual machines configured with less minimum memory than start-up memory. To configure a **Smart Paging File Location**, modify the path of the **Smart Paging File Location** under the **Management** section of the VM settings.

Configuring Non-Uniform Memory Access support

For larger multiprocessor and multi-socket systems, the correct configuration of **Non-Uniform Memory Access** (**NUMA**) settings can mean an increase in the performance of a single VM, of co-hosted VMs, and of an entire Hyper-V host.

NUMA is a computer system architecture used in multiprocessor systems, where some memory regions have smaller access latencies and others have greater access latencies. Each processor, for example, might have a portion of system memory connected to it that provides faster access, while other memory regions are accessed with greater latency. If the amount of memory dedicated to a processor spans the dedicated low-latency memory region, a processor must write and read from memory regions with a larger latency. With NUMA settings, you can ensure that the amount of memory reserved for a processor does not span the faster access regions.

If you align the sockets and nodes of a VM to the hardware a VM is running on, you can improve the VM performance. To match the virtual NUMA topology to the hardware topology, click the **Use Hardware Topology** button:

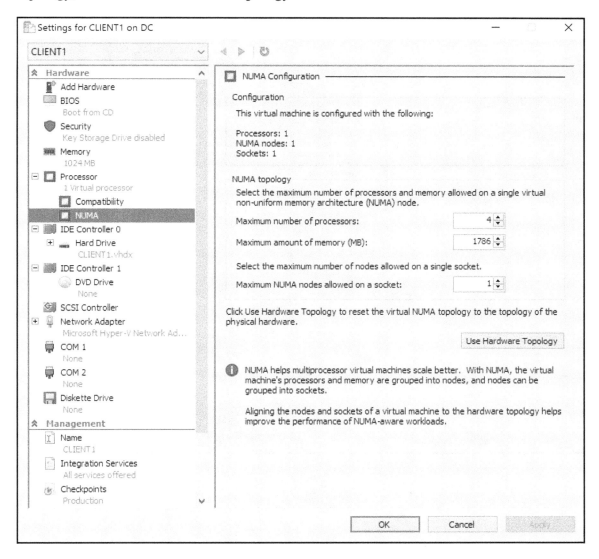

To allow virtual machines to span NUMA nodes, open the **Hyper-V Manager** and click **Hyper-V settings** in the menu on the left. Select **NUMA Spanning** from the left pane to configure the settings:

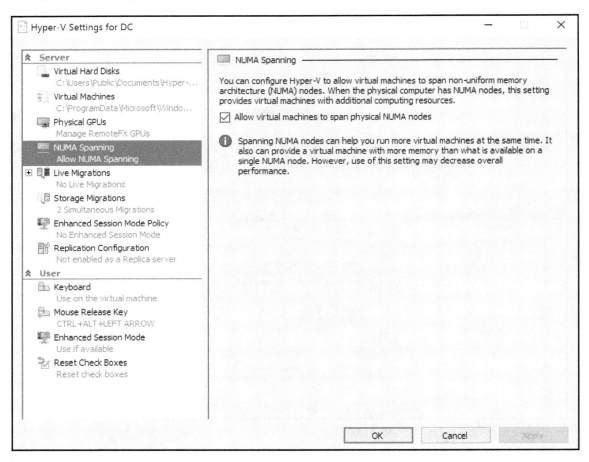

Configuring resource metering

Resource metering is a feature that enables a virtual machine to report its performance counters, which can be used to analyze virtual machine resource metering and apply the readings for specific business needs. This can be achieved using PowerShell or through a virtualization WMI provider. For example, if a VM is a part of a public cloud data center, in order to bill a customer, you need to know how much memory, network traffic, CPU time, and other resources the customer has used. The following metrics can be tracked for a specific period:

- The average CPU usage
- The average physical memory usage
- The minimum memory usage
- The maximum memory usage
- The maximum amount of disk space allocated to a virtual machine
- The total incoming network traffic for a virtual network adapter
- The total outgoing network traffic for a virtual network adapter

To perform resource metering management in PowerShell, type the following commands:

```
# Enable resource metering
Enable-VMResourceMetering -VMName VM_NAME

# Disable resource metering
Disable-VMResourceMetering -VMName VM_NAME

# Display resource utilisation
Measure-VM -VMName VM_NAME

# Display detailed resource metering in a formatted list
Measure-VM -VMName VM_NAME | Format-List
```

The output of these commands looks as follows:

```
PS C:\WINDOWS\system32> Measure-VM -VMName "MCSA-WS2016"

VMName       AvgCPU(MHz) AvgRAM(M) MaxRAM(M) MinRAM(M) TotalDisk(M) NetworkInbound(M) NetworkOutbound(M)
------       ----------- --------- --------- --------- ------------ ----------------- ------------------
MCSA-WS2016  201         3072      3072      3072      1956864      0                 0


PS C:\WINDOWS\system32> Measure-VM -VMName "MCSA-WS2016" | Format-List

VMId                              : 3a946d0d-da10-49fe-a0ad-742dc5941fe0
VMName                            : MCSA-WS2016
CimSession                        : CimSession: .
ComputerName                      : SK-SURFACE
MeteringDuration                  :
AverageProcessorUsage             : 161
AverageMemoryUsage                : 3072
MaximumMemoryUsage                : 3072
MinimumMemoryUsage                : 3072
TotalDiskAllocation               : 1956864
AggregatedAverageNormalizedIOPS   : 0
AggregatedAverageLatency          : 0
AggregatedDiskDataRead            : 1
AggregatedDiskDataWritten         : 2
AggregatedNormalizedIOCount       : 310
NetworkMeteredTrafficReport       : {Microsoft.HyperV.PowerShell.VMNetworkAdapterPortAclMeteringReport,
                                    Microsoft.HyperV.PowerShell.VMNetworkAdapterPortAclMeteringReport,
                                    Microsoft.HyperV.PowerShell.VMNetworkAdapterPortAclMeteringReport,
                                    Microsoft.HyperV.PowerShell.VMNetworkAdapterPortAclMeteringReport...}
HardDiskMetrics                   : {Microsoft.HyperV.PowerShell.VHDMetrics, Microsoft.HyperV.PowerShell.VHDMetrics,
                                    Microsoft.HyperV.PowerShell.VHDMetrics, Microsoft.HyperV.PowerShell.VHDMetrics...}
AvgCPU                            : 161
AvgRAM                            : 3072
MinRAM                            : 3072
MaxRAM                            : 3072
TotalDisk                         : 1956864
```

Managing Integration Services

Integration Services are software that runs on guest virtual machines and provides enhancements, better integration, and additional features. There are six Integration Services available currently:

- **Operating system shutdown**: This enables the user to shut down the client operating system without logging on to it, either through Hyper-V Manager or the command line
- **Time synchronization**: This synchronizes the clock on the VM with the clock on the Hyper-V host

- **Data Exchange**: This enables the guest VM to communicate with the Hyper-V host via VMBus
- **Heartbeat**: The Hyper-V host tracks the signal that the VM generates periodically to indicate its health state
- **Backup (volume shadow copy)**: This enables the user to back up a VM
- **Guest services**: This enables data transfers

These services can be seen in the following screenshot:

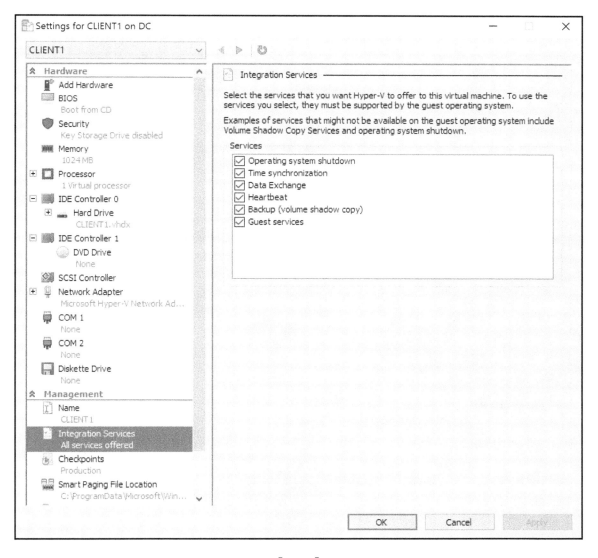

Implementing Enhanced Session Mode

Enhanced Session Mode Policy allows additional actions in interaction with virtual machines, such as clipboard features (cutting and pasting), volume and device mapping, and audio redirection. Enhanced Session Mode needs to be enabled to provide support for guest virtual machines running Windows Server 2016, Windows Server 2012 R2, Windows 10, and Windows 8.1

To enable Enhanced Session Mode from the Hyper-V Manager, open the Hyper-V settings and click on the **Enhanced Session Mode Policy**. Click the **Allow enhanced session mode** setting checkbox:

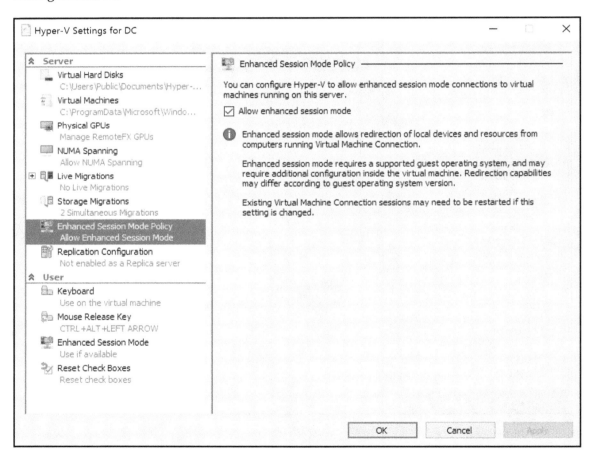

Exporting and importing VMs

The ability of Hyper-V to export and import virtual machines means that you can move or copy virtual machines from one Hyper-V host to another or to make multiple copies of the same virtual machines to the same host.

Exporting a virtual machine is a very simple process:

1. Open the **Hyper-V Manager**
2. In the pane on the left, click **Export**
3. Type the path or browse for the folder
4. Click **Export**:

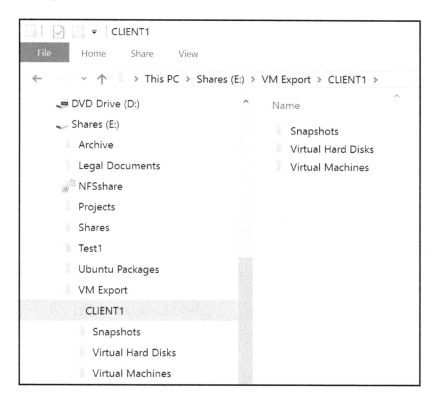

The **Export** action creates three folders: `Virtual Machines`, `Virtual Hard Disks`, and `Snapshots`. Importing a virtual machine involves a few more steps than exporting a virtual machine, but it is also a simple process.

To import a virtual machine, follow these steps:

1. Open **Hyper-V Manager**.
2. In the pane on the left, click **Import Virtual Machine**.
3. The **Import Virtual Machine** window will open. Click **Next**.
4. In the **Locate Folder** screen, type the path or browse for the folder of the virtual machine you want to import. Click **Next**.
5. Select the virtual machine to import. Click **Next**.
6. In the **Choose Import Type** screen, you have three options to choose from:
   - **Register the virtual machine in-place (use the existing unique ID)**: This option leaves the files you are importing where they are and registers the exported VM using the same ID.
   - **Restore the virtual machine (use the existing unique ID)**: This option copies the exported VM into a new location and registers the VM using the same ID.
   - **Copy the virtual machine (creates a new unique ID)**: This option copies the exported files using the new ID:

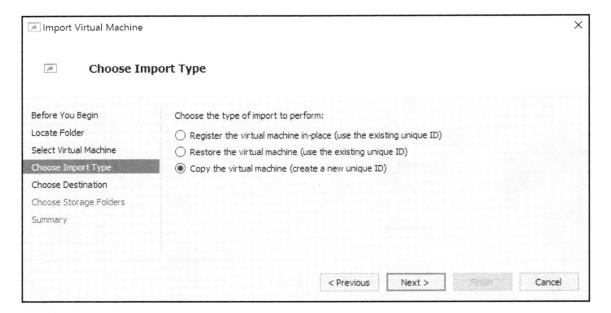

It is important to note that each VM has its own unique identifier number, or ID. Two VMs that use the same ID cannot run on the same Hyper-V host, so registering a VM or restoring a VM on the same server from where it was exported results in an error. Copying the VM, on the other hand, generates a new ID, so both VMs can run on the same host at the same time.

Configuring Hyper-V storage

When talking about storage in Hyper-V, the first term that comes to mind is likely to be VHDs. These versatile files act as hard disks and store your valuable data. Hyper-V supports both VHD and VHDX, which we addressed in `Chapter 3`, *Configuring and Implementing Storage*, when we described storage in Windows Server 2016. Hyper-V supports different VHD and VHDX types:

- **Fixed size**: As the name implies, the size of the disk is determined at the moment of creation and its size does not change. This type of disk allocates storage space that is equal to its nominal size, regardless of how much actual virtual disk space you are using. For example, if you create a 100-GB fixed-size virtual disk, it will occupy 100 GB of storage space even if the virtual disk does not store any files. The advantage of these kinds of disks is that the storage space allocated is potentially contiguous, and since it doesn't change in size, virtual-disk file fragmentation does not occur, resulting in faster disk I/O operations.
- **Dynamically expanding**: Contrary to fixed virtual disks, dynamically-expandable disks change their size as you populate them with data. The advantage is that this type of disk does not allocate the full nominal storage size, but increases in size over time. This, however, potentially increases the fragmentation of the file. Another drawback is that they are somewhat slower than fixed disks due to resizing and the possible fragmentation.
- **Differencing**: A differencing disk must be associated with another disk, called a **parent disk**. A differencing disk is also called a child disk and stores the changes, or the differences, on the parent disk. One parent disk can have multiple child disks and the biggest advantages of this are that it can carry out quick rollbacks, it can save storage space, and similar systems can be deployed quickly.
- **Physical disk or pass-through**: In this case, the virtual machine has direct access to the physical disk, while having exclusive access over other virtual machines. Advantages include fast access and data transfer speed, but this comes at the expense of reserving a physical disk for one virtual machine at a time.

Hyper-V also supports a third virtual hard disk format, called VHD Set, which uses a new `.VHDS` file type. VHD Set is a virtual disk format that is suitable for a shared virtual disk model, and is intended for use in guest clusters. It supports Hyper-V Replica, the online resizing of shared virtual disks, and application-consistent checkpoints.

To recap, Hyper-V supports two virtual disk formats, VHD and VHDX. The following table compares the VHD and VHDX file formats, and presents the pros and cons of each file format:

VHD	VHDX
512-byte logical sector size	4,096-byte logical sector sizes
Maximum size is 2 TB	Maximum size is 64 TB
No protection of data	Data-corruption protection
Cannot be resized live	Can be resized live
Supported by Microsoft and other vendors, such as Citrix and Oracle	Supported by Microsoft
Potential data-alignment issues	Improved alignment
No custom metadata support	Custom metadata support
Supported by Windows Server 2008, Windows Server 2012, and Windows Server 2016	Supported by Windows Server 2016 and Windows Server 2016

Creating VHD and VHDX files using Hyper-V Manager

To create a virtual hard disk using Hyper-V manager, follow these steps:

1. Open the **Hyper-V Manager**.
2. In the **Actions** pane on the left, click **New**, then select **Hard disk**.
3. A **New Virtual Hard Disk Wizard** will open. Click **Next** to skip the introductory screen.

4. In the **Choose Disk Format** screen, select the virtual disk type: **VHD**, **VHDX**, or **VHD Set**. Click **Next**:

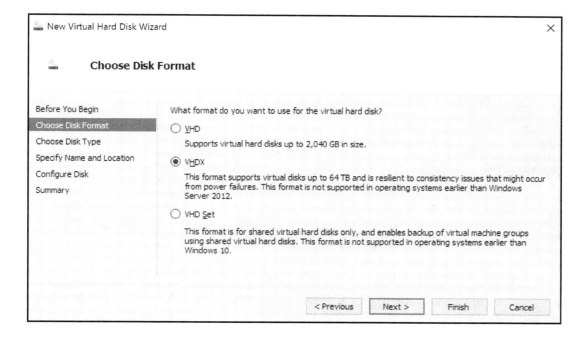

5. Choose the disk type. If your selection in a previous step was **VHD**, **Fixed size** is automatically selected. If your pick was **VHDX**, **Dynamically expanding** is selected. If you chose **VHD Set**, the **Differencing** type is not supported, leaving you with only two choices. Click **Next**:

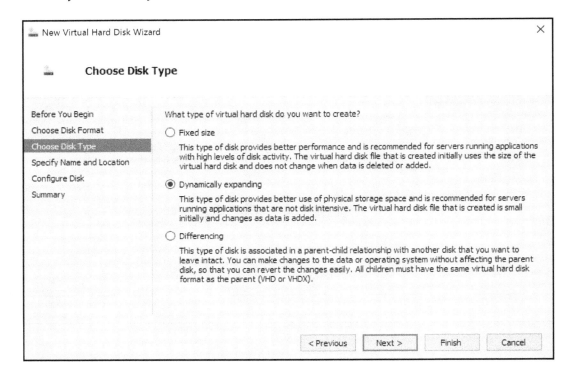

6. Specify the name and the location of the virtual disk. Click **Next**.
7. On the **Configure Disk** screen, you can choose from the following options:
   - **Create a new blank virtual hard disk**
   - **Copy the contents of the specified physical disk**

- **Copy the contents of the specified virtual hard disk**:

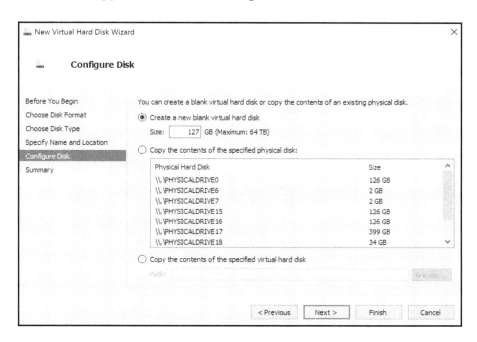

8. On the **Summary** screen, review your selections and click **Finish**.

After you have created a virtual hard disk, you can attach it to a virtual machine or any Windows Server 2016 or Windows 10 operating system.

To attach a VHD or VHDX to a VM, follow these steps:

1. Open **Hyper-V Manager**.
2. In the pane in the middle, select a VM.
3. Open **VM Settings** (right-click on a VM or click on **Settings** in the pane on the right).
4. If a VM is a Generation 1 VM, then you have the option to attach a disk to an **IDE Controller** as well as to an **SCSI Controller**. If a VM is a Generation 2, the **SCSI Controller** is the only option to attach a virtual hard disk. You can have only four IDE devices. Hyper-V in Windows Server 2016 supports up to four Virtual SCSI Controllers and each Virtual SCSI Controller supports up to 64 devices.

5. In the pane on the left, click **SCSI Controller**.

6. In the pane on the right, select **Hard Drive** and click **Add**.

7. The newly-added hard drive is shown in the left pane under **SCSI Controller**. In the pane on the left, select the newly added **Hard Drive**:

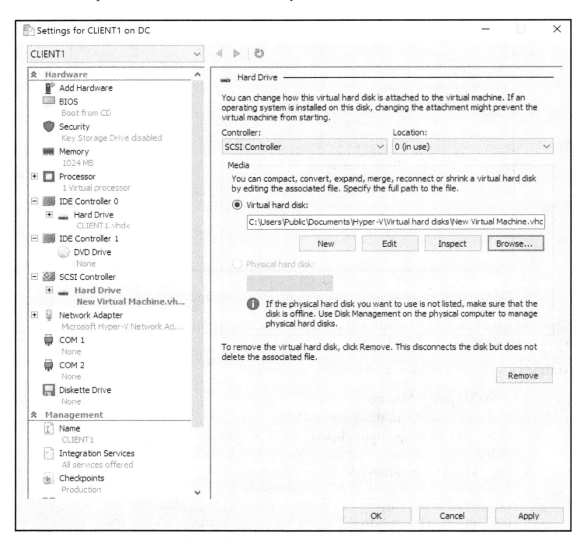

8. In the pane on the right, you can create, edit, or inspect a virtual hard disk. Browse and select a previously created virtual hard disk and click **Apply**.

Editing virtual hard disks

You can perform additional management tasks on virtual hard disks by using the **Edit Disk** option in Hyper-V Manager.

To edit and manage a virtual hard disk, follow these steps:

1. Open **Hyper-V Manager**.
2. In the **Actions** pane on the right, click on **Edit Disk**.
3. The **Edit Virtual Hard Disk Wizard** will open. Click **Next** to skip the introductory screen.
4. On the **Locate Disk** screen, locate the virtual hard disk you want to edit and review the warnings about the disk editing procedure. Click **Next**.
5. The **Choose Action** screen will appear. You can choose from one of the following options:
     • **Compact**: This reduces the size of the virtual hard disk. For example, it shrinks the dynamically expanding disk after data deletion.
     • **Convert**: This converts a virtual hard disk into a different format and type.

- **Expand**: This expands the size and capacity of the virtual hard disk:

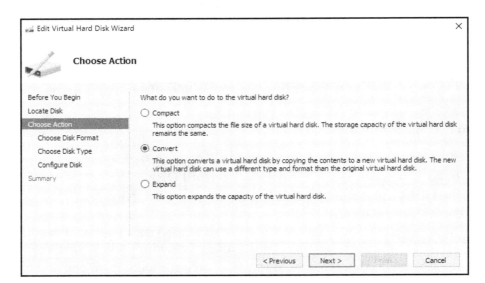

6. Click **Finish** to complete the process and close the window.

Configuring Hyper-V networking

You completed the first step of the configuration of Hyper-V networking when you installed the Hyper-V server role. You would have chosen the network interface that was used to create a virtual switch, through which a virtual machine communicates with the outside world.

Configuring Hyper-V virtual switches

Hyper-V supports three types of virtual switches: External, Internal, and Private:

- **External virtual switches enable virtual machines to connect to a physical network**, and if the physical network has internet accessibility, the VM can connect to the internet as well. Therefore, you would use external virtual switch in a production environment, to make virtual machines and their services available to users.

- **Internal virtual switches do not provide access to a physical network**. They use a virtual switch that can be only used by virtual machines on the host and they provide connectivity between the host and the VMs running on that host. You would primarily use internal switches in development and testing scenarios where you need to have access to the host computer to provide mutual file access or service access.

- **Private virtual switches do not provide access to a physical network** and can be only used by the virtual machines that run on the host. An example where you would use this switch is for testing and development purposes, where the virtual machines running on the host need to be completely isolated from the host and external network:

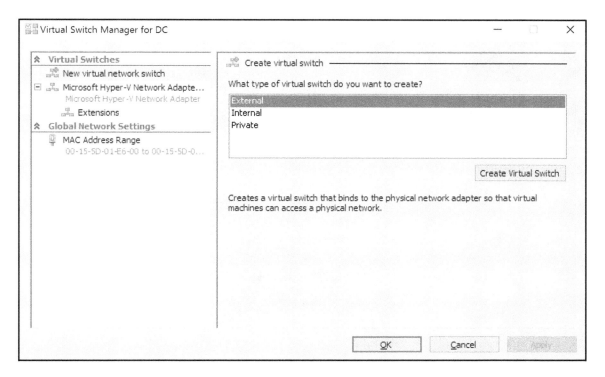

The process required to create any of these three switches is the same. Follow these steps to create an External virtual switch:

1. Open **Hyper-V Manager**.
2. In the **Actions** pane in the right, click **Virtual Switch Manager**. The **Virtual Switch Manager** screen will open.

3. In the pane on the left, select **New virtual network switch**.

4. In the pane on the right, select **External** and click the **Create Virtual Switch** button.

5. At the top of the pane on the right, enter the name of the virtual switch name and add a description if desired.

6. You can then select a connection type, or the type of virtual switch to create:

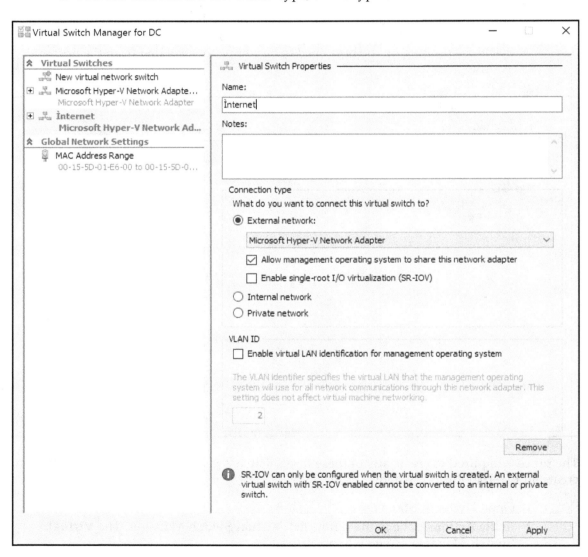

7. The **External network** option has additional configuration options:
    - The drop-down menu allows you to choose a network adapter that the virtual switch will be bound to.
    - The **Allow management operating system to share this network adapter** checkbox allows hosts to communicate with this physical adapter.
    - The **Enable single-root I/O virtualization (SR-IOV)** checkbox allows network traffic to bypass the software switch layer of the Hyper-V virtualization stack.
8. If you are using virtual LANs, check the **Enable virtual LAN identification for management operating system** setting to use VLANs on this network as well.
9. Click **OK** or **Apply** to create a virtual switch.
10. After you have created a virtual switch, you can use the switch in the VM settings.

Adding and removing virtual network interface cards (vNICs)

Hyper-V in Windows 2016 supports a maximum of 12 virtual network adapters per virtual machine. Generation 2 virtual machines support the addition or removal of virtual network adapters while a VM is running. To add or remove a virtual network adapter to a Generation 1 virtual machine, a VM must be shut down.

Follow these steps to create a network adapter:

1. Open the VM settings
2. In the pane on the left, click **Add Hardware**
3. In the pane on the right, select **Network Adapter** and click **Add**

4. From the **Virtual Switch** drop-down menu, choose a virtual switch to connect to:

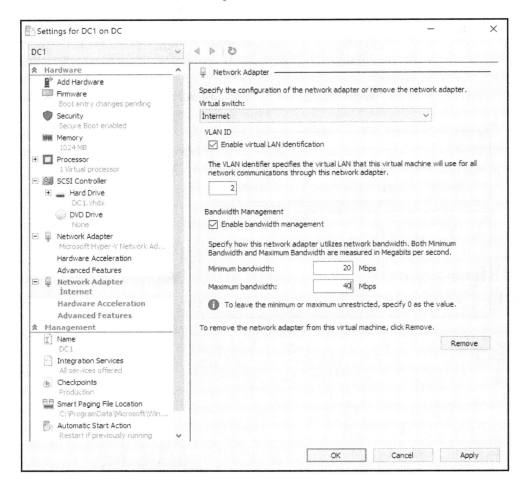

5. For VLAN support, click **Enable virtual LAN identification** and enter the VLAN ID

6. To reserve the network bandwidth for a network adapter, select the **Enable bandwidth management** checkbox

7. Click **OK** or **Apply** to create a network adapter and **Remove** to delete a network adapter

Configuring advanced virtual network adapter features

To configure advanced network adapter features, open the VM settings and select a network adapter in the pane on the left:

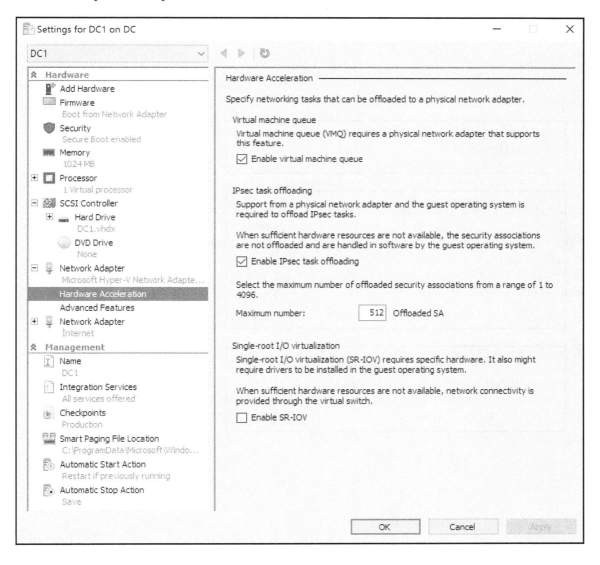

Enable the **Virtual Machine Queue (VMQ)** to take advantage of the network adapter's ability to use DMA to transfer packets directly to the VM's shared memory, and to implement other networking performance enhancements. IPSEC Task Offloading, for example, provides performance enhancements by offloading services for IPSec data processing to supported network interface cards. **Single Root I/O Virtualization (SR-IOV)** provides performance improvements for virtualized networks.

Summary

In this chapter, we learned about Hyper-V as the virtualization solution in Windows Server 2016. We looked at the hardware and software requirements of Hyper-V, before configuring its installation and configuration. This included installing the Hyper-V server role and management tools, performing remote management of Hyper-V hosts, using PowerShell Direct, and configuring nested virtualization. We then looked at configuring virtual machines, as well as exporting and importing them. We concluded by creating virtual disk configurations of virtual switches and more advanced virtual network features.

In the next chapter, we will cover Windows Containers, introduce the container concept, and determine the requirements for Windows Containers. We will install and configure the Windows Server Container host, install and configure Docker on Windows, configure container images, and create containers. We will also see how to manage Windows Containers and Container networking, and how to manage container images using DockerHub and Dockerfile.

Questions

1. What is the Virtual Machine Manager (VMM) or the Hypervisor?
    1. A Windows Management console for managing virtual machines
    2. A software layer that sits on top of the hardware
    3. A software layer separating child partitions
    4. A software layer separating the host partition and the child partition

2. What are the Hyper-V hardware requirements? Choose all that apply.
   1. UEFI
   2. 64-bit processor
   3. 32-bit processor
   4. Second Level Address Translation (SLAT)
   5. TPM
   6. Data Execution Prevention (DEP)

3. You have a server, SRV1, running Windows Server 2012 R2. You have a second server, SRV2, running Windows Server 2016. Hyper-V is running on SRV2. All the latest patches and updates to the operating system have been applied to SRV1. You want to be able to manage Hyper-V on SRV2 from SRV1. What do you need to do?
   1. Install Remote Server Administration Tools (RSAT) on SRV1
   2. Install Remote Server Administration Tools (RSAT) on SRV2
   3. Run Windows Update on SRV2
   4. Upgrade SRV1 to Windows Server 2016
   5. Run Windows Update on SRV1

4. You want to use PowerShell Direct to manage remote virtual machines. Which two commands should you use?
   1. `Enable-PSSessionConfiguration`
   2. `Invoke-Command`
   3. `Get-PSSession`
   4. `Enter-PSSession`
   5. `Import-PSSession`

5. You plan to use nested virtualization. Which PowerShell cmdlet should you use?
   1. `Get-VMProcessor`
   2. `Set-VMBios`
   3. `Set-VMProcessor`
   4. `Set-VMHost`
   5. `Set-VMFirmware`

6. You have a Windows Server 2016 computer running the Hyper-V server role. You have 10 virtual machines. You have an Active Directory Domain Services (AD DS) role installed on the VM1 virtual machine. You notice that the VM9 virtual machine cannot join the Active Directory Domain on VM1. All VMs have been successfully added to an AD domain on VM1. You want to be able to join the VM9 virtual machine to the AD domain on VM1. What should you do?
    1. Reinstall VM9
    2. Add VM to a workgroup
    3. Enable Secure Boot on VM1
    4. Enable Enhanced Session Mode Policy
    5. Configure Integration Services on VM1

7. You have a Hyper-V host running 100 virtual machines. You have configured a secure, encrypted connection using Internet Protocol Security encryption between users and virtual machines. You notice that the CPU on virtual machines is higher than normal when users transfer large files to and from virtual machines. You want to reduce the CPU usage on virtual machines. What should you do?
    1. Enable DHP Guard
    2. Enable IPSec Task Offloading
    3. Enable MAC Address Spoofing
    4. Enable Device Naming

8. What are the characteristics and advantages of VHDX file format? Choose all that apply.
    1. 8,192-byte logical sector size
    2. Data-corruption protection
    3. 2 TB maximum size
    4. Can be resized live

9. You are configuring the Hyper-V server storage. You want to choose the virtual disk type that offers the best performance. Which disk type should you choose?
    1. Fixed size
    2. Dynamically expanding
    3. Pass-through
    4. Differential

10. You are configuring a virtual machine on a Hyper-V host. You notice that you cannot copy text from the host to the virtual machine. You want to be able to copy text from the virtual machine to the host and vice versa. What should you do?
    1. Configure Enhanced Session Mode Policy
    2. Enable Dynamic Memory
    3. Configure NUMA Spanning
    4. Enable Data Exchange

Further reading

To learn more about the topics covered in this chapter, we suggest the following topics for further reading:

- **Supported Linux and FreeBSD virtual machines for Hyper-V on Windows**: https://docs.microsoft.com/en-us/windows-server/virtualization/hyper-v/supported-linux-and-freebsd-virtual-machines-for-hyper-v-on-windows
- **Hyper-V feature compatibility by generation and guest**: https://docs.microsoft.com/en-us/windows-server/virtualization/hyper-v/hyper-v-feature-compatibility-by-generation-and-guest
- **PowerShell Direct – Running PowerShell inside a virtual machine from the Hyper-V host**: https://blogs.technet.microsoft.com/virtualization/2015/05/14/powershell-direct-running-powershell-inside-a-virtual-machine-from-the-hyper-v-host/
- **Installing or Uninstalling Roles, Role Services, or Features**: https://docs.microsoft.com/en-us/windows-server/administration/server-manager/install-or-uninstall-roles-role-services-or-features
- **Working with Hyper-V and Windows PowerShell**: https://docs.microsoft.com/en-us/virtualization/hyper-v-on-windows/quick-start/try-hyper-v-powershell
- **Hyper-V PowerShell Commands**: https://docs.microsoft.com/en-us/powershell/module/hyper-v/?view=win10-ps

5
Understanding Windows Containers

Windows Server 2016 comes with a very important feature—Windows Containers. Deploying containers gives you the ability to create an isolated environment for an application. Windows Server 2016 has two types of containers—Windows Containers and Hyper-V containers. In this chapter, you will learn about containers and how to deploy and manage both container types in Windows Server 2016.

In this chapter, we will cover the following topics:

- An introduction to containers
- Deploying Windows Containers
- Managing Windows Containers

An introduction to containers

Before you start using Windows Containers, you need to understand their purpose. In this section, we'll look at the pros and cons of using containers, and which scenarios are beneficial so that we can move from classic virtual machines to containers.

Understanding the concept of containers

The history of containers started a long time ago but as a concept, it was adopted by Microsoft in Windows Server 2016. The main purpose of containers is to provide an isolated environment for an application. The space used by containers is completely separated from other containers or operations on the operating system, so containerized applications will not affect other applications, nor will be they affected by other applications themselves. If one of the containers are using too much CPU or network bandwidth, then other containers on same host will be affected and performances will be decreased. Containers are known as the **next evolution in virtualization**.

Virtual machines are independent operating systems with dedicated resources, that are designed to be used for a long time period. Due to virtual machine desing, any kind of application can be placed on virtual machines, but that require additional layer of management. Unlikely of virtual machines, containers are more flexible than virtual machines and have significantly smaller footprint. Full OS management is excluded from containers, because all containers on same host share host kernel. Containers also require applications that are intended to be containerized.

Windows Server 2016 supports two different types of containers:

- **Windows Server Containers**: These provide application isolation by using the process and the namespace. This type of container shares an OS kernel with the container host and all other containers that run on the host.
- **Hyper-V containers**: These extend the isolation that Windows Server Containers provide by running a VM. The container host OS kernel is not shared with other Hyper-V containers in this type of container.

Like virtual machines, containers have an operating system. Filesystems are supported, as well as network access to resources on containers. What significantly differentiates containers from virtual machines is the technology behind them.

Before you start playing around with containers, you need to learn about the key concepts of the container architecture:

- **Container host**: The physical or virtual computer that has configured the Windows Containers feature to host containers
- **Container image**: The reference image that will be used for creating new containers

- **Container OS image**: The OS image is one of the layers in the container image and the first layer in the container
- **Sandbox**: The container layer that holds changes made to the container
- **Container repository**: The place for storing the container image and its dependencies

You can manage containers using PowerShell or by using the open source Docker platform.

Containers in Windows

As we mentioned earlier, Windows Server 2016 comes with two different types of containers—Windows Containers and Hyper-V containers. In this section, both Windows Container types will be described so that you can decide which is the appropriate type for you.

Windows Server Containers

Windows Server Containers allow you to run multiple isolated apps on the same computer, but they do not offer security-enhanced isolation. Unlike physical or virtual computers, where only a single user mode per kernel is supported, containers allow you to have more than one user mode per kernel. The Windows Server Containers user mode allows Windows processes and app processes to run in the container, isolated from the user mode of other containers. Windows Server Containers are preferred in scenarios where you need to use a stateless application. This means that the host OS and the application trust each other. You should ensure that the application that you deploy in a container is stateless and doesn't have a GUI, because GUIs are is not supported in containers. Windows Server Containers are also good candidates for rapid deployments. As we mentioned earlier, each container consists of a few layers, and this is a good way of deploying applications where packages are created using a layered approach. For example, if you create a container image that has **Internet Information Services (IIS)** installed with ASP.NET, developers can use that image without changing the configured layers.

Windows Server Containers require the following:

- The Windows container role, which is available on the following systems:
    - Windows Server 2016 (Full or Server Core)
    - Nano Server
    - Windows 10 (Anniversary Update)

- For Hyper-V containers, the Hyper-V role needs to be installed
- Windows Server Container hosts must have the Windows OS installed on the C:\ drive

Hyper-V containers

Virtual machines provide an isolated environment for running applications, but unlike containers, virtual machines provide a full OS with kernel and user modes. Like virtual machines, Hyper-V containers are child partitions of the host OS. However, unlike virtual machines, Hyper-V containers don't have a full OS. Hyper-V containers have an optimized, stripped-down version of Windows Server OS, with security-enhanced isolation between Hyper-V containers on the same container host. Hyper-V containers use container images like Windows Server Containers, and automatically create virtual machines by using that image. Hyper-V containers start faster than virtual machines, as well as Nano Servers. In general, Hyper-V containers use Windows Containers inside virtual machines, but with better security isolation.

Each Hyper-V container has its own copy of the Windows OS kernel and memory assigned directly to them. Hyper-V containers are the preferred virtualization model in multi-tenant environments. For example, you might want to offer your customers a multi-tenant platform for hosting web applications and ensure that their code and applications will not interfere with other tenants.

Hyper-V containers require the following:

- Nested virtualization
- 4 GB RAM for the virtualized Hyper-V host
- The role, which is available on the following systems:
    - Windows Server 2016
    - Windows 10 (Anniversary Update)

- The container host VM, which can be any of the following:
    - Windows Server 2016 (Full or Server Core)
    - Nano Server
    - Windows 10 (Anniversary Update)
    - Processor with Intel VT-x and EPT technology
- A Hyper-V VM with configuration version 8.0 or later
- At least two virtual processors for the container host VM

Deploying Windows Containers

Once you understand the concept of Containers, you can start deploying them. In this section, you will learn how to prepare the infrastructure for Containers, how to install and configure Docker on Windows, and how to deploy Windows Containers and Hyper-V containers.

Installing and configuring a Windows Server Container host

The first step in deploying Containers is to deploy the container host. This host can be Windows Server 2016, Full or Core, or Nano Server. Of course, this procedure can vary, depending on the host and container types.

 In this section, our focus will be on the Windows Server 2016 (Desktop Experience) virtual machine as a container host.

Preparing the virtual machine to be a container host for Windows Containers

If you want to use a container host for Windows Containers only, you need to do the following:

1. Install the Windows Container feature. This step is mandatory, because you cannot do any work with containers without this feature installed. This can be done using the Server Manager:

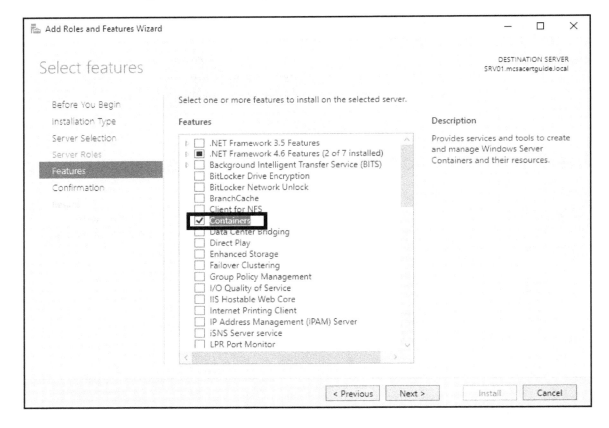

Alternatively, if you want to use PowerShell, you can run the following command:

```
Install-WindowsFeature Containers
```

2. Create a virtual switch. Containers, like virtual machines, connect to a virtual switch for network communication. All virtual switch types are supported, that is, `Private`, `Internal`, `External`, and `NAT`. You can do this by using the Hyper-V manager or PowerShell via the following command:

```
New-VMSwitch -Name ContainerNetwork -SwitchType Private
```

This needs to be done on the virtualization host that hosts a virtual machine, which will be the container host.

 If the type is **Network Address Translation** (**NAT**), you must also use the `-NATSubnetAddress` switch, with the IP range as a parameter in the format `172.16.0.0/12`.

3. If your virtual switch is of the NAT type, you need to configure NAT settings. This can be done using the following PowerShell command:

```
New-NetNat -Name ContainerNat -InternalIPInterfaceAddressPrefix
"172.16.0.0/12"
```

4. Configure the MAC address spoofing. If your container host is virtualized, you need to enable MAC address spoofing using the Hyper-V manager or PowerShell. In Hyper-V manager, you need to change the settings of the container host virtual machine. The following screenshot shows the settings window where you can enable this:

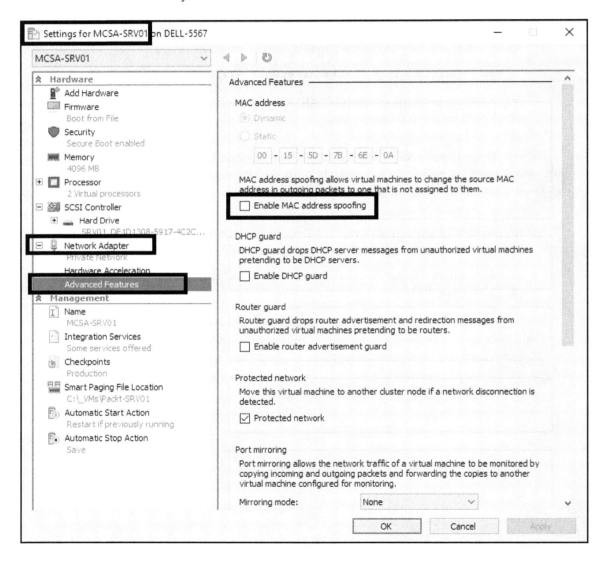

Using PowerShell, the following command will enable the desired option:

```
Get-VMNetworkAdapter -VMName MCSA-SRV01 | Set-VMNetworkAdapter -
MacAddressSpoofing On
```

Preparing the virtual machine to be a container host for Hyper-V containers

If you decide to prepare your container host for Hyper-V containers, a few more steps need to be carried out in addition to all the steps for the Windows container:

1. Enable the Hyper-V role. This step is mandatory and can be done using Server Manager or the following PowerShell command:

```
Install-WindowsFeature Hyper-V -IncludeAllSubFeature -
IncludeManagementTools
```

2. Enable nested virtualization. To enable a Hyper-V role on a virtual machine, you need to enable nested virtualization. This can be done using the following PowerShell command:

```
Set-VMProcessor -VMName MCSA-SRV01 -ExposeVirtualizationExtensions
$true
```

 The virtual machine that will be the container host needs to have at least two virtual processors.

Installing the package provider

Once you have prepared your container host, the next step is to deploy the container from the base image. Base images are not included in Windows Server 2016, and the package provider needs to be used to retrieve and manage base images for deployments. All package providers, except `PowerShellGet`, need to be installed on demand. Once the package provider is installed and imported, you can start deploying the containers.

The Windows PowerShell `Find-PackageProvider` cmdlet will give you a list of all the package providers that are available for installation. There are many package providers and you need to select one using the PowerShell `Install-PackageProvider` cmdlet. If the package provider that you want to use is already installed, you just need to import it into PowerShell using the `Import-PackageProvider` cmdlet.

Package providers can refer to different sources or repositories. The most common include `PSGallery`, `PackageManagement` (also known as OneGet), and `NuGet`.

The following screenshot shows the output of the preceding command:

```
Administrator: Windows PowerShell                                               —    □    ✕
PS C:\Users\Administrator.MCSACERTGUIDE> Install-PackageProvider NuGet

The package(s) come(s) from a package source that is not marked as trusted.
Are you sure you want to install software from 'https://oneget.org/nuget-2.8.5.208.package.swidtag'?
[Y] Yes  [A] Yes to All  [N] No  [L] No to All  [S] Suspend  [?] Help (default is "N"): Y

Name                      Version         Source          Summary
----                      -------         ------          -------
nuget                     2.8.5.208       https://onege... NuGet provider for the OneGet meta-package manager


PS C:\Users\Administrator.MCSACERTGUIDE> _
```

Installing Docker on Windows

Docker is a collection of open source tools and solutions that provide a common model for packaging or containerizing application code in a standardized unit for software development. This unit is also known as a Docker container and includes everything necessary to run it. Support for Docker comes with Windows Server 2016, which provides a built-in, native Docker daemon for Windows Server hosts. The host daemon is a light environment that communicates with the Docker client. The Docker client is responsible for running commands to build, ship, and run Docker containers. Docker containers are based on open standards. This allows containers to run on all major Linux distributions and Microsoft operating systems. Docker containers can run on any computer, on any infrastructure, and in any cloud.

The Docker Engine for Windows Server requires Windows Server 2016. The Windows Server Docker Engine doesn't support cross-platform containerization, which means that Windows Containers require a Windows Docker host, and Linux containers require a Linux Docker host. Containers in Windows can be managed using the Docker tool or PowerShell, but Containers that are created with PowerShell cannot be managed with the Docker toolset or vice versa.

Windows Server 2016 does not include the Docker Engine, and you need to install and configure it. As we mentioned previously, Docker consists of the Docker Engine and the Docker client.

To install Docker, you need to observe the following steps:

1. Install the `NuGet` package provider
2. Install the Docker module from `PSGallery`
3. Install the Docker installer package
4. Restart your computer

All of these steps need to be done using the following Powershell commands:

```
Install-PackageProvider -Name Nuget -Force
Install-Module -Name DockerMsftProvider -Repository PSGallery -Force
Install-Package -Name docker -ProviderName DockerMsftProvider
Restart-Computer-Force
```

If you are not able to install the latest Docker package version, you need to add the `-RequiredVersion` switch and the version number as a parameter. In my case, I used version 17.06. At the time of writing this book, the latest version is 18.09.

After these steps, you will have a functional Docker Engine on Windows Server 2016 as a container host.

Installing container images

Once you have installed Docker on Windows Server, the next step in the containerization process is preparing container images for container deployment. Although you can do this using the PowerShell `Find-ContainerImage`, `Save-ContainerImage`, and `Install-ContainerImage` cmdlets, after installing the `ContainerImage` package provider, the focus of this chapter will be on using Docker commands.

The Docker command that you can use to list Docker images is as follows:

```
docker images
```

This will show you all the Docker images that you have downloaded on your container host.

If you want to search all of the available Microsoft Docker images, you need to run the following command:

```
docker search Microsoft
```

The following screenshot shows the output of the preceding command:

```
Administrator: Windows PowerShell                                                                        —   □   ×

PS C:\Users\Administrator.MCSACERTGUIDE> docker search microsoft
NAME                                     DESCRIPTION                                      STARS    OFFICIAL    AUTOMATE
D
microsoft/dotnet                         Official images for .NET Core and ASP.NET ...    1348                 [OK]
microsoft/mssql-server-linux             Official images for Microsoft SQL Server o...    1049
microsoft/aspnet                         Microsoft IIS images                             811                  [OK]
microsoft/windowsservercore              The official Windows Server Core base image      632
microsoft/aspnetcore                     Official images for running compiled ASP.N...    571                  [OK]
microsoft/nanoserver                     The official Nano Server base image              466
microsoft/iis                            Microsoft IIS images                             348
microsoft/mssql-server-windows-developer Official Microsoft SQL Server Developer Ed...    282
microsoft/mssql-server-windows-express   Official Microsoft SQL Server Express Edit...    275
microsoft/aspnetcore-build               Official images for building ASP.NET Core ...    267                  [OK]
microsoft/azure-cli                      Official images for Microsoft Azure CLI          154                  [OK]
microsoft/powershell                     PowerShell for every system!                     142                  [OK]
microsoft/vsts-agent                     Official images for the Visual Studio Team...    115
microsoft/dynamics-nav                   Official images for Microsoft Dynamics NAV...    103
microsoft/dotnet-samples                 .NET Core Docker Samples                         66                   [OK]
microsoft/bcsandbox                      Business Central Sandbox                         53
microsoft/mssql-tools                    Official images for Microsoft SQL Server C...    49
microsoft/oms                            Monitor your containers using the Operatio...    41                   [OK]
microsoft/cntk                           CNTK images from github.com/Microsoft/CNTK...    38                   [OK]
microsoft/wcf                            Microsoft WCF images                             28
microsoft/dotnet-nightly                 Preview images for .NET Core and ASP.NET C...    20                   [OK]
microsoft/dotnet-framework-build         The .NET Framework build images have moved...    16                   [OK]
microsoft/mmlspark                       Microsoft Machine Learning for Apache Spark      7
microsoft/aspnetcore-build-nightly       Images to build preview versions of ASP.NE...    3                    [OK]
microsoft/cntk-nightly                   CNTK nightly image from github.com/Microso...    2
PS C:\Users\Administrator.MCSACERTGUIDE> _
```

Once you have decided on what you want to download to the local repository, you need to run the following command:

```
docker pull <imagename>
```

In my example, I ran the following command to install an image that hosts IIS on Windows Server Core:

```
docker pull microsoft/iis:windowsservercore
```

The following screenshot shows the output of the preceding command:

```
Administrator: Windows PowerShell                                                                        —   □   ×

PS C:\Users\Administrator.MCSACERTGUIDE> docker pull microsoft/iis:windowsservercore
windowsservercore: Pulling from microsoft/iis
3889bb8d808b: Downloading [>                                            ]   8.092MB/4.07GB
bf261bf8d7bc: Downloading [>                                            ]   540kB/1.565GB
ab9da938c285: Downloading [=========>                                   ]   25.84MB/139.3MB
43bf4c0c5220: Waiting
812860398ee3: Waiting
■
```

Some of the images are too big and installing them can take a long time. For example, the size of the aforementioned image is more than 11 GB.

Once you have installed the Docker image, the `docker images` command allows you to see which images are available on your local repository:

Creating Hyper-V and Windows Server Containers

The last step in this process is creating an image. As we mentioned earlier, containers can be created and started as Windows Containers or Hyper-V containers. To create containers, you need to use the `docker run` command, with different switches depending on the container type.

If you want to create a Windows container called `IIS-Standard`, based on the downloaded image, you need to run the following command:

```
docker run --name IIS-Standard -d -p 80:80 microsoft/iis:windowsservercore
```

For a Hyper-V container, you need to run a similar command, with one more switch that defines the isolation level:

```
docker run --name IIS-Hyper-V -d -p 80:80 --isolation=hyperv
microsoft/iis:windowsservercore
```

If you want to check which Containers have been created and are running on the host, you need to run the `docker ps` command:

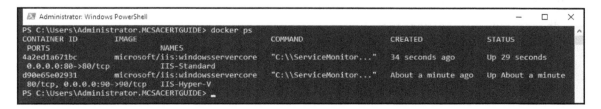

You now have two different types of container live on Windows Server 2016.

Managing Windows Containers

In the previous section, we learned how to prepare our infrastructure for containers and how to deploy Windows Containers and Hyper-V containers. This section will cover managing Windows and Hyper-V containers.

Container networking

Networking is an important part of implementing containers. Containers on a Windows server, as we mentioned earlier, have a similar function to virtual machines. Each container needs to have a network adapter that needs to be connected to the Hyper-V virtual switch. There are five different virtual switches that can be created through Docker:

- **NAT**: The default network, named NAT, which is created by Docker Engine when it first starts up.
- **Overlay**: The network driver creates a distributed network between multiple Docker daemons to enable Swarm services to communicate together.
- **Transparent**: Allows Containers to connect directly to the physical network.
- **L2Bridge/L2Tunnel:** Provides L2 address translation. Your containers can have the same IP subnet as the container host.

There are a few commands that are useful for Docker networking.

If you want to view Docker networks, you need to run the following command:

```
docker network ls
```

Network details can be listed using the following command:

```
docker network inspect
```

The following command can be used if you want to create a container with a specific network configuration:

```
docker run <containername> --net=<networkname>
```

Managing Windows Containers

Once created, containers also need to be managed. Managing containers includes creating, starting, stopping, and removing containers, along with many other tasks. You can use the following Docker commands to manage containers:

- The following command lists installed images on your container host:

  `docker images`

- The following command creates a container by using a container image:

  `docker run:`

- The following command commits the changes you made to the container and creates a new container image:

  `docker commit:`

- The following command stops a running container:

  `docker stop:`

- The following command removes an existing container:

  `docker rm:`

- The following command downloads and installs images from the Docker repository:

  `docker pull:`

- The following command runs a command in a running container:

  `docker exec:`

- The following command copies files to a container:

  `docker cp:`

- The following command lists created containers:

  `docker ps:`

All of these Docker commands have a lot of parameters that can be used to perform actions on containers.

For more information on Docker commands, go to the following link: `https://docs.docker.com/engine/reference/commandline/docker/`.

Managing container images using Docker Hub and Dockerfile

Docker Hub provides a centralized resource for container images, and is managed by the Docker company. It provides the following features and functions:

- **Image repositories**: Contains images stored in repositories
- **Organizations and teams**: Provides private repositories for collaboration
- **Automated builds**: Automates the building and updating of images from GitHub or Bitbucket, directly on Docker Hub
- **Webhooks**: Allows you to trigger an event or action when an image or updated image is successfully pushed to the repository
- **GitHub and Bitbucket integration**: Allows you to add the Docker Hub and your Docker images to current workflows

To interact with repositories on Docker Hub, you need to create a Docker ID at `https://hub.docker.com/`. Then, you can run the `docker login` command and log in to Docker Hub. With a valid Docker ID, you will be able to pull and push images from numerous Docker Hub repositories.

The process of creating container images can be automated. Docker Engine includes tools that provide many benefits, such as storing container images as code, CI, and the rapid recreation of container images. The components in Docker Engine that are responsible for automation are the Dockerfile and the `docker build` command. The Dockerfile is a text file that contains instructions detailing how to create a new container image. The Docker Engine command, `docker build`, consumes and processes the Dockerfile. The Dockerfile is a simple file, and provides a list of commands that need to be executed during the creation of container images, as shown in the following code:

```
# Sample Dockerfile

# Indicates that the windowsservercore image will be used as the base
image.
FROM microsoft/windowsservercore

# Metadata indicating an image maintainer.
```

```
LABEL maintainer="vladimir@mcsacertguide.local"

# Uses dism.exe to install the IIS role.
RUN dism.exe /online /enable-feature /all /featurename:iis-webserver
/NoRestart

# Creates an HTML file and adds content to this file.
RUN echo "This is container image created by Dockerfile" >
c:\inetpub\wwwroot\index.html
```

Once you save the Dockerfile, you can use the `docker build` command to start creating container images:

```
docker build -t mcsa-iis -f .\iis.txt .
```

When a container image is created, you should see the following message:

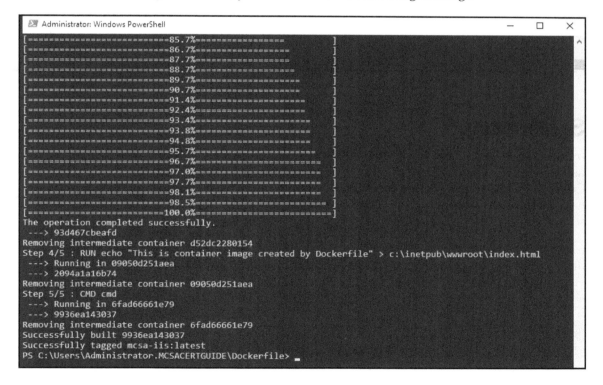

If you list Docker images using the `docker images` command, you will see that you have a new container image available for deployment:

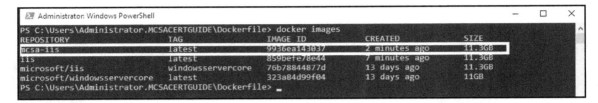

The new container image with fully installed IIS is ready for deployment, and each container that's installed that runs this image will have a custom welcome page in IIS:

Summary

In this chapter, you have learned about the concept of containers and the pros and cons of using them. You have also learned how to prepare your infrastructure for Windows Containers and Hyper-V containers, how to deploy each of these two container types, and how to manage containers using Docker, Docker Hub, and Dockerfile. Containers are, for sure, the future of virtualization.

In the next chapter, you will learn about some important concepts for implementing a highly available infrastructure. You will look at disaster recovery and high availability in Hyper-V and how to implement Storage Spaces Direct and network load balancing.

Questions

1. What is the first step in configuring a Hyper-V container host?
    1. Installing Hyper-V
    2. Installing the container feature
    3. Enabling nested virtualizations
    4. Configuring a virtual switch

2. Which network is created by default when the Docker Engine starts for the first time?
    1. Overlay
    2. Ethernet
    3. Internal
    4. NAT

3. Can a Nano Server be a container host?
    1. Yes
    2. No

4. Which switch needs to be used to create a Hyper-V container?
    1. `--isolation=hyperv`
    2. `--hypervcontainer=true`
    3. `--isolation=vmisolation`
    4. None

5. Which Docker command lists created Containers?
    1. `docker container`
    2. `docker rm`
    3. `docker ps`
    4. `docker pull`

6. Which Docker command lists available images for installation?
    1. `docker images`
    2. `docker pull`
    3. `docker search`
    4. `docker build`

7. Which type of file is a Dockerfile?
    1. `.ps1`
    2. `.bat`
    3. `.txt`
    4. `.bash`

8. Does Windows Server 2016 include Docker Engine by default?
    1. Yes
    2. No

Further reading

For further reading about Docker, please check the following links:

- `https://docs.microsoft.com/en-us/virtualization/windowsContainers/about/`
- `https://docs.docker.com/network/`
- `https://docs.docker.com/engine/reference/commandline/docker/`
- `https://docs.docker.com`

6
High Availability

One of the most important parts of a highly available Windows Server 2016 infrastructure solution is failover clustering, that will be covered and detailed explained in `Chapter 7`, *Implementing Clustering*.

Almost every organization has a business-critical IT solution. An outage of file, mail, or database servers can affect the whole organization and result in data or money loss and damage the reputation of the business. Because of this, high availability is the most important part of planning and implementing IT solutions. In this chapter, you'll learn about the concepts of disaster recovery and high availability and how to implement these solutions.

We will cover the following topics in this chapter:

- Disaster recovery and high availability in Hyper-V
- Implementing Storage Spaces Direct
- Implementing Network Load Balancing

Disaster recovery and high availability in Hyper-V

This section will describe the high availability and disaster recovery solutions that are built into Windows Server 2016. You'll learn how to implement Hyper-V Replica and about both live and storage migrations.

Implementing Hyper-V Replica

Disaster recovery is an important part of IT solutions. Although backups can be a solution for saving and storing data in different locations and can act as a disaster recovery solution, it's a time-consuming process. There are many solutions and third-party companies that can provide disaster recovery for you, but if you're running Hyper-V Server on Windows Server 2012 or later, you can use Hyper-V Replica. Hyper-V Replica enables running virtual machines to be replicated efficiently to a secondary host across a WAN or a LAN link. Primary and replica copies of virtual machines will be synchronized at regular intervals that can be configured in Windows Server 2016.

Hyper-V Replica technology consists of the following components:

- **Replication engine**: Represents the core of Hyper-V Replica and is responsible for configuration, replication, and failover functionalities
- **Change tracking**: Component which tracks changes that are occurring on VMs primary copy
- **Network module**: This element provides a secure and efficient way to transfer virtual machine replicas between hosts (Primary and Replica)
- **Hyper-V Replica Broker role**: This role is configured in failover clustering when we want to enable replication on VMs that are clustered

Hyper-V Replica is a feature that needs to be enabled on the virtual machine level.

In Windows Server 2016, you can configure Hyper-V Replica and increase the availability of business-critical virtual machines. Replication frequency in Windows Server 2016 Hyper-V Replica can be configured to intervals of 30 seconds, 5 minutes, or 15 minutes. In earlier versions of Windows Server, the only option was intervals of five minutes. With Windows Server 2012 and newer Windows Server operating systems, you can enable Extended Replica and extend the replication to the third server. The server that's running the primary copy of the virtual machine replicates the virtual machine to the replica server, and the replica server then replicates the virtual machine to the extended replica server.

To implement Hyper-V Replica, you require the following:

- Hyper-V role on Windows Server 2016
- Enough storage on the primary and replica servers
- Network connectivity between the primary and replica servers

- Firewall rules to be correctly configured to enable replication between the primary and replica servers (ports 80 and 443)
- X.509v3 certificate to support mutual authentication with certificates if desired

Hyper-V Replica doesn't need be installed separately, because it's a part of the Hyper-V role in Windows Server 2016. It's fully supported on a standalone Hyper-V Server and doesn't need to be configured on a domain-joined Hyper-V Server. Hyper-V Replica just needs to be enabled and configured, using the following steps:

1. In Hyper-V Manager, enable the Hyper-V server as a replica server
2. Configure the Hyper-V settings, such as **Authentication and ports** and **Authorization and storage**, as follows:

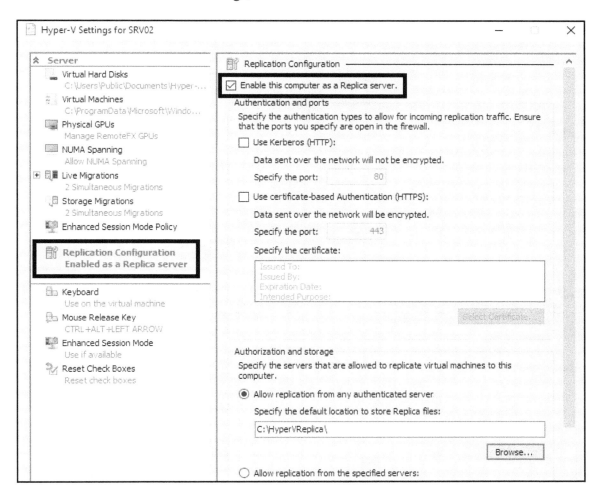

3. Start the wizard for enabling virtual machine replication, and specify the following:
   - The replica server name
   - The connection parameters
   - The replication **Virtual Hard Disks** (**VHDs**)
   - The replication frequency
   - The additional recovery points
   - The initial replication method

This is shown in the following screenshot:

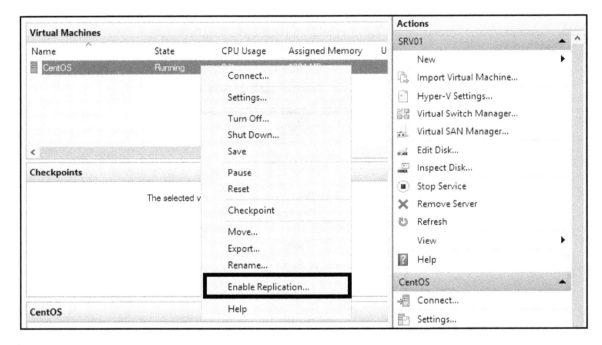

4. Once the initial replication is done, you'll be able to see the same virtual machine on the secondary host, but in the **Off** state, as follows:

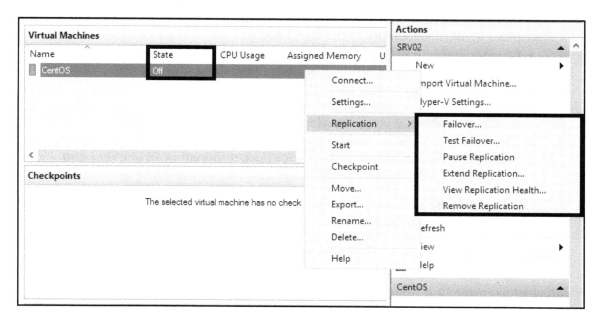

Live migration

One of the biggest advantages in high availability and clustering solutions in Windows Server is a process called live migration. Hyper-V allows you to move virtual machines to another host without shutting down. If you've implemented a failover cluster, the process will seamlessly move virtual machines from one node to another node in cluster. If you haven't implemented a failover cluster and you want to move from the *live* virtual machine to another host, the live migration process will perform the storage migration process. However, at the end, the result will be same: the virtual machine will be on another host.

In scenarios where you have implemented a failover cluster, live migration guarantees that a virtual machine will be migrated automatically from one to another in case of one node failure. If you haven't implemented failover cluster and virtual machines are on standalone Hyper-V servers, you can perform live migration if you want to move from one Hyper-V server to another, without interrupting virtual machine functionality.

The live migration process consists of four steps:

- **Migration setup**: The source node creates a TCP connection with the target host. Live migration will create a temporary virtual machine on the target host in order to allocate memory to the target host.
- **Guest-memory transfer**: The guest memory is transferred iteratively to the target host while the virtual machine is still running on the source.
- **State transfer**: Virtual machine migration includes a state transfer phase. Hyper-V needs to stop the source, transfer the state of the virtual machine to the target host, and restore the virtual machine on the target host.
- **Cleanup**: This is the last step in the live migration process. It involves shutting down the virtual machine on the source host, terminating all workers, and completing the migration.

During the state transfer phase, Hyper-V must pause the virtual machine during the final state transfer. Also, all "dirty pages" in the state partition will be migrated. Dirty pages represent the last remaining files of the virtual machine memory that need to be migrated.

If you want to enable Live Migration, you need to meet following requirements.

- By default, Live Migration is disabled, and need to be enabled
- The source and target hosts must have installed Hyper-V role and management tools
- The source and target hosts should have identical processor architectures
- User accounts must be members of the Local Administrator group
- Authentication method need to be choose between Kerberos and CredSSP and configured
- The source and target hosts must be part of same domain or different domains that trusts each other
- Different and separate network should be used for Live Migration

Live migration can be enabled using Hyper-V Manager or the PowerShell `Enable-VMMigration` cmdlet:

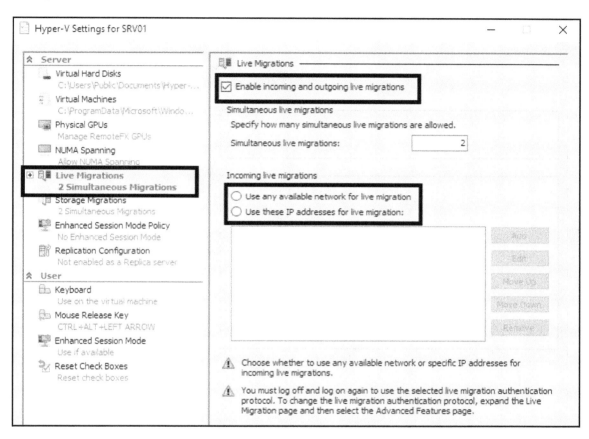

The PowerShell command, by default, checks **Use these IP addresses for live migration**, even if the lists of IP addresses aren't populated. To configure all available networks to be used for migration, you need to run the following PowerShell command:

```
Set-VMHost -UseAnyNetworkForMigration $true
```

Live migration can be initiated using Hyper-V Manager or PowerShell. If you want to use Hyper-V Manager to move a virtual machine, you need to select the **Move** option from the virtual machine options:

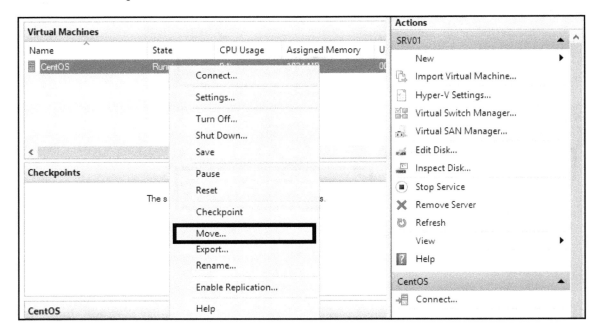

Then, you need to select which type of migration you want and the destination:

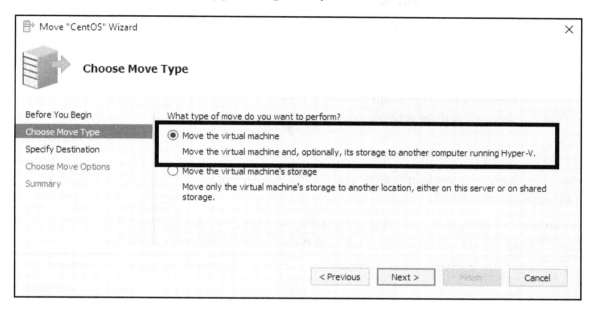

The PowerShell command for moving a virtual machine to another host, if the virtual machine files are stored on the **Server Message Block (SMB)**, is as follows:

```
Move-VM <VMName> <RemoteServerName>
```

If the virtual machine files are stored locally on a host, as mentioned, the storage migration process will be initiated in order to move all virtual-machine-related files to a new host. In this scenario, you need to use the following PowerShell command:

```
Move-VM <VMName> <RemoteServerName> -IncludeStorage -DestinationStoragePath
<DestinationPath>
```

Configuring authentication for migration

To perform live migration, you need to configure authentication. As mentioned, there are two possible authentication options: Kerberos and CredSSP. By default, once you enable live migration, CredSSP is selected as the authentication method. They have the following differences:

- Kerberos lets you avoid having to sign in to the server, but requires constrained delegation to be set up
- CredSSP lets you avoid configuring constrained delegation, but requires you sign in to the source server

Once you decide on the best option, you can configure this using Hyper-V Manager or a PowerShell command.

If you want to change this configuration using the Hyper-V Management console, you need to configure the **Live Migrations** advanced features under **Hyper-V Settings**:

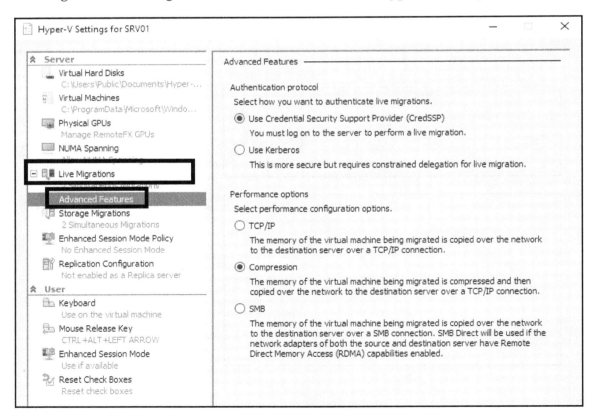

The following PowerShell command will configure the authentication according to your request:

```
Set-VMHost -VirtualMachineMigrationAuthenticationType
<AuthenticationProtocol>
```

Storage migration

In some scenarios, you might need to move virtual machine files to another location. This might be the case, for example, if you've implemented faster storage and you want to move your business critical machines to that storage. Up until Windows Server 2012, this process resulted in downtime of the virtual machine, because it had to be turned off. You had to export and import the virtual machines. With Windows Server 2012 and Windows Server 2016, you can move storage more easily, because of a feature called storage migration, which is implemented natively in the server OS.

Storage migration performs this seamlessly for the user and virtual machine by copying the virtual hard disk. When the process starts, Hyper-V starts copying the hard disk(s) to another location. During the process, the virtual machine is live and fully functional. Every change that occurs on the virtual machine during storage migration will be written to the source and the destination disk as well. Once the disk copy process is complete, Hyper-V switches virtual machines to use the destination location and associates the new virtual disk with the virtual machine. The last step in the process is deleting the source VHD/VHDX files and the virtual machine configuration.

In the storage migration process, you can select one of three possible options:

- **Move all of the virtual machine's data to a single location**
- **Move the virtual machine's data to different locations**
- **Move only the virtual machine's virtual hard disks**

These can be seen in the following screenshot:

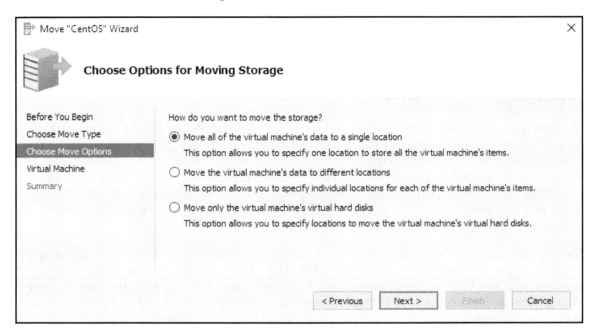

Storage migration can be done using Hyper-V Manager or the PowerShell Move-VMStorage cmdlet. If you want to use the Hyper-V Manager to move the virtual machine, you need to select the **Move the virtual machine's storage** option and then select the type of moving that you want:

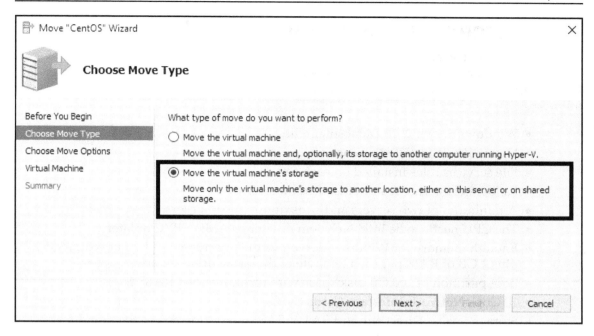

The following PowerShell command needs to be used if you want to initiate storage migration using PowerShell:

```
Move-VMStorage <VMName> -DestinationStoragePath <DestinationPath>
```

Implementing Storage Spaces Direct

Storage Spaces Direct is the Microsoft implementation of software-defined storage that comes with Windows Server 2016. This technology uses servers with local-attached drives to create highly available storage for a smaller price than traditional **Storage Array Network** (**SAN**) solutions. Storage Spaces Direct can be deployed in two different architecture, **Converged** and **Hyper-Converged**. Converged is used in scenarios where you want to use separate clusters for storage and compute, while Hyper-Converged give you the ability to use same cluster for storage and compute. In this section, you'll learn what is required for Storage Spaces Direct and how to implement this technology on Windows Server 2016.

Requirements for Storage Spaces Direct

Although you can use any almost any hardware to configure Storage Spaces Direct, Microsoft has a list of recommended vendors. Don't worry, all known vendors, such as Dell, Lenovo, HP, and Supermicro, are supported. However, the basic requirements are as follows:

- Windows Server 2016 Datacenter edition
- Hyper-V role installed on each server
- File services roles installed on each server
- Failover clustering feature installed on each server
- A minimum of two servers and a maximum of 16 servers
- The CPU needs to be Intel Nehalem or later or AMD EPYC or later
- Enough memory for Windows Server, virtual machines, and other workloads, plus 4 GB of RAM per each terabyte of the cache drive capacity
- Boot partition of 200 GB disk space with recommended RAID 1
- 10 Gbps **Network Interface Cards** (**NICs**)
- Storage Spaces Direct support SATA, SAS, and NVMe drives that are directly attached to each server
- All disks that you're going to add to Storage Spaces Direct must be unformatted

Once you meet all of the necessary requirements for Storage Spaces Direct, you can start by enabling and configuring this technology, which will be covered in the next sections.

Enabling Storage Spaces Direct

Storage Spaces Direct was designed to cover both converged and hyper-converged scenarios:

- **Converged**: Storage and compute are in separate clusters. The converged implementation of Storage Spaces Direct provides network-attached storage over SMB3 file shares.
- **Hyper-converged**: There's one cluster for compute and storage. This deployment option runs Hyper-V virtual machines directly on the servers that provide the storage.

Once you meet all prerequisites and decide which deployment is appropriate for you, you can start enabling this technology. The starting point for this task is installing Windows Server 2016 and joining to the domain. Once you complete this step, you can go to the next step, which is installing all of the necessary roles to each server.

Installing all necessary roles

On each server, the following roles need to be installed:

- Failover clustering
- Hyper-V
- File Server (if you want to host any file shares, such as for a converged deployment)
- Data-Center-Bridging (if you're using RoCEv2 instead of iWARP network adapters)
- RSAT-Clustering-PowerShell
- Hyper-V-PowerShell

You can do this using Server Manager or the following PowerShell command:

```
Install-WindowsFeature -Name "Hyper-V", "Failover-Clustering", "Data-Center-Bridging", "RSAT-Clustering-PowerShell", "Hyper-V-PowerShell", "FS-FileServer" -IncludeAllSubFeature -IncludeManagementTools
```

In this command, all necessary features for any deployment type are included.

Validating and creating the cluster

Cluster validation is an important task and can be done using the Failover Cluster Manager or PowerShell.

Before moving on to this step, ensure that your drives are empty and not formatted.

If you want to do this using the GUI, go to the Failover Cluster Manager and carry out the following steps:

1. Open **Validate Configuration** in the **Action** pane
2. Add the servers for validation
3. Select **Run only test I select** and click **Next**
4. Select **Storage Spaces Direct** for validation
5. Start the validation process

If you want to do this using PowerShell, you need to run the following command:

```
Test-Cluster -Node <ServerName1, ServerName2> -Include "Storage Spaces
Direct", Inventory", "Network", "System Configuration"
```

If the validation passes successfully, you can create a cluster using the Failover Cluster Manager wizard or by using the following PowerShell command:

```
New-Cluster -Name <ClusterName> -Node <ServerName1, ServerName2> -NoStorage
```

Enabling Storage Spaces Direct

When you create a cluster successfully, the next step is enabling Storage Spaces Direct. This can only be done using the following PowerShell command:

```
Enable-ClusterStorageSpacesDirect -CimSession <ClusterName>
```

This command will put the storage system into Storage Spaces Direct mode and do the following:

- Create a single large pool called something like **S2D on Cluster1**
- Configure the Storage Spaces Direct caches
- Create two tiers as default tiers

This command might take several minutes. Once it's finished, the system will be ready for the volumes to be created.

 You can also use the node name instead of the cluster name, to avoid DNS replication delays that may occur.

Creating volumes

The last step in Storage Spaces Direct enabling is creating volumes. This can be done using the Failover Cluster Manager or the PowerShell `New-Volume` cmdlet. If you want to do this using this GUI, you need to go through the following steps:

1. Select **New Virtual Disk**:

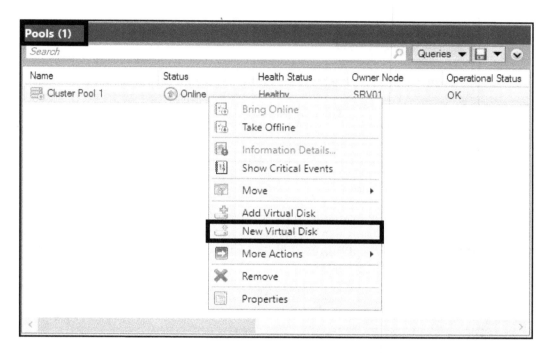

2. Select the storage pool in which the disk will be created
3. Enter the disk name

4. Define the disk size:

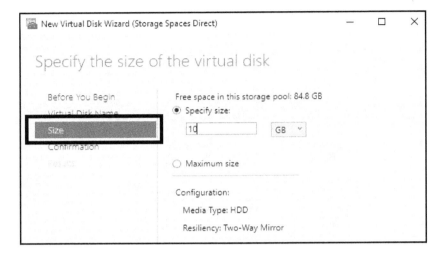

5. Confirm the disk creation

Once the disk is created, it'll be available in the Failover Cluster Manager console. You can work with the disk just as you can work with all other cluster disks. After these steps, you can say that you've enabled and configured Hyper-Converged Storage Spaces Direct on Windows Server 2016:

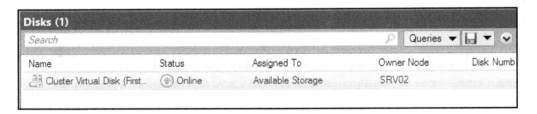

If you want to do the same thing using PowerShell, you need to run the following command:

```
New-Volume -FriendlyName <VolumeName> -FileSystem <NTFS | ReFS> -
StoragePoolFriendlyName S2D* -Size <GB | TB>
```

Implementing Network Load Balancing

Network Load Balancing (**NLB**) is a feature on Windows Server that's responsible for balancing the network traffic between a set of servers. Before you deploy NLB, you need to know in what scenarios it can be used. In this section, you'll learn what NLB is, what's its purpose, and how to install and configure it.

An introduction to NLB

Network Load Balancing is a scalable Windows Server feature that provides network traffic distribution and can be installed on all editions of Windows Server 2016. The Windows Server NLB cluster can have between 2 and 32 nodes that can be added or removed at any time after configuration. NLB is suitable for stateless applications, such as web applications. It isn't an appropriate solution, however, for traditional databases and file servers. One of the features of NLB is that it isn't failure-aware. If one of the nodes goes offline for any reason, requests will no longer be forwarded to that node. Once the node comes back online, it'll be automatically added to the balance.

When you configure an application to use NLB, the application's IP address will be the IP address of the NLB cluster. Each node in the cluster will have that IP address configured as an additional address in order to receive packets. All nodes in a cluster will receive the incoming packet, but only one of the nodes will respond. NLB forwards traffic to nodes based on their activity. With this feature, NLB ensures that the least active node at that moment will receive a new packet.

Prerequisites for NLB

Before you install NLB, you need to know that there are some requirements that you must meet:

- **All hosts in an NLB cluster must be in the same subnet**: This is recommended because NLB won't achieve convergence if the latency between nodes is above 250 ms
- **All network adapters in an NLB cluster must be configured to use either unicast or multicast**: Mixing these traffic types isn't supported
- **Only the TCP/IP, IPv4, and IPv6 protocols are supported in NLB**: All other protocols aren't supported
- **IP addresses of nodes in an NLB cluster must be static**: Dynamic Host Configuration Protocol (DHCP) will be disabled automatically for all network adapters that are used in an NLB cluster

Once you meet all of the prerequisites, you can start installing and configuring NLB on your servers.

 If your NLB nodes only have one network interface, the cluster operation mode needs to be multicast. Unicast mode requires at least two network interfaces.

Installing NLB nodes and creating an NLB cluster

Installing NLB is a straightforward process that can be done using the Server Manager or PowerShell. All nodes that are part of an NLB cluster need to have the NLB feature installed. If you want to install this feature using PowerShell, you need to run the following command:

```
Install-WindowsFeature NLB -IncludeAllSubFeature -IncludeManagementTools
```

If you want to install NLB on all nodes at the same time with one command, you can run the following PowerShell command:

```
Invoke-Command -ComputerName <ServerName> -ScriptBlock {Install-
WindowsFeature NLB -IncludeAllSubFeature -IncludeManagementTools}
```

When you've installed the NLB feature on all desired servers, you can create an NLB cluster. This can be done using the Network Load Balancing Manager or PowerShell. If you want to create an NLB cluster using the **Network Load Balancing Manager**, you need to open the console and select **New Cluster**:

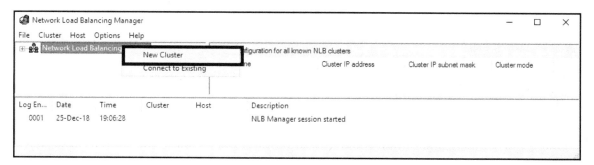

Then, you just need to follow the wizard and configure the parameters:

- On the **New Cluster: Connect** page, select one of the servers on which the NLB feature is installed to be the NLB cluster host
- On the **New Cluster: Host parameters** page, define the host priority, the IP address, and the default state
- On the **New Cluster: Cluster IP address** page, click on **Add** and add the IP address and the subnet mask that will be assigned to the new cluster
- On the **New Cluster: Cluster parameters** page, define the cluster name and the cluster operation mode from unicast, multicast, or **Internet Group Messaging Protocol** (**IGMP**) multicast
- On the **New Cluster: Port rules** page, define the port and protocol rules

When the cluster is configured, only one host is configured as a node in the cluster. Each new node needs to be added after the cluster is configured. To do this, go to the Network Load Balancing Manager, expand the option for an NLB cluster and select **Add Host to Cluster**. This procedure is similar to that you used for creating a cluster.

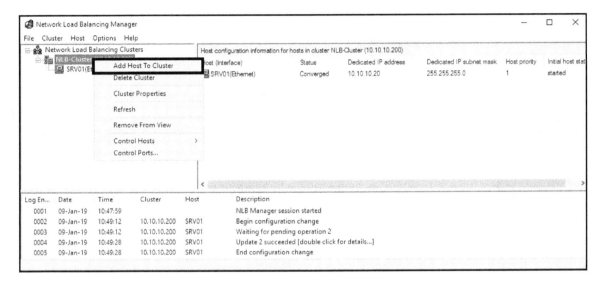

The PowerShell commands that need to be used to create an NLB cluster and add another host in the cluster are as follows:

```
New-NlbCluster -InterfaceName <InterfaceName> -OperationMode <Multicast |
Unicast> -ClusterPrimaryIP <ClusterIPAddress> -ClusterName <ClusterDNSName>

Add-NlbClusterNode -InterfaceName <InterfaceNameOnFirstNode> -NewNodeName
<ServerName> -NewNodeInterface <InterfaceNameOnNewNode>
```

The DNS record for the NLB cluster name and the IP address won't be added automatically and need to be added manually.

Configuring NLB clustering and nodes

Configuring NLB clusters involves defining how nodes in a cluster will respond to incoming traffic. NLB distributes traffic based on the port and the protocol. Traffic distribution can be defined by the configuration port rules and the affinity settings.

Port rules

Port rules define how the NLB cluster directs requests to specific IP addresses, ports, and protocols. Depending on your application, you can define that only traffic that comes to a specific port will be balanced. By default, there's only one rule that covers all ports from `0-65536`. Port rules can be configured as follows:

- **Multiple hosts**: All NLB nodes respond according to the weight assigned to each node
- **Single host**: The NLB cluster directs traffic to the node that's assigned the highest priority

Affinity settings

Affinity defines how the NLB cluster distributes request from clients. Affinity settings will be applied only if you've configured port rules for multiple hosts:

- **None**: In this mode, all cluster nodes respond to all client requests. Affinity mode is suitable for stateless applications.
- **Single**: With this affinity mode, a single cluster node manages all requests from a single client. This is also known as a **sticky connection**.
- **Network**: When you set this mode, a single node will respond to all requests from a class C network.

Network settings

The network part is important when you plan to implement an NLB cluster. As mentioned earlier in this section, the NLB cluster can use either the unicast or the multicast cluster operation mode:

- **Unicast**: All cluster hosts use the same unicast MAC address. When you use the unicast mode with a single network adapter, only nodes in the same subnet can communicate with each other. If you use the unicast mode with two or more network adapters on a node, one adapter is used for dedicated cluster communications and the other adapter is used for management tasks.
- **Multicast**: Each cluster host keeps its original MAC address, but additional multicast MAC addresses will be assigned to nodes. You must use multicast mode when each host has only one network adapter. Sometimes, with multicast mode, you need to configure the static **Address Resolution Protocol (ARP)** on your router or switch, in order to prevent switch flooding.
- **Internet Group Management Protocol (IGMP) multicast**: IGMP multicast mode is a special multicast mode. This mode prevents the switch flood, because traffic is forwarded only through switch ports that are configured in the NLB cluster.

The downside of IGMP multicast mode is that it requires switch hardware, which supports this functionality.

Summary

In this chapter, you've learned about the concept of high availability and its purpose. You've learned how to implement high availability solutions using Windows Server 2016, such as live and storage migration in Hyper-V, and how to implement and configure Hyper-V Replica. You're now familiar with Storage Spaces Direct and the Microsoft implementation of software-defined storage. Finally, you learned what the Network Load Balancing cluster is and how to implement and configure NLB.

Chapter 7, *Implementing Clustering*, will cover why we need clusters and what type of clusters can be configured. We'll describe the procedure of cluster configuration in detail for the most popular cluster scenarios.

Questions

1. What's the shortest interval for Hyper-V Replica synchronization?
    1. 5 seconds
    2. 60 minutes
    3. 5 minutes
    4. 30 seconds

2. Is live migration available on standalone Hyper-V servers?
    1. Yes
    2. No

3. In which state do drives need to be for Storage Spaces Direct?
    1. Formatted in NTFS
    2. With two partitions minimum
    3. Unformatted
    4. Converted to Dynamic disk

4. What's the maximum number of NLB cluster nodes?
    1. 16
    2. 1
    3. 64
    4. 32

5. What's the Storage Spaces Direct deployment that supports computing and storage at the same time?
    1. Converged
    2. Super Storage Spaces Direct
    3. Hyper-converged
    4. Advanced software-defined storage

6. The affinity settings None, Single, and Network are NOT supported in which port rule?
    1. Multiple hosts
    2. Single hosts

7. What's the maximum number of servers in a Storage Spaces Direct cluster?
    1. 2
    2. 4
    3. 16
    4. 32

8. Can storage migration move all virtual machine data to another location?
    1. Yes
    2. No

9. Can live migration move virtual machines to another Hyper-V server?
    1. Yes
    2. No

Further reading

For further reading, please check the following links:

- https://docs.microsoft.com/en-us/windows-server/storage/storage-spaces/storage-spaces-direct-overview
- https://docs.microsoft.com/en-us/windows-server/networking/technologies/network-load-balancing
- https://social.technet.microsoft.com/wiki/contents/articles/36705.hyper-v-replica-step-by-step-virtual-machine-replication.aspx
- https://docs.microsoft.com/en-us/windows-server/virtualization/hyper-v/manage/live-migration-overview

Implementing Clustering
7

One of the building blocks of a highly available Windows Server 2016 infrastructure solution is failover clustering. In this chapter, we'll explain how to implement and configure failover clustering and failover settings, virtual machine monitoring, workload migrations, and how to monitor clustered environments.

Failover clustering is a technology that provides you with the ability to implement services in a highly available manner. Many organizations that have business-critical services rely on failover clustering technology in order to achieve better availability and service stability.

In this chapter, you'll learn how to plan and implement a failover cluster service, how to manage and configure services in a failover cluster, and how to make your virtual machines clustered.

We'll cover the following topics in this chapter:

- Planning and implementing failover clustering
- Managing a failover cluster
- Hyper-V failover clusters

Planning and implementing failover clustering

Each implementation of a highly available solution, regardless of whether you need a high availability service or virtual machine, must start with the planning phase. After the planning phase, implementation and configuration are required in order to make the environment ready for use. This section will cover those processes and you'll be able to learn how to plan, implement, and configure a failover cluster in Windows Server 2016.

Planning a failover cluster

Failover clustering is a technology that will be whenever you want to configure services in a highly available manner. Before you implement failover clustering, you need to identify the services or applications that you want to use. Failover clustering is best for stateful applications, such as databases, but Hyper-V virtual machines are also good candidates for failover clustering. This technology is limited to IP-based protocols and suitable only for IP-based applications. Both IPv4 and IPv6 are supported.

Although it isn't mandatory, most failover clustering scenarios require shared storage to provide consistent data to a service after failover. Other setups, such as **SQL AlwaysOn** and Exchange **database availability group** (**DAG**), don't need shared storage, but still fully rely on failover clustering components. There are five different shared storage options that are available in Windows Server 2016 and can be used for this technology:

- **Shared serial-attached SCSI (SAS)**: This is the lowest-cost option. It isn't flexible; two cluster nodes must be close physically.
- **Internet Small Computer Systems Interface (iSCSI)**: This is a type of **Storage Area Network** (**SAN**) that transmits SCSI commands over IP networks. This option offers good performance, especially when a 10 Gbps medium is used with enabled **jumbo frames**. iSCSI is more expensive than shared SAS, but still cheaper than other solutions.
- Fibre Channel (FC): FC SANs have better performance than iSCSI SANs but are more expensive. Also, FCs require specialized knowledge and hardware to implement.
- **Shared virtual hard disk**: From Windows Server 2012 R2, you can use a shared virtual hard disk as the VM guest-clustering storage.
- **Scale-Out File Server:** From Windows Server 2012 R2, you can use SMB 3.0 as storage for some failover cluster roles, specifically SQL Server and Hyper-V.

Failover clustering requirements

Like all other technologies, failover clustering has requirements that need to be met in order to provide a stable environment for a highly available service.

Storage requirements

The following are some of the storage requirements:

- Using dynamic disks isn't recommended, so you should use basic disks
- Disks must be formatted with **New Technology File System** (**NTFS**) or **Resilient File System** (**ReFS**)
- You should isolate storage devices by using one cluster = one **Logical Unit Number** (**LUN**)
- **Multi Path I/O** (**MPIO**) is recommended in order to enable network redundancy
- CSV or a file server cluster is highly recommended for storing virtual hard disks

Hardware requirements

To meet the availability and support requirements, the failover clusters must be aligned with the following hardware requirements:

- The hardware should be certified for Windows Server.
- Each node should have the same or similar hardware.
- If you use SAS or FC storage, the storage device controllers must be identical and should have the same firmware installed.
- If you use an iSCSI storage connection, each cluster node must have their network adapter dedicated to storage communication only. A gigabit adapter or faster is highly recommended.
- Each node in a cluster must pass all validation tests.
- Each node should have the same processor architecture.

Network requirements

Network components also need to meet specific requirements:

- Each network adapter on the nodes must be identical
- Each network adapter on the nodes should have the same IP protocol version and speed
- The network that you use for a failover cluster should be redundant in order to avoid a single point of failure
- All network adapters should have the same IP address assignment method—static or DHCP

- To implement failover clustering, each node should have three network adapters—one for communication with the storage, one for communication with the network, and one for communication between nodes for evaluating the heartbeat
- Each of the networks must use a unique subnet
- Network adapters should support **Receive Side Scaling** (**RSS**) and **Remote Direct Memory Access** (**RDMA**) technologies

Although NIC Teaming can be used for network redundancy, MPIO should be your preferred option. NIC Teaming can cause package dropping in some scenarios.

Heartbeat is a basic mechanism for synchronizing two nodes and detecting server failures. Heartbeat monitors the data flow on a network that is shared by servers.

Software requirements

Software requirements are also important for the correct functioning of a failover cluster:

- **Active Directory** (**AD**) domain controllers must be on Windows Server 2008 or later
- Domain and forest functional levels must be on Windows Server 2008 or later
- The DNS server must be on Windows Server 2008 or later
- The application that is planned for high availability should support Windows Server 2016
- Each node should run the same edition of Windows Server 2016
- Each node must have the failover clustering role installed

Once you meet all requirements, you can start implementing a failover cluster.

Implementing a failover cluster

Once you've met all the prerequisites, you can move on to the next step, which is validating the configuration.

Validating the cluster configuration

The validation wizard performs multiple tests on the failover cluster configuration and settings. The wizard needs to be started before you create a cluster. You can create a cluster without validation, but this isn't recommended. The validation wizard must certify each of cluster nodes that will participate in the failover cluster, by performing tests for the cluster, the inventory, the network, the storage, and the system. Validation will help you to identify any issues in the hardware or software configuration. This can be done using the **Microsoft Failover Cluster Manager** (**MSFCM**) console as follows:

1. Open the **Failover Cluster Manager** console
2. Click on **Validate Configuration...** in the **Actions** pane
3. On the **Select Servers** or a **Cluster** page, add all nodes that need to be validated
4. On the **Testing Options** page, select the test type that you want to perform
5. On the **Confirmation** page, click **Next** and the validation tests will start

If you want to use PowerShell to perform the validation tests, run the following command:

```
Test-Cluster –Node <ServerName1, ServerName2> –Include
Storage,Inventory,Network,"System Configuration"
```

Once the validation test is done and everything is fine, you can start by creating the cluster.

Creating the cluster

Depending on the application that needs to be configured as highly available, the cluster configuration might be different. However, the cluster creation process is the same, regardless of the application.

The cluster can be created using the Failover Cluster Manager or PowerShell:

1. Open the **Failover Cluster Manager** console
2. Click on **Create Cluster...** in the **Actions** pane
3. On the **Select Servers** page, add all servers that will be cluster nodes
4. On the **Access Point for Administering the Cluster** page, define the IP address and the cluster DNS name
5. On the **Confirmation** page, verify the parameters and click next if you want to proceed with creating the cluster

On the **Confirmation** page, be aware of the **Add all eligible storage to the cluster** checkbox. By default, the checkbox is checked, but it needs to be unchecked in some scenarios.

If you want to use PowerShell to create a cluster, you need to use the following command:

```
New-Cluster -Name <ClusterName> -Node <ClusterNodes> -StaticAddress
<IPAddress>
```

 The IP address for the cluster can be selected from the subnet that the network adapters have configured as the default gateway. If the adapter doesn't have a default gateway configured, the subnet won't appear as an option.

When the cluster is created, you can start to evaluate the necessary configuration for your service or application that will be configured as a clustered application.

Cluster quorum

The cluster quorum is really important for proper cluster functioning. The quorum function is responsible for voting in a cluster. Each cluster will be fully functional if 50.1% of nodes are up. Let's say we have a three-node cluster. If one node is down and two nodes are up, the cluster has a quorum because 66.6% of the nodes are up. If you have a two-node cluster, however, and one node goes down, the second node will work properly, even though only 50% of the nodes are up. However, if the network connectivity between nodes goes down and both nodes stay up, both nodes will declare themselves to be the primary node, which can cause a big problem in the data and the application. To avoid this scenario, you need to configure **Quorum Witness**. Witness only has a valid vote in scenarios where there are even numbers of nodes that can vote.

In Windows Server 2016, as well as earlier versions Windows Servers, there are four quorum modes:

- **Node Majority**: Each node that's available can vote
- **Node and Disk Majority**: Each node can vote, as can a designated disk witness
- **Node and File Share Majority**: Each node can vote, as can a designated file share witness
- **No Majority: Disk Only**: The cluster has quorum if one node is available and in communication with a specific disk in the cluster storage

Dynamic Quorum, as a new mode, was introduced in Windows Server 2012. Based on the nodes which appear online, this mode will dynamically adjust the quorum votes. Part of the Dynamic Quorum that came with Windows Server 2012 is Dynamic Witness. The witness will only vote if its vote is needed. Dynamic Quorum is set as a default configuration in Windows Server 2016 and there are three types of witness that you can choose from:

- **Disk witness**: Primary and most used in different scenarios.
- **File share witness**: Used as an alternative when there is no shared storage or when you can't use a disk as a witness.
- **Azure Cloud witness**: New functionality in Windows Server 2016. Microsoft Azure Blob Storage may be used to read or write a blob file.

A Cluster Quorum can be created using the Failover Cluster Manager console or PowerShell:

1. Open the **Failover Cluster Manager** console and right-click on the previously created cluster.
2. Select **More Actions** and then **Configure Cluster Quorum Settings...**:

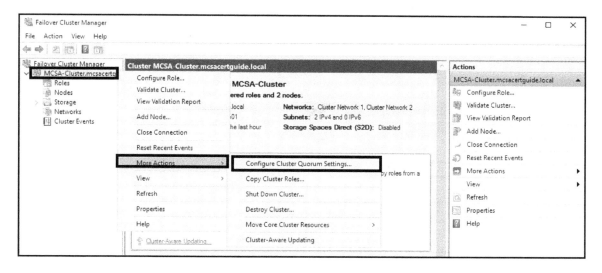

Then you just need to follow the wizard and configure the quorum settings based on your needs.

Managing a failover cluster

The configured failover cluster is just the first step in the process to make a service or application highly available. The next step is configuring the cluster and preparing to cluster a service or application, regardless of whether that's a file server, which is fully supported in failover clustering, or SQL Server, which has its own clustering mechanism that fully relies on failover clustering. In this section, you'll learn how to configure and maintain a failover cluster.

Configuring storage

Most clustered applications require one of the types of shared storage that were described previously in this chapter. If, for example, you add iSCSI shared storage on each cluster node after you create a cluster, the failover cluster won't be aware of the attached storage and you'll need to add the storage manually. You can do that using the Failover Cluster Manager console or PowerShell:

1. Open the **Failover Cluster Manager** console
2. Expand **Storage** under the created cluster, right-click on **Disks**, and select **Add Disk**:

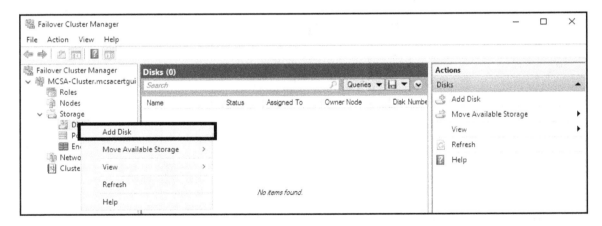

3. On the **Add Disks to Cluster** page, select the desired disk and click **OK**

If you want to do this using PowerShell, run the following command:

```
Get-ClusterAvailableDisk | Add-ClusterDisk
```

 Note that cmdlet Add-ClusterDisk can't define what disk will be added to the cluster, so you need to bind two different cmdlets.

When this task is complete, you can proceed with adding a clustered role.

Configuring clustered roles

In this section, we'll be covering how to install a file server as a clustered role. Each cluster node must be connected to shared storage before you start configuring the cluster application.

Several roles are supported in failover clustering in Windows Server 2016, such as a file server or a Hyper-V server. When you've installed and configured all prerequisites and you've decided which clustered role you want to install, you can start the process. The prerequisite for this step is to install the role on all failover cluster nodes. To be sure that you don't forget to install the role on all nodes, the best thing to do is to use PowerShell:

```
Invoke-Command -ComputerName ClusterNode01,ClusterNode02 -ScriptBlock
{Install-WindowsFeature DNS -IncludeAllSubFeature -IncludeManagementTools}
```

Once you've installed the role on each cluster node, you can start to configure the clustered application. Like other operations, this can either be done using the Failover Cluster Manager console or using PowerShell:

1. Open the **Failover Cluster Manager** console
2. Right-click on the previously created cluster and select **Configure Role...**
3. On the **Select Role** page, select the desired role (in this scenario, **File Server**)
4. On the **File Server Type** page, select one of the types
5. On the **Client Access Point** page, define the IP address and the DNS name of the clustered role
6. On the **Select Storage** page, select one or more of the available clustered disks
7. On the **Confirmation** page, click **Next** and the role configuration will be started

If the failover cluster **Virtual Computer Object** (**VCO**) doesn't have access to create a computer object in a specific organizational unit, you need to create a computer object with a specific name that will be used for the clustered role. Otherwise, the role will be configured, but will constantly be in the failed state.

The PowerShell command that needs to be used for this task is as follows:

```
Add-ClusterFileServerRole -Name <RoleName> -StaticAddress <IPAddress> -
Storage <ClusterDiskName>
```

Finally, we can see that **File Server** is configured as a clustered role:

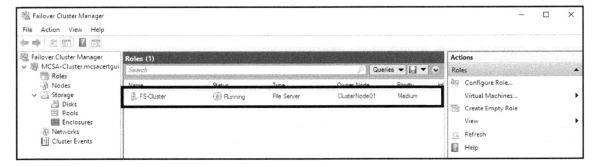

Configuring the network

Unlike storage, where you need to configure a shared (or local) disk as a cluster disk, the failover cluster can discover each newly added network to a node and add it to a cluster. Of course, if the same network isn't configured on all nodes, the network won't be useful in the cluster. Once you add and configure a network adapter on each node, you'll be able to configure the cluster network.

As mentioned earlier, three unique network adapters and subnets, properly configured on each node, are highly recommended. The first network will be used for communication with other network services, the second one for cluster communication only, and the third one must be dedicated for communication with the storage. By default, the first added network will be configured for the communication with rest of network, as well for the cluster communication. Every subsequent network will be automatically configured for cluster communication only.

If you need to change these setting, you can do this using the Failover Cluster Manager console as follows:

1. Open the **Failover Cluster Manager** console
2. Click on **Networks** under the created cluster:

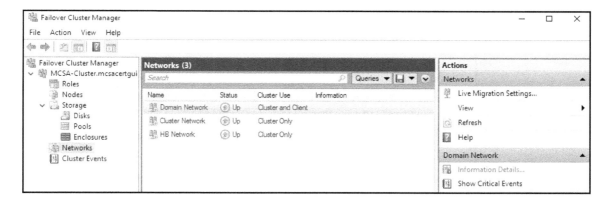

3. You'll see all networks in the cluster and be able to edit the properties of each network:

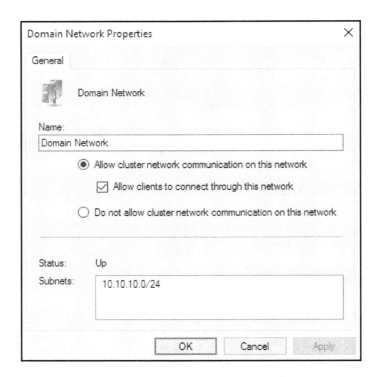

 In the **Actions** pane, under **Networks**, you'll see **Live Migration Settings**. This needs to be used to select which network should be dedicated to live migration.

Configuring failover and preference settings

Each clustered role can be configured with different settings. These settings include failover properties and the preferred owner. If you open the Failover Cluster Manager console, right-click on the role, and select **Properties**, you'll see the role settings in two tabs—**General** and **Failover**.

On the **General** tab, you can define which node will be the preferred node for the role, or you can leave all nodes unchecked. You can also configure the priority for starting the clustered role again after a failure:

On the **Failover** tab, you can configure how the cluster role handles failover and failback. By default, if the role fails to failover more than once in six hours, it will remain in the failed state. Failback is, by default, prevented:

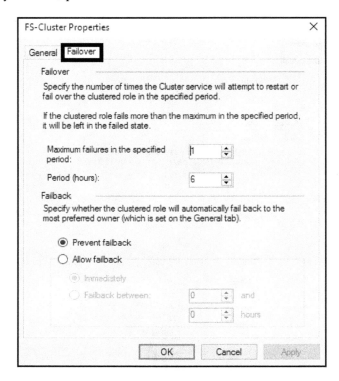

Cluster-aware updating

Like other systems, failover cluster nodes need to be updated with patches. The process is simple but a bit different to updating other Windows Servers. For a smooth update process, you need to do the following:

1. Gracefully failover all clustered roles to other nodes
2. Update the node
3. Restart the node to apply updates
4. Failback the clustered roles to the updated node

 You need to be aware that other nodes must have enough resources to host all clustered roles from the node that needs to be updated. This is particularly important if you have clustered virtual machines.

Then, the same process needs to be applied to each failover cluster node. This process can be automated. In Windows Server 2012, Microsoft implemented **Cluster-Aware Updating** (**CAU**). This is a feature for automatically updating cluster nodes and allowing administrators to update all failover cluster nodes without user interaction. During the process, CAU will take each failover cluster node offline, install the updates, restart the node if necessary, bring the node back online, and then move to update the next node in a cluster.

To configure this feature, you need to use the Failover Cluster Manager console as follows:

1. Open the **Failover Cluster Manager** console
2. Right-click on the previously created cluster, select **More Actions**, and click on **Cluster-Aware Updating**

If you're starting this for the first time, you need to configure CAU by clicking on **Configure cluster self-updating options**:

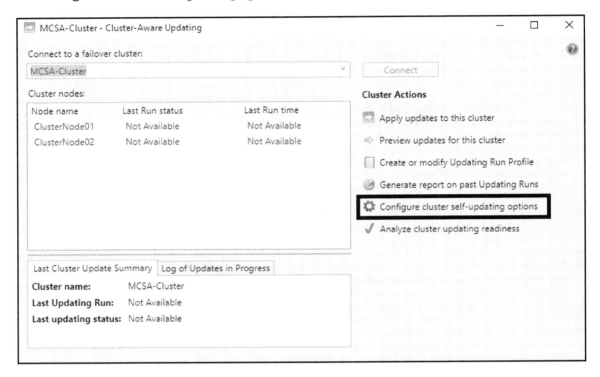

This will open new wizard for configuring CAU:

1. On the **Add Clustered Role** page, check **Add the CAU clustered role, with self-updating mode enabled, to this cluster**, and click **Next**
2. On the **Self-updating schedule** page, define the schedule that you want
3. On the **Advanced Options** page, you can define some more advanced options, such as the node order or the default value for the node reboot timeout after an update
4. On the **Additional Options** page, select any additional options if necessary
5. On the **Confirmation** page, click **Apply** to proceed with configuring CAU

Once CAU is enabled and configured, your failover clustered nodes will be updated automatically.

Backing up and restoring a cluster

With failover clustering, your environment is configured as highly available. You should also, however, make sure you take care of backing up your cluster, in case it encounters a failure. To achieve this, you can use Windows Server Backup or any non-Microsoft backup solution. If you use Windows Server Backup, this feature needs to be installed on each node in the cluster. For a successful backup, you need to be aware of the following:

- The cluster must be running and must have a quorum
- You must back up all clustered applications
- If you have SQL Server in the cluster, you must back up the SQL databases and configuration
- If you have application data on a cluster disk, you need to back up the data as well

If you need to restore the cluster, there are two known types of restoration:

- **Nonauthoritative restore**: This restores a single node in case of failure or damage
- **Authoritative restore**: Use this when you must restore the cluster configuration

 Backup and restore procedures must be tested before you use them in production.

Hyper-V failover clusters

As mentioned earlier in this chapter, the failover cluster feature is really important if you want to achieve high availability in your organization. In the previous section, we covered the configuration of file server as a highly available service. However, in the virtualization era, clustered virtual machines can provide a big benefit to your business. In this section, we'll learn what's important for clustered virtual machines and how to prepare the infrastructure.

Hyper-V cluster components and requirements

In the virtualization era, you need to know how virtual machines can be clustered. There are two different approaches—**host clustering** and **guest clustering**. Before you start planning and implementing a clustering solution, you need to know what the difference between these clustering approaches is:

- **Host clustering**: Virtual machines are highly available and don't need any special configuration.
- **Guest clustering**: Virtual machines are cluster nodes and services or application on them need to be cluster-aware. Also, shared storage is mandatory.

Although, in Windows Server 2016, you can enable nested virtualization, nodes in Hyper-V cluster should be physical servers. Also, physical servers need to have both physical and virtual networks. Be aware that each node in a Hyper-V cluster should have at least three network adapters—one for network communication, one for cluster communication, and one for storage communication. If you want to implement redundant networks, you need to double the network adapters per purpose. It's very important to create the same virtual networks on all physical hosts that participate in one cluster. If a virtual machine fails over to an other node and the virtual networks are not named and configured properly, the virtual machine won't be useful. Storage is also an important component of VM clustering. You can select one of the options that we described earlier in this chapter, but storage needs to be shared.

Regarding the software requirements, all nodes in a Hyper-V cluster need to be Windows Server 2016 Standard, Datacenter, or Microsoft Hyper-V Server 2016. All nodes should have the same service packs and patches installed and have the same drivers and firmware.

Implementing Hyper-V failover clusters

Implementing Hyper-V failover clusters is similar to implementing clustered roles. Each node that you intend to be part of the Hyper-V cluster needs to have the Hyper-V role and the failover cluster feature installed. As mentioned previously, all nodes should be the same or similar with regards to both hardware and software requirements. Once you meet all prerequisites, you can start with the implementation of the Hyper-V cluster.

The process of validating and creating a cluster is the same as described earlier and won't be repeated in this section.

Configuring a Cluster Shared Volume (CSV)

CSV is one of the most important parts of a Hyper-V cluster. CSV allows multiple cluster nodes to have read-write access at the same time and to the same disk that's added as a cluster disk. If you've configured a Hyper-V cluster, each node will, most likely, host some virtual machines. To achieve high availability, virtual machine files need to be stored on a shared location. With CSV, virtual machines can be moved quickly to other nodes without changing disk ownership, and so the possibility of damage is significantly decreased.

CSV isn't mandatory for a Hyper-V cluster, but CSV implementation has some benefits:

- Reduced LUNs for the disks
- Improved use of disk space
- Single location for VM files
- No specific hardware requirements

CSV needs to be created when you create a failover cluster. A cluster disk that will be promoted to CSV must be available as shared storage. CSV should be configured before you make virtual machines highly available, although you can perform storage migration and move virtual machine files to CSV later on. When you promote a cluster disk to CSV, the drive letter will be removed, and CSV will appear as a local folder, C:\ClusterStorage\VolumeX, on each cluster node.

CSV configuring can be done using the Failover Cluster Manager console or PowerShell by following these steps:

1. Go to the **Failover Cluster Manager** console
2. Expand **Storage** under the created cluster

3. Right-click on the cluster disk that you want to promote to CSV and select **Add to Cluster Shared Volumes**:

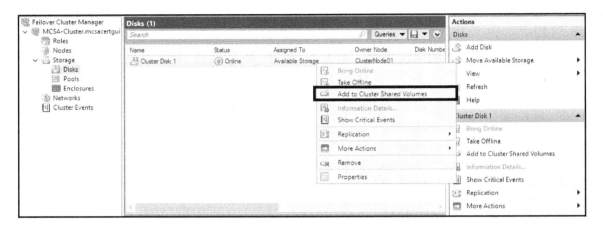

The PowerShell command that needs to be used for this action is as follows:

```
Get-ClusterResource <DiskName> | Add-ClusterSharedVolume
```

Configuring virtual machines in a Hyper-V failover cluster

If you've created and configured a Hyper-V cluster and you've configured CSV, you can start creating highly available virtual machines. Basically, the process of creating virtual machines that need to be highly available is almost the same as creating virtual machines in Hyper-V. You need to use CSV as a storage location for the virtual machine and configure it as a cluster role using the Failover Cluster Manager as follows:

1. Go to the **Failover Cluster Manager** console
2. Right-click on **Roles** and select **Configure Role**
3. On the **Select Role** page, select **Virtual Machine**
4. On the **Select Virtual Machine** page, check the virtual machines that you want to be clustered and click **Next**
5. On the **Confirmation** page, click **Next** and the machine will be added as a cluster role

If you want to use PowerShell to perform this action, you need to use the following command:

```
Add-ClusterVirtualMachineRole -VMName <VMName>
```

Once you've created virtual machines as cluster roles, the virtual machine settings need to be changed using the Failover Cluster Manager console, as shown in the following screenshot:

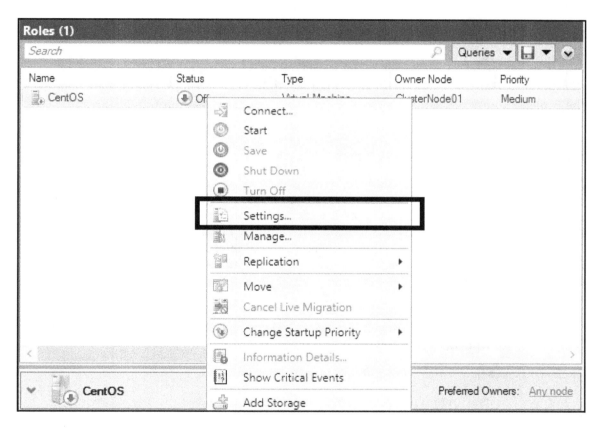

If you try to make changes on the virtual machine using **Hyper-V Manager**, you'll receive a warning message like this:

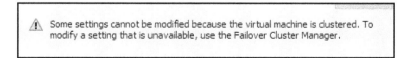

Configuring health protection

Network health protection came with Windows Server 2012 R2. Network teaming is one of the options that can increase network redundancy, but there are more possible network issues that can affect your high availability. Network health protection allows virtual machines to be live migrated to other cluster nodes if the network connectivity is disconnected. As mentioned, live migration increases the availability of virtual machines by moving it automatically in case of failure, instead of performing manual migration. Every 60 seconds, a virtual machine checks whether the cluster resources needed for its functioning are available on the host where the virtual machine is located. If the virtual machine discovers that the cluster resources have been disconnected, the virtual machine will check that resources needed are available on other nodes and it'll initiate live migration. Each network adapter per virtual machine can control this feature. By default, the **Protected network** setting is enabled for all virtual network adapters.

Configuring VM monitoring

Before Windows Server 2012, failover clusters weren't able to monitor an application that was running in virtual machines. Now, however, this is possible. If a service in a virtual machine stops responding, the failover cluster can take actions such as restarting the virtual machine or moving to other nodes to restore the service. For this feature, the cluster node and virtual machine must run Windows Server 2012 or later and have integration services installed. This can be done using the Failover Cluster Manager console or PowerShell by following these steps:

1. Open the **Failover Cluster Manager**
2. Expand **Roles**, right-click on the desired virtual machine, and select **Configure Monitoring**

Then, you can select the service that you want to monitor.

If you want to use PowerShell to perform this action, you need to run the following command:

```
Add-ClusterVMMonitoredItem -VirtualMachine <VMName> -Service <ServiceName>
```

Summary

In this chapter, you've learned about high availability and disaster recovery in Window Server 2016. You've learned what Hyper-V Replica is and how to implement it; how to configure live and storage migration in a non-domain environment; how to prepare, implement, and configure the failover cluster; how to configure clustered roles; and finally, how to prepare and implement your environment for highly available virtual machines.

Questions

1. Can you monitor virtual machine services in a failover cluster?
    1. Yes
    2. No

2. Which PowerShell cmdlet needs to be used to create new cluster?
    1. `New-FailoverCluster`
    2. `Add-Cluster`
    3. `Add-FC`
    4. `New-Cluster`

3. Which roles need to be installed as prerequisites on servers that will be nodes in Hyper-V cluster? (Select all that are applicable.)
    1. Hyper-V
    2. Failover cluster
    3. AD DS
    4. File Server

4. Which roles need to be installed as prerequisites on servers that will be nodes in a cluster? (Select all that are applicable.)
    1. Hyper-V
    2. Failover cluster
    3. Role that will be clustered
    4. DNS

5. Will the failover cluster automatically detect a new network in a cluster?
    1. Yes
    2. No

6. Will the failover cluster automatically detect a new disk in a cluster?
    1. Yes
    2. No

7. Which two PowerShell cmdlets need to be used to add a new disk in a cluster?
    1. `Get-Disk`
    2. `Add-Disk`
    3. `Get-ClusterAvailableDisk`
    4. `Install-Disk`

8. Can Azure blob storage be a witness in a failover cluster on Windows Server 2012?
    1. Yes
    2. No

Further reading

For further reading regarding this topic, check the following links:

- **What's new in Failover Clustering**: `https://docs.microsoft.com/en-us/windows-server/failover-clustering/whats-new-in-failover-clustering`
- **Create a failover cluster**: `https://docs.microsoft.com/en-us/windows-server/failover-clustering/create-failover-cluster`
- **Plan for Hyper-V scalability in Windows Server 2016**: `https://docs.microsoft.com/en-us/windows-server/virtualization/hyper-v/plan/plan-hyper-v-scalability-in-windows-server`

8
Monitoring and Maintaining Server Environments

Once installed and configured, Windows Server 2016 is functional for production in most scenarios. Each server, however, needs to be monitored and maintained during its life cycle. Windows Server 2016 has built-in roles and services that can help you to achieve this goal. In this chapter, you'll learn how to implement **Windows Server Update Services** (**WSUS**) and use it to manage system updates. You will also learn how to install and configure Windows Server Backup, how to protect services with this feature, and how to monitor Windows Server 2016 using built-in tools.

We'll cover the following topics in this chapter:

- Implementing Windows Server Update Services
- Configuring Windows Server Backup
- Monitoring Windows Server Installations

Implementing Windows Server Update Services

WSUS is a role that can help you to update your infrastructure easily. In this section, you'll learn how to install, configure, and manage the WSUS server in your environment.

Designing and installing WSUS

The WSUS role is included in Windows Server 2016 and can obtain updates from Microsoft Update servers and then distribute them throughout your organization. The updates that WSUS can obtain are applicable to all Windows operating systems, for both client and server, and most common Microsoft products. WSUS can be implemented as a single server, which is the most common scenario in smaller organizations. In larger organizations, WSUS can be implemented in a WSUS hierarchy model, where one of the WSUS servers will download updates from Microsoft Update and distribute them to downstream WSUS servers. The updates will then be distributed to the clients. Computers that are WSUS clients can be organized into groups for simplified management.

Before you install the WSUS server, you need to decide which WSUS implementation is best for your organization. WSUS can be implemented in a few different deployment models:

- **Single WSUS server**: This is the most basic implementation. One WSUS server will obtain updates from Microsoft Update and distribute them to the clients.
- **Multiple WSUS servers**: This is the most common scenario for large organizations. WSUS servers can be deployed on each site, for example, and those servers will obtain updates from the upstream WSUS server.
- **Disconnected WSUS servers**: In this scenario, the WSUS server isn't connected to the internet. The server will obtain updates using a removable drive generated on another WSUS server.

The WSUS server hierarchy, in the multiple WSUS server model, allows you to do the following:

- Download updates to downstream servers that are closer to clients
- Download updates from Microsoft Update once and distribute them to other WSUS servers
- Separate WSUS servers based on location or language
- Scale WSUS for a large organization

The WSUS server hierarchy consists of two types of servers:

- **Upstream servers**: These connect directly to Microsoft Update to obtain updates.
- **Downstream servers**: These receive updates from a WSUS upstream server. You can implement downstream servers in two different modes:
    - **Autonomous mode**: Obtain updates from upstream servers and manage WSUS locally
    - **Replica mode**: Receive updates, computer groups, and approvals from an upstream server

Before you install the WSUS server, you need to know that a WSUS server requires the following:

- **Internet Information Services (IIS)**
- Microsoft .NET Framework version 4.6 or newer
- Microsoft Report Viewer version 2008 Redistributable or newer
- SQL Server 2012 with **service pack 1 (SP1)**, SQL Server 2012, SQL Server 2008 R2 SP2, SQL Server 2008 R2 SP1, or WID

The installation of a WSUS role is a simple process that can be done using Server Manager or PowerShell.

If you haven't installed IIS and .NET Framework already, these will be installed automatically during the WSUS role installation.

The PowerShell command for installing the WSUS server is as follows:

```
Install-WindowsFeature UpdateServices-Services,UpdateServices-WidDB -
IncludeAllSubFeature -IncludeManagementTools
```

If you want to use the SQL Server database, you need to install `UpdateServices-DB`.

Configuring WSUS

An automatic computer update consists of two different steps: configuring the WSUS server and configuring the computers. These steps aren't related from a configuration perspective, meaning that it doesn't matter what you configure first, but the automatic update process will be fully completed once you finish both steps.

Configuring the WSUS server

When you install the WSUS server role, you need to configure the role before you start to use it. Once you start the post-deployment wizard, you need to follow the wizard and configure the WSUS server as follows:

1. On the **Choose Upstream Server** page, select the source for obtaining updates
2. On the **Specify Proxy Server** page, define a proxy if you have one, click **Next**, and **Start Connecting**
3. On the **Choose Products** page, check the products that need to be updated with WSUS
4. On the **Choose Classification** page, select the types of update that will be downloaded for products
5. On the **Configure Sync Schedule** page, define a schedule for synchronization

When you configure all of these settings, you'll be able to open the WSUS console and start managing it once the computers are registered to WSUS. When you open the WSUS console for the first time, you'll see a setup page, as shown in the following screenshot:

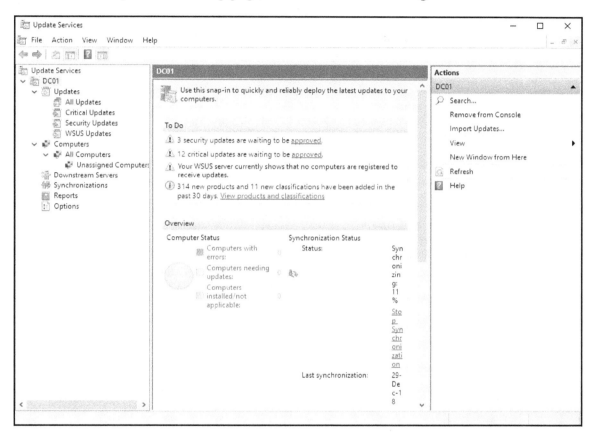

 Connecting to the upstream server can take some time and you need to be patient.

Configuring computers

By default, client computers will obtain all updates from Microsoft Update. If you want to configure clients to obtain updates from the WSUS server, you need to configure the Group Policy with the appropriate settings. The GPO settings for WSUS shown in the following screenshot are located in **Computer Configuration** | **Policies** | **Administrative Templates** | **Windows Components** | **Windows Update**:

Setting	State	Comment
Defer Windows Updates		
Do not display 'Install Updates and Shut Down' option in Sh...	Not configured	No
Do not adjust default option to 'Install Updates and Shut Do...	Not configured	No
Enabling Windows Update Power Management to automati...	Not configured	No
Turn off auto-restart for updates during active hours	Not configured	No
Always automatically restart at the scheduled time	Not configured	No
Specify deadline before auto-restart for update installation	Not configured	No
Configure Automatic Updates	Not configured	No
Specify intranet Microsoft update service location	Not configured	No
Automatic Updates detection frequency	Not configured	No
Do not allow update deferral policies to cause scans against ...	Not configured	No
Remove access to use all Windows Update features	Not configured	No
Do not connect to any Windows Update Internet locations	Not configured	No
Allow non-administrators to receive update notifications	Not configured	No
Do not include drivers with Windows Updates	Not configured	No
Turn on Software Notifications	Not configured	No
Allow Automatic Updates immediate installation	Not configured	No
Turn on recommended updates via Automatic Updates	Not configured	No
No auto-restart with logged on users for scheduled automat...	Not configured	No
Re-prompt for restart with scheduled installations	Not configured	No
Delay Restart for scheduled installations	Not configured	No
Reschedule Automatic Updates scheduled installations	Not configured	No
Enable client-side targeting	Not configured	No
Allow signed updates from an intranet Microsoft update ser...	Not configured	No

There are a lot of settings that can be configured, but the most important settings are the following:

- **Configure Automatic Updates**: You need to define whether automatic updates will be enabled and how they'll be configured. Select downloading and installing methods and a schedule for updates, as shown in the following screenshot:

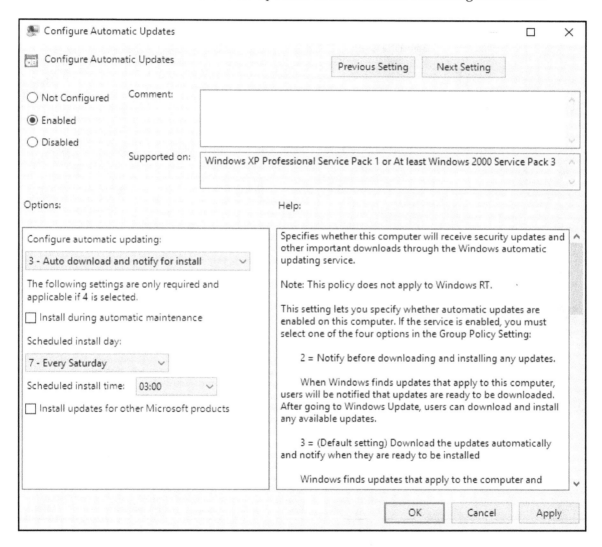

- **Specify intranet Microsoft update service location**: Define the URL with FQDN or the IP address of the WSUS server in the `http://10.10.10.10:8530` format, as shown in the following screenshot. Adding a port number at the end isn't mandatory but is recommended:

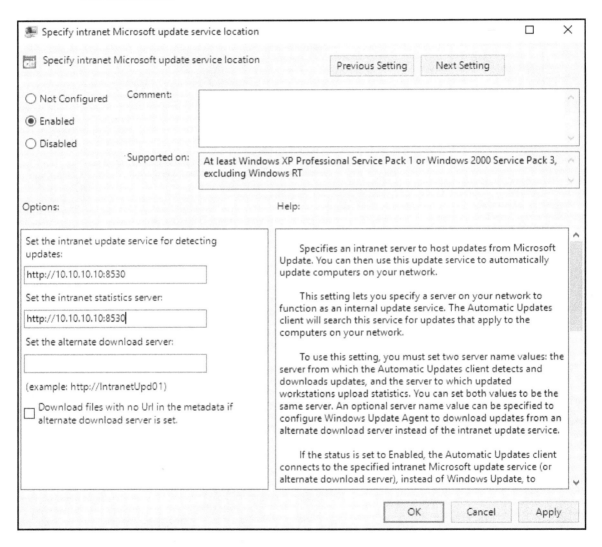

Once you configure GPO with WSUS settings and click **Apply**, the computers in an organization will be configured to use WSUS as an update location.

Managing patch management

Once you've configured WSUS Server and defined the GPO that will configure computers, patch managements can be fully automated. In most scenarios, however, all management tasks need to be done manually. This includes configuring computer groups, synchronization, approving updates, and so on.

Configuring computer groups

For easier management, configuring computer groups is highly recommended. You can create a new group using the **Update Services** management console:

1. Open the **Update Services** management console
2. Expand **Computers**
3. Right-click on **All Computers** and select **Add Computer Group...**:

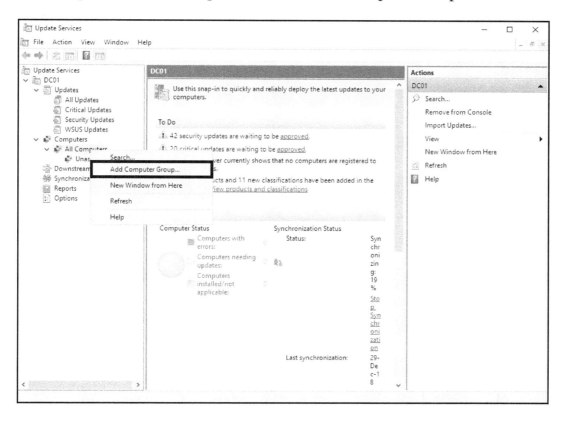

To add a computer to a specific group, you need to do the following:

1. Open the **Update Services** management console
2. Expand **Computers**
3. Open **Unassigned Computers**, right-click on the desired computer, click on **Change Membership...**, and select the appropriate computer group:

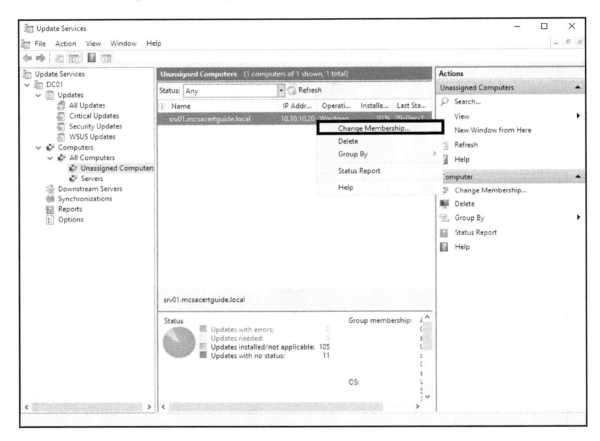

Alternatively, you can do this using PowerShell cmdlets: `Get-WsusComputer` and `Add-WsusComputer`:

```
Get-WsusComputer -NameIncludes <ComputerName> | Add-WsusComputer -
TargetGroupName <TargetGroupName>
```

Approving updates

By default, WSUS doesn't automatically approve updates to computers. Although it's possible, this isn't recommended. The best practice is to approve updates first to a group of a few test computers, then to a few pilot production computers, and then, if there are no issues, approve updates to all production computers. This approving flow can reduce the risk of possible unexpected issues caused by updates. If you've approved and applied updates that are causing issues, you can use WSUS to remove them. The process of approving updates for removal is same as for installing them:

1. Open the **Update Services** management console
2. Expand **All Updates** under **Updates**
3. Select update(s), right-click them, and select **Approve...**:

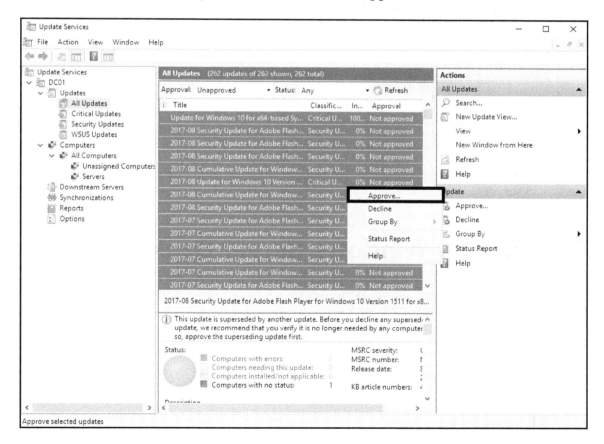

4. On the **Approve Updates** page, select the desired action from the group drop-down menu:

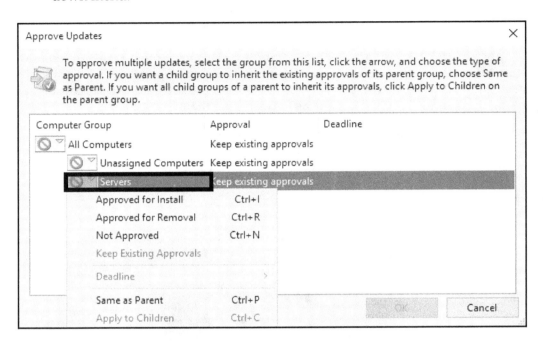

Once the approval process is finished, computers will be able to download updates from the WSUS server.

Configuring Windows Server Backup

Due to the importance of data protection, some backup mechanisms need to be involved in the life cycle of every organization. Windows Server Backup is a built-in mechanism for backing up Windows operating systems. In this section, we'll cover the implementation of Windows Server Backup and backup strategies in general.

Implementing Windows Server Backup

Windows Server Backup, as a native backup solution in Windows Server 2016, can be used to back up the following:

- The full server
- Selected volume(s)
- Individual files and folders
- The system state
- Virtual machines on the Hyper-V host
- **Cluster Shared Volume (CSV)**

Windows Server Backup can also restore a bare-metal server or a system state, as well as individual files and folders. In addition to Windows Server 2016, you can use Azure Online Backup, a cloud-based backup that allows you to back up your files off-site. Windows Server Backup is a single-instance solution. You can't use one Windows Server Backup to backup a complete infrastructure or multiple servers as you can with other solutions such as Veeam or Data Protection Manager.

Windows Server Backup is a feature in Windows Server and you can use Server Manager or PowerShell to install it. When you've installed Windows Server Backup, you can start backing up your data.

Backing up and restoring data

Because there are many scenarios in which you can use Windows Server Backup, the details of these tasks can vary. In this section, a few of these situations will be described.

Backing up files and folders

The simplest scenario is when you want to back up local files and folders. If you've already installed the Windows Server Backup feature, you need to follow these steps:

1. Go to the **Windows Server Backup** console
2. Select **Local Backup** and then, in the **Actions** pane, select your desired option:

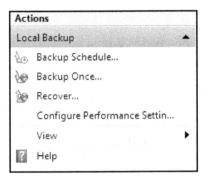

I've selected **Backup Schedule...** in this example.

3. Select **Backup Schedule**:
    1. On the **Select Backup Configuration** page, select **Custom**
    2. On the **Select Items for Backup** page, click on **Add Items** and select the items that you want to back up
    3. On the **Specify Backup Time** page, define the backup schedule
    4. On the **Specify Destination Type** page, select one from the three possible options:
        - Back up to a hard disk that's dedicated to backups
        - Back up to a volume
        - Back up to a shared network folder
    5. On the **Confirmation** page, click **Finish**

In Windows Server Backup, using a dedicated disk for backup is highly recommended. Using a network location is the least recommended option. If you decide to use a network location, you need to be aware that incremental backups aren't possible; every new backup will overwrite previous backups.

Depending on your selected destination type, the next page will be different and you'll need to define a disk or network location for the backup.

Restoring files and folders

If you need to restore a file or folder in the case of failure, the procedure is very easy:

1. Go to the **Windows Server Backup** console
2. Select **Local Backup** and then, in the action pane, select **Recover**
3. On the **Getting Started** page, define where your backup files are stored
4. On the **Select Backup Date** page, select an appropriate date for restoring the files
5. On the **Recovery Type** page, select the type of data that needs to be restored
6. On the **Select Items to Recover** page, select the data that you want to restore
7. On the **Specify Recovery Options** page, define where the data will be recovered and what to do with the existing data
8. On the **Confirmation** page, click on **Recover** and your data will be restored

Backing up system images

The process of backing up system images is similar to backing up files and folders:

1. Go to the **Windows Server Backup** console
2. Select **Local Backup** and **Backup Schedule**
3. On the **Select Backup Configuration** page, select **Full Server**
4. On the **Specify Backup Time** page, define the schedule for backup
5. On the **Specify Destination Type** page, you need to select one of the three possible options

6. On the **Confirmation** page, click **Finish**:

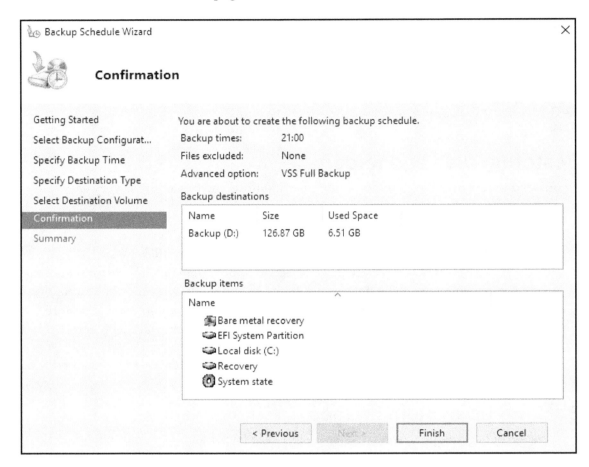

Restoring a system image

Restoring system images is different from restoring files and folders. There are two different ways to restore a system state from a backup and revert an entire computer to a previous state.

Using the Window Server Backup console

1. Go to the **Windows Server Backup** console
2. Select **Local Backup** and then, in the **Actions** pane, select **Recover**
3. On the **Getting Started** page, define where your backup files are stored
4. On the **Select Backup Date**, select an appropriate date to restore the files
5. On the **Recovery Type** page, select **System State**
6. On the **Select Location for System State Recovery** page, select either the original or an alternative location
7. On the **Confirmation** page, click on **Recover** and your data will be restored

 System State backup will take a lot of time to recover. The system will restart after it finishes to apply the changes.

Using installation media

In the event of a hardware failure or something similar, when you can't access your system but you have backup files, you need to restore the system state using installation media by following these steps:

1. Boot the installation wizard from the Windows Server 2016 installation media
2. On the **Windows Setup** page, select **Repair Your Computer**
3. On the **Choose an Option** page, select **Troubleshoot**
4. On the **Advanced Option** page, select **System Image Recovery**
5. On the **System Image Recovery** page, choose the target operating system

A new wizard will open. You will need to select one of the following options:

- Use the latest system image or select a system image
- Format or re-partition disks

Once you confirm, system image restoration will start.

Backup strategy

Nowadays, backups are a very important part of the lifecycle of an organization. Accidental data loss, disaster scenarios, ransomware, and other dangerous situations can be less stressful if you have a backup solution implemented. Although no one can say for certain which is the best backup solution, there are various best practices you can follow while implementing a backup solution:

- **Backup location**: Selecting a backup destination depends on many factors. If you decide to use Windows Server Backup as a solution, the best possible option for backup storage is a dedicated disk. The disk needs to be either a local disk or an iSCSI disk attached to the server. Windows Server Backup will remove the letter and re-format the disk to store all backed up files to that disk.
- **Backup retention**: This depends on your business; there are no set rules to follow. Most organizations use a retention period of 30 days with a plan in which one full backup is performed weekly and incremental backups are performed intermittently. In general, backup retention is closely connected with the **Recovery Time Objective (RTO)** and **Recovery Point Objective (RPO)** in your organization's business Continuity Plan.
- **Cloud backup**: Nowadays, cloud backup is the most flexible and secure backup option. As a native solution in Windows operating systems, you can use Azure Backup. There are many benefits from using cloud backups, including the possibility of using off-site backups, resistance to ransomware, and long-term retention of data.

Monitoring Windows Server

Monitoring is another very important part of an organization's life cycle. Monitoring can help you to prevent some services, application failures, or downtime. For example, you can monitor your CPU or RAM usage, and configure a trigger that will inform you when the CPU or RAM exceeds the configured limits. Windows Server, by default, has some built-in monitoring tools that should be used. In this section, you'll learn about the purpose of these tools and how to use them.

Performance Monitor

Performance Monitor is a tool that can be used to collect and analyze performance-related information about your servers. Based on this information , you can decide whether you need to add more servers in the farm to optimize your workload.

Performance Monitor is also a useful tool if you want to establish baselines that can then be used later on for analyzing data. By using a **Data Collector Set**, which is part of Performance Monitor, you can track server usage trends or evaluate capacity planning.

A Data Collector Set is a custom set of performance counters, event traces, or system configuration data. You can configure a Data Collector Set to run at a scheduled time. This can be useful for analysis and comparison with older data. For example, you can configure a Data Collector Set to run everyday at 8 a.m. and work for the next 24 hours. After a few days, you'll have collected performance-related information for the counters that are selected and you can compare the results in order to check whether there are any usage patterns or bottlenecks. In many scenarios, Performance Monitor is the first step in troubleshooting a low-performing service or application.

Data Collector Set can contain the following types of collectors:

- **Performance counters**: Provide server performance data
- **Event trace data**: Gives details about system activities and events
- **System configuration information**: Enables you to record the present condition of registry keys and changes to those keys

A Data Collector Set can be created from a template or by selecting individual data collectors. To configure a Data Collector Set you can use the Performance Monitor console or PowerShell cmdlets. To create Data Collector Set for collection data logs, you need to perform the following steps:

1. Go to the **Performance Monitor** console
2. Expand **Data Collector Sets**
3. Right-click on **User Defined**, select **New**, and then select **Data Collector Set**
4. On the **How would you like to create this new Data Collector Set** page, define the name and type of the Data Collector Set
5. On the **What type of data do you want to include** page, define whether you want to create Data Logs or a Performance Counter Alert
6. On the **Which performance counters would you like to log** page, define the counters that you want to monitor
7. On the **Where would you like the data to be saved** page, define the location for storing a Data Collector Set
8. On the **Create the data collector set** page, select whether you want to edit properties, save, or start a Data Collector Set

Event Viewer

Event Viewer is a Windows Server component that can show you a recorded logs of events that occur on Windows Server. The collected logs are categorized into four sections:

- Security
- Application
- System
- Setup

Event Viewer is based on the MMC console and the basic setup page is shown in the following screenshot:

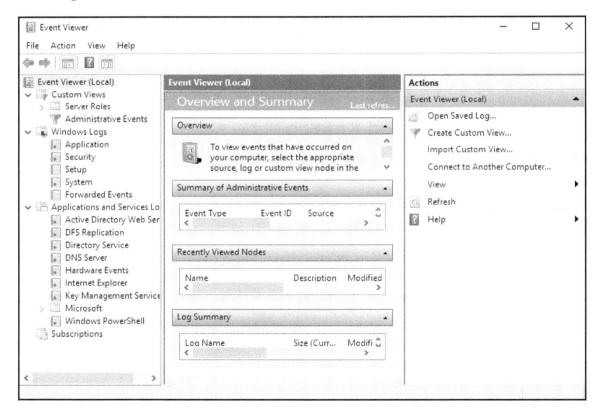

Each of these sections provides access to filtered logs. For example, logs created during login will be stored in the **Security** section, while Windows Update logs will be stored in the **Setup** section.

Event Viewer gives you the ability to create custom logs. This is a very useful option due to the amount of data that can be stored on the server. Custom views allow you to filter a view by queries and sort the events that you want to analyze. Custom logs can be saved, exported, or imported for analysis purposes. Custom logs can be filtered based on the following:

- The time of the event
- The event level (error, critical, or warning)
- Event IDs
- The user or computer context

By default, there's one hard-coded custom view called **Administrative Events**. New custom events can be created using the Event Viewer management console as follows:

1. Go to the **Event Viewer** management console
2. Click on **Create Custom View** in the **Actions** pane
3. Define what needs to be included in the custom view and click **OK**

The following screenshot shows the **Create Custom View** window:

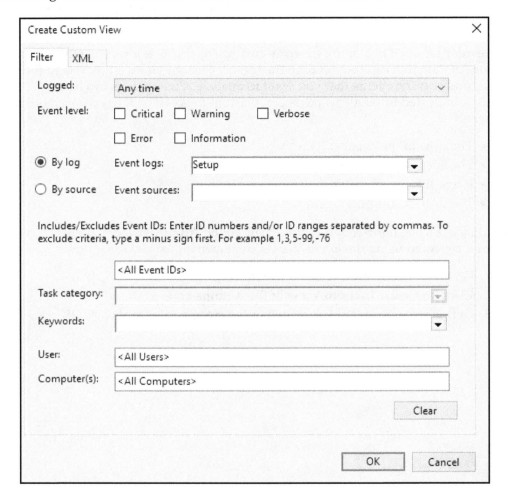

Another very important functionality of Event Viewer in Windows Server 2016 is Event Subscription. This feature enables a single server to collect copies of events from other servers in an environment, by using Windows Remote Management (**WinRM**). Subscriptions can be collector-initiated or source computer-initiated:

- **Collector-initiated**: This model identifies all computers from which the collector will receive and pull events
- **Source-initiated**: In this subscription model, source computers push events to the collector

To use event subscription, you must configure the forwarding and collecting computers so that they use the WinRM service and **Windows Event Collector service (wecsvc)**. Both of these services must keep running on PCs that are participating in the forwarding and collecting process

On the source computer, you need to run the following command:

```
winrm quickconfig
```

On the collector computer, you need to run the following command:

```
wecutil qc
```

Once you've configured the necessary services, you need to configure the subscription using the **Event Viewer** management console:

1. Go to the **Event Viewer** management console
2. Right-click on **Subscription**, and select **Create Subscription**
3. Define parameters and click **OK**

The following shows the **Subscription Properties** screen:

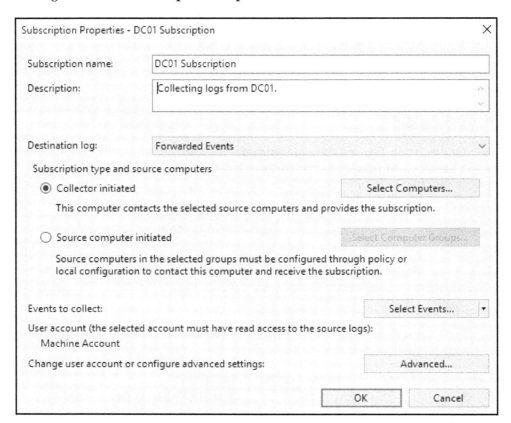

The computer account for the collector computer needs to be added to the Event Log Readers group. Otherwise, you'll receive an **Access Denied error, code 0x5**.

Server Manager

Server Manager provides a centralized location that allows you to store and view event logs from other computers. It also provides monitoring solutions for remote servers without accessing them directly. You can simply use the **Server Manager** console and click on **Add other servers to manage** on the dashboard, as shown in the following:

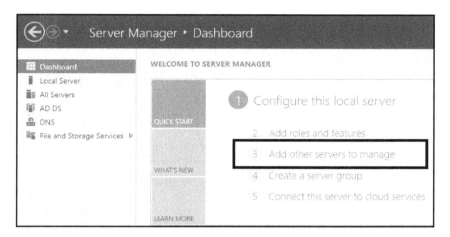

Once the servers are added to the list, they will be visible on the **All Servers** page:

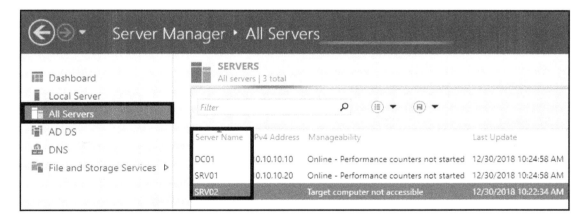

Configuring alerts

In **Performance Monitor**, you can configure alerts. You need to create a Data Collector Set that will contain performance counters for alerting purposes, as well as for performance analysis purposes, as described previously. You can do this using the **Performance Monitor** management console. Follow these steps:

1. Go to the **Performance Monitor** console
2. Expand **Data Collector Sets**
3. Right-click on **User Defined**, select **New**, and then select **Data Collector Set**
4. On the **How would you like to create this new Data Collector Set** page, define the name and type of the Data Collector Set
5. On the **What type of data do you want to include** page, select **Performance Counter Alert**
6. On the **Which performance counters would you like to monitor** page, define the counters that you want to monitor and set limits
7. On the **Create the data collector set**, select whether you want to edit properties, save, or start a Data Collector Set

Once you create a Data Collector Set for alerting purposes, you need to edit the properties, and define an action when the counters exceed the defined threshold, by configuring **Alert Action** or **Alert Task**:

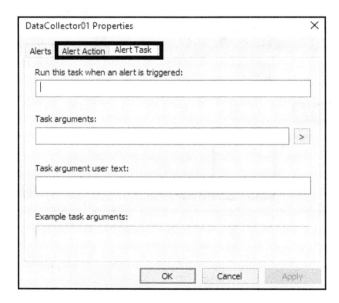

Summary

In this chapter, you've learned how to monitor and maintain a pre-installed and configured Windows Server. You've learned how to control and automate Windows Updates; how to back up and restore files, folders, and system states using Windows Server Backup; and how to monitor Windows Server using Performance Monitor and Event Viewer.

Questions

1. What's the best way to configure WSUS clients?
    1. Group Policy
    2. Manual configuring
    3. Editing registry keys
    4. Implementing changes by startup script

2. What are the characteristics of the WSUS hierarchy?
    1. Upstream server
    2. Replica server
    3. WID database server
    4. Downstream server

3. By default, is automatic approval configured?
    1. Yes
    2. No

4. How can we restore a system state?
    1. Windows Server Backup console
    2. Installation media
    3. Server Manager console
    4. MMC

5. Can Windows Server Backup back up multiple servers?
    1. No
    2. Yes

6. Can Windows Server Backup back up Hyper-V virtual machines?
    1. Yes
    2. No

7. Can Data Collector Set be used for alerting purposes?
    1. Yes
    2. No

8. What kind of model does the collector-initiated event subscription approach use?
    1. Pull
    2. Push
    3. Two-way
    4. One-way

9. Can Server Manager monitor multiple servers?
    1. Yes
    2. No

Further reading

For more information about the topics covered in this chapter, use the following links.

- https://docs.microsoft.com/en-us/windows-server/administration/windows-server-update-services/get-started/windows-server-update-services-wsus
- https://blogs.technet.microsoft.com/filecab/tag/windows-server-backup/
- https://docs.microsoft.com/en-us/windows-server/administration/windows-commands/wbadmin
- https://docs.microsoft.com/en-us/previous-versions/windows/it-pro/windows-server-2008-R2-and-2008/cc766130(v=ws.11)
- https://blogs.technet.microsoft.com/askds/tag/event-logs/

Assessments

Chapter 1: Installing Windows Server 2016

1. SRV1
2. Software-Defined Networking, Storage Spaces Direct
3. VHD files, Server pools
4. `Install-WindowsFeature`
5. `slmgr.vbs -ato`, `slmgr.vbs -ipk`
6. `netdom`, `Add-Computer`
7. `slmgr.vbs`, `dism.exe`
8. Windows Server 2016 Standard, Windows Server 2016 Datacenter, Windows Server Core
9. Activate computers in groups of 5
10. License conversion

Chapter 2: Windows Server Imaging and Deployment

1. Faster server deployment, Lower operational costs, Easier backup, Server consolidation
2. CPU usage, Memory requirements, Disk usage
3. MAPT
4. False
5. False
6. IP address range scanning, LDAP, SNMP, WMI
7. Run `Sysprep.exe`
8. `Sysprep.exe /oobe`

9. `Add-WindowsDriver -Path c:\mountedimage -Driver c:\drivers, DISM.exe /image:c:\mountedimage /Add-Driver /driver:c:\drivers\`

10. `DISM.exe /mount-image /imagefile:c:\sources\install.wim /mountdir:c:\mount`

Chapter 3: Configuring and Implementing Storage

1. Security, Self-healing, Support for larger file sizes
2. Fixed size, Dynamically expanding
3. Install Server for NFS
4. SMB Share - Advanced, NFS Share - Advanced
5. Enable caching of shares on SRV2, Enable BranchCache on the file share on SRV2
6. Create a virtual disk, Create a storage pool
7. Single parity, Two-way mirror, Three-way mirror
8. URL address
9. `3260`
10. Enable throughput optimization, Enable background optimization

Chapter 4: Getting to Know Hyper-V

1. A software layer that sits on top of the hardware
2. 64-bit processor, Second Level Address Translation (SLAT), Data Execution Prevention (DEP)
3. Upgrade SRV1 to Windows Server 2016
4. `Invoke-Command`, `Enter-PSSession`
5. `Set-VMProcessor`
6. Configure Integration Services on VM1
7. Enable IPSec Task Offloading
8. Data corruption protection, Can be resized live
9. Pass-through
10. Configure Enhanced Session Mode Policy

Chapter 5: Understanding Windows Containers

1. Installing the container feature
2. NAT
3. Yes
4. `--isolation=hyperv`
5. `docker ps`
6. `docker search`
7. `.txt`
8. No

Chapter 6: High Availability

1. 30 seconds
2. Yes
3. Unformatted
4. 32
5. Hyper-converged
6. Single hosts
7. 16
8. Yes
9. Yes

Chapter 7: Implementing Clustering

1. Yes
2. `New-Cluster`
3. Hyper-V, Failover cluster
4. Failover cluster, Role that will be clustered
5. Yes

6. No
7. Add-Disk, Get-ClusterAvailableDisk
8. No

Chapter 8: Monitoring and Maintaining Server Environments

1. Group Policy
2. Upstream server, Downstream server
3. No
4. Windows Server Backup console, Installation media
5. No
6. Yes
7. Yes
8. Pull
9. Yes

Index